# More 101 Best Home-Based Businesses for Women

## Priscilla Y. Huff

## Prima Publishing

*Dedicated to Chip, my entrepreneurial partner; Ray, Tom, and Brandon, entrepreneurs in the making; and Jordan and Sierra Jade, entrepreneurs of the next century. Also with love to the memory of my father, Ernest R. Yost, who taught me the value of persistence, faith, and hard work.*

PRIMA PUBLISHING and colophon are registered trademarks of Prima Communications, Inc.

Disclaimer: The business ideas presented herein are not a guarantee of monetary success. The information is based on research, examples, and advice from business experts, trade associations, and women business owners. Every attempt was made to ensure accuracy, and neither the author nor the publisher can be held responsible for any errors or changing circumstances. All featured businesses, franchises and business opportunities, publications, products, services, and suppliers are mentioned here for informational purposes only. Their inclusion does not represent an endorsement on the part of the author or publisher.

**Library of Congress Cataloging-in-Publication Data**

Huff, Priscilla Y.
    More 101 best home-based businesses for women / Priscilla Y. Huff.
        p.   cm.
    Includes bibliographical references and index.
    ISBN 0-7615-1269-1
    1. Home-based businesses.   2. Women-owned business enterprises—Management.   3. New business enterprises—Management.
I. Huff, Priscilla Y.   101 best home-based businesses for women.
HD62.38.H843 1998
658'.041—dc21                                                        97-43994
                                                                                CIP

       99  00  01  02  HH  10  9  8  7  6  5  4  3  2
Printed in the United States of America

---

**How to Order**
Single copies may be ordered from Prima Publishing, P.O. Box 1260BK, Rocklin, CA 95677; telephone (916) 632-4400. Quantity discounts are also available. On your letterhead, include information concerning the intended use of the books and the number of books you wish to purchase.

---

**Visit us online at http://www.primapublishing.com**

# Contents

# Preface

This is my fifth book about home-based and small businesses, and each time I do the research and interviews for one of my books, I am amazed at the creativity and ingenuity that women entrepreneurs employ when they start their businesses. They possess an inner drive combined with limitless energy and enthusiasm that sustain them in their quest for success. While they all hope to make money with their businesses—and many make a substantial yearly income—they also love what they do and are not afraid to help others along the way. These women (and men) want to give their children a better life and leave a legacy for them. Whether knowingly or not, they are also becoming role models for their children—demonstrating that your life work can be your occupation, too, and that you need not be "trapped" in a job or career that you hate.

A keynote speaker at a women's entrepreneur conference said the challenge for a woman in the next century will be to find a "balance" in her life among her personal needs, family, faith, and work. Today, business ownership is helping women do just that. Even though an entrepreneur averages more hours a week than if he or she held a "regular" job, the women I interviewed still liked the flexibility they had owning their own businesses. One woman volunteers by helping slow readers in a nearby elementary school; another who owns a thriving soap-making business still has time to design and make clothes for her grandchildren; and I, like many of the "sandwich" generation, have time to help both my elder parents and children with many of life's crises, both large and small.

Even though many employers have become more sympathetic to those who are caregivers, it still is empowering to know that we women business owners have more control and say over our lives. To be fair, I also have had women tell me that they have no interest in owning a business and would not like that responsibility. I have no argument with them, because entrepreneurship is not for everyone. It takes stamina, persistence, and a willingness to constantly learn what is needed to be successful. An entrepreneur also cannot be afraid to fail—experts say sometimes it takes as many as three business start-ups before one becomes successful.

Whatever you choose to do—work for a company, be a full-time homemaker, or become an entrepreneur—be proud of yourself and respect others, no matter what they do for a living. In giving respect, you promote understanding, which will help us all live and work together in harmony. Impossible? Maybe, but something we can all strive for as the next century dawns.

It is my wish that this book (and my previous ones) will suggest possibilities and give you options of entrepreneurial ideas that you may not have considered before.

With all my heart, I give you *more* 101 best wishes in all the ventures on which you embark!

# Part I

# Getting Started

# 1

# Home Business Today (and Tips for Tomorrow)

*If women's businesses keeping growing as they have been, we can imagine owning half the assets in the world.*
—Rona Feit, Horizon speaker at Paris Organization for Economic and Cooperative Development meeting, April 1997

The home and small business trend across America is growing each year at rates that far exceed projected estimates. IDC/Link, a New York City consultancy, estimated last year that forty-seven million Americans stayed home to work—and their numbers are still growing! Women are a big part of this movement, according to the National Foundation for Women Business Owners (NFWBO), which says home-based businesses owned by women are making a substantial economic contribution. In the United States, these businesses provide full-time employment for nearly six million people, and part-time work for an additional eight million. As of 1996, nearly 8 million women-owned businesses were operating in the United States, generating nearly $2.3 trillion annually in revenues to the economy, more than the gross domestic product of most small countries.

Why are women starting businesses at twice the rate as men (according to the U.S. Small Businesses Administration)? The reasons are as varied as the women who start them. Here are some of the most common:

❖ They need money but want to be able to have a flexible work schedule to fit their families' needs.
❖ For one reason or another, they find themselves single but with no marketable skills and do not want to do factory or office work.
❖ Their children are grown.
❖ Even with two full-time paychecks, working couples cannot seem to get ahead of their bills.
❖ They want a better life for their children.
❖ They are tired of trying to please a company or boss and want to try to run their own businesses.
❖ They want to do work they enjoy.
❖ They want the opportunity to help their community in some way with their businesses.
❖ They want to be able to be creative in their work.
❖ Some of the hottest jobs prospects predicted for the next century for women do not have a very high earning potential.

Fill in your reason(s) for wanting to start a business: I want to start a business because _____
_____.

Of course, everything has pros and cons, and before you start a business, you should be realistic. Even though the average home business earns $50,000 a year compared with the average worker's salary of about $26,000 a year, a home or small business will probably take at least two years to show a profit. Financial experts say ideally you should have savings that will cover at least six months to two years of household and projected business expenses if you decide to start your business full-time. Alternatives are to start a business part-time until your profits are substantial enough for you to "quit your day job" or to rely temporarily on the financial support of a partner.

## What Are Some Other Myths About Home-Based Businesses?
### Myth 1
*A home-based business has no overhead.*
**Reality:** Often as much as 50 percent of a home-based business's billing rate will go toward covering overhead costs, but the good news is that you can deduct from your income tax a percentage of your household and related bills if you work from your home. You can check with your accountant, bookkeeper, or local IRS office for guidelines about these tax deductions.

### Myth 2
*I will not need child care if I work from home.*
**Reality:** True, a home business allows you the flexibility of working your own hours, but it is still difficult, if not impossible, to conduct a conference call with a two-year-old in the same room! Truth is, a majority of entrepreneurial moms have some sort of child care arrangement—using either a spouse or baby-sitter to care for the children in the home while they work for a block of time or taking their children to a day care or sitter for a few hours a day or week. Even older children can be demanding and sometimes resentful of your business's demands. It is best to realistically discuss your business idea with your family and think carefully about the number of hours you will actually be able to put into your business.

### Myth 3
*If I have a home business, I will have time to clean house, continue to volunteer at church and school, cook delectable meals, taxi the kids to all their activities, and have a meaningful, personal relationship with a "significant other."*
**Reality:** This is really a fantasy world! A home-based or small business demands more hours than a regular job, especially in the start-up phases. Unless you are a "superwoman" or "supermom" (I know I am not!), then you will have to prioritize the important parts of your life and phase yourself out of all but the most significant people and activities with which you are involved. As my mother always told me, "I have no formula for success, but I do know that you will fail if you try to please everyone!"

On a positive note, you can use your business to help your community by giving jobs or internships to youth, mentoring a struggling entrepreneur, donating your product and/or services to a charity auction, and in many other ways. You not only get to help others but it is also good (often free) publicity for your business. Women business owners in the United States are more likely than male entrepreneurs to participate in volunteer activities and to encourage their employees to volunteer, according to the NFWBO.

## Myth 4
*I have a great idea that I know will make me lots of money, and I hope to start it next week.*
**Reality:** Business experts say that the amount of time and research a person puts into a business idea relates directly to the success of that business. I do not mean to dampen your enthusiasm, but one of the biggest mistakes a new entrepreneur makes is going ahead too soon, before thoroughly investigating the business and its trade. One woman who has a successful food delivery franchise took a full year to research the business before she invested a single dollar.

You can make a list of business ideas that interest you, look to see what businesses like those exist in your community, talk to other women entrepreneurs, and even work for a time in a business that is similar to the idea that interests you. Phyllis Gillis, author of *Entrepreneurial Mothers*, said at a seminar I attended, "If you think you might like to bake special desserts for caterers or restaurants, bake a hundred pies in a week to see if that is what you really want to do fifty weeks a year!" Working in a business that interests you can also give you valuable skills and business knowledge to apply later on to your own business.

Check, too, to see whether a potential market for your business exists in your community. My sister-in-law tried to start a personal provider service—running errands and shopping for people. Unfortunately, the people in her community aren't interested in hiring someone to do their shopping. My sister-in-law now advertises in a community that is only a few miles away but has a higher percentage of professional couples who are more likely to use her business's services.

When you believe you have a good idea and a potential market, then you can begin to write a business plan to set your goals, financial needs, and so forth. You will have a much better idea of what your business will offer and who your customers will be. You may wish you could start tomorrow, but taking the time to research and plan your business idea will pay off, literally, and your business will be much more likely to succeed.

**Myth 5**
*If I work from home, I can be much more casual in both how I dress and how I treat my customers.*
**Reality:** Yes, you can dress in your T-shirt and sweatpants while you make business calls (unless you have a home office that receives customers), but how you treat your customers should be as professional as any business protocol dictates. Do you respond promptly to customer requests? Do you have professional-looking promotional materials? Can your customers depend on your product and service? How can customers and business associates reach you if you are not in your home office? Do you belong to any professional trade groups or associations?

In other words, you can work from your home office, but you should always follow professional procedures and ethics as if you were working from the office of a CEO of a major corporation. After all, you are the CEO of your business, even if you are the only employee. Just remember to act like one, or no one will take your business seriously.

### Your Business Idea and the Next Century

Whether you have already selected a business or are still in the process of choosing one, you will want to consider some tips on bringing your business into the next century as well as what will be among the predicted hottest businesses for the next century. Here are some that futurists say will be in demand:

♣ Business services: Employee training, home office products, outsourcing of office services, desktop publishing, marketing services, meeting planner

❖ Creative businesses: Educational products and materials (toys, homeschooling aids, distant education), crafts teacher, photographer, custom sewing, arts and music services

❖ Computer businesses: Court scopist (an independent court reporter or "note reader"), Internet services, information specialist, medical billing, transcription, software development, database designer

❖ Personal and home services: Financial planning, security products, child and elder care, home delivery services, personal errands and shopping, referral services, cleaning

❖ Food items: Specialty foods (sauces, condiments, healthful snack foods), fresh water delivery, foodaceuticals (foods that promote health and general well-being), personal chef, catering

❖ Health-related businesses: Personal fitness trainer, massage therapist, aromatherapy, home health care, herbalist, homeopathic medicine

❖ Green/environmental businesses: Garden-related products, herbs, special landscaping, recycling (services, products), chemical-free produce

❖ Mature adult services: Retirement and financial planning, career planning and job counseling, personal organizer, insurance claims specialist, resettling specialist

❖ Miscellaneous: Exporting (markets in India, China, Latin and South America), mail order, self-publishing, adventure travel, new sports

Here are some tips for bringing your business into the next century:

1. Keep informed of the ongoing movements in your field and business by reading trade publications as well as books and journals that cover future trends (see recommended books at the end of this chapter).

2. Listen to your friends, family, neighbors, and most of all your customers, who will tell you about their needs, problems, and so forth. What are their hobbies, concerns, and future goals for themselves and their families? What are their leisure activities?

3. Keep up with current advances in both home office technology and that which pertains to your trade and business.
4. Have your eyes and ears open for new "niches" and customer markets that may open up and present new opportunities for your business.

### Entrepreneurship and Failure

*I feel the most important requirement in success is learning to overcome failure. You must learn to tolerate it, but never accept it.*
—Reggie Jackson

Entrepreneurs exhibit some common characteristics: determination, discipline, drive, persistence, and fearlessness about mak-

---

## Tips on Getting the Respect Your Business Deserves

The National Foundation for Women Business Owners says that "the greatest challenge of business ownership for women is being taken seriously." Here are some tips to help you:

✤ Set up a room, or even a desk in a corner, designated just for your business. Separate your work space from the rest of the house with screens or partitions so that when you are in your "office," your family and others will know you are working. It also helps your mindset in shifting from household chores to business tasks when you are in your business area.

✤ Find a block (or segments) of time that you can regularly set as business hours. Politely let others know these are your business hours, and you will get back to them—unless it is an emergency—when you are finished working.

ing mistakes. Some people never even try to fulfill their dreams because they are afraid they will fail. As I mentioned in my last book (*101 Best Small Businesses for Women*), a mistake is only foolish if you fail to learn from it. I believe this also pertains to failure of a business. An ongoing study of entrepreneurs by the Entrepreneurial Research Consortium (ERC), coordinated by Babson College professor Paul D. Reynolds, has found that it takes an average of three business start-ups by a new entrepreneur before one business succeeds and sustains itself.

A quote by Benjamin Disraeli reads, "As a general rule, the most successful people in life are those who have the best information." Thus, read, take courses if needed, talk to other entrepreneurs, and ask questions and more questions until your get all the information you need.

---

❖ Carry business cards and an appointment book with you at all times. When your friends ask you for lunch, open up your book to write in your luncheon date.

❖ Get an answering machine or voice mail to handle calls when you are away from your office or otherwise occupied. Promptly respond to messages. Doing so tells people they are important to you. Update your outgoing message daily, if only to change the date. Be the professional your business needs.

❖ Have a business plan and check it regularly to see whether you are close to following the time schedule you have allotted to reach your goals. Keep focused on the tasks at hand, but also look toward the future possibilities your business might achieve. Have a business vision.

❖ Convey confidence in yourself and your business, even if you do not yet feel it inside. Your customers will be more likely to trust you with their business, and others will respect you as a savvy entrepreneur.

## Tips on Dealing with Business Failures

*They fail, and they alone, who have not striven.*
—Thomas Bailey Aldrich

American loves a comeback, an against-all-odds story. Here are some tips to help you if you feel your business is floundering or has failed:

❖ Your first or even second business may not have succeeded, but evaluate your mistakes, learn from them, and try again—this time with a successful venture.

❖ Persist until your business idea succeeds. Refuse to give up. See if it can go toward a different, untapped market.

❖ Concentrate and focus on your business goals and vision. Look forward, not backward.

❖ Be proud of what you have accomplished and learned along the way.

❖ Help some other faltering entrepreneur along the way. It has its own rewards.

❖ Don't be afraid to start more than one business venture at the same time.

### Additional Information

**Recommended Reading**

*The Joy of Self-Employment: Entrepreneurship and Education in a Changing World* by Todd Leigh Mayo (New York: Pinnacle Press, 1997).

*When She Goes to Work, She Stays Home: Women, Technology and Home-Based Work* by International Specialized Book Services (Portland, OR: 1991).

*Chaos or Community? Seeking Solutions, Not Scapegoats for Bad Economics* by Holly Sklar (Boston: South End Press, 1995).

*Who Stole the American Dream?* by Donald L. Barlett and James B. Steele (Philadelphia: Philadelphia Inquirer, 1996 [newspaper series/paperback]).

*Clicking: 16 Trends to Future Fit Your Life, Your Work, Your Business* by Faith Popcorn and Lys Marigold (New York: HarperCollins, 1996).

*Trends 2000: How to Prepare for and Profit from the Changes of the 21st Century* by Gerald Celente (New York: Warner, 1997).

## Organizations

Trends Research Institute, Salisbury Turnpike, Rhinebeck, NY 12572; publishes *The Trends Journal*.

Worldwatch Institute, 1776 Massachusetts Ave., N.W., Washington, DC 20036-1904; publishes *Worldwatch*.

# 2

# Guidelines for Running a Business from Home

*And when her biographer says of an Italian woman poet, "during
some years her Muse was intermitted," we do not wonder at the fact
when he casually mentions her ten children.*
— Anna Garlin Spencer

After an occasional particularly bad day when I was a substitute
teacher (which I did for eight years to help earn money for my
family, and which I could do while I worked part-time at
my writing and publishing business), I would dream of the day
I would be able to quit and work at my business full-time. It
was hard to be patient, but working part-time at teaching and
coaching also gave me the time to research, read, take business
courses, attend conferences, and learn more about the writing
and self-publishing industry. You may also be anxious to start
your business, but taking the time to save your money and doing
the necessary preparation beforehand will help increase the
chances that your business will succeed in the first months and
years of operation.

## Considerations Before Starting a Business

### Where Will You Work?

Using an extra bedroom, a large closet, a corner of a room, a basement, or even constructing an addition are all possibilities for setting a space apart from the rest of your residence. Sure, you can work from your kitchen table—as so many of those home-based opportunity ads headline—but the reality is that it is best to set up an area solely devoted to your business, one that should not be entered by other family members without your permission. You need this office area to run your business as a professional. Other areas can be used, if needed, for production, but an office is the "hub" of your business, a place for the boss and secretary (you!). To qualify for any tax deductions, the home office generally must be set aside exclusively for the business. Check with your accountant or tax adviser for details.

### How Will Your Business Affect Your Family?

A new business will make demands on you that may sometimes interfere with family activities and schedules. Be honest with yourself and your family, discussing the ramifications and also listening to their concerns. Emphasize the positive aspects, including how your business can benefit them. Do not make unrealistic promises, though. Set guidelines for them and yourself as far as work hours and off hours. Schedule regular times with your family, or else your business will consume you.

My family actually likes it when I am on a deadline with a manuscript. We eat out more often, and I could care less how the kids' rooms look. (For more tips on working at home with children, see the sidebar on page 14.)

### How Will You Furnish Your Office?

With a business plan (see the next chapter), you will list the needed furnishings and equipment. The type of business, of course, will dictate what specialized equipment your will need, but ordinary office equipment such as desks, chairs, lamps, and so forth, can be leased or purchased new. Check garage sales and in the classified ads of your local newspapers to get some

# Tips for Living with Your
# Home Business and Children

❖ Reward your children and spouse when you have business successes (or when you just want to thank them for their patience) by treating them to a special treat—a movie or dinner out, for example.

❖ Take regular breaks with your children. It is good for you to relax a few moments and good for your family to do something fun.

❖ Network with other working moms, and possibly take turns having each other's children over to help give some uninterrupted working time to one another.

❖ Let your children help in the business (if they want), and pay them accordingly as you would any other employee. Check with your accountant about tax deductions concerning salaries paid to your children.

❖ Keep your work space separate from your family, so your business records and equipment will not be disturbed, and they will recognize you are at work when you are in your office.

❖ Have an answering machine or voice mail system to take calls if a sudden emergency or minor "crisis" should occur with your children.

❖ Have a box of toys, games, and snacks near your phone in case you need to occupy your children when you are on a business call.

❖ Enjoy your family and your business, and do not worry about being "superwoman," trying to do everything. Do not be in the business mode twenty-four hours a day. Spend time with your family, and take time for yourself. That is one of the benefits of having a home business: flexible hours.

good bargains. Do not skimp, though, on your office chair, lighting, and any major equipment purchases such as a computer, printer, and copier. These are essential, and you will want to take your time to shop and compare. Pick a printer that can help you with your graphics. Also be sure of your warranties and service plans.

You will also want to have a separate telephone line with an answering system so customers can still reach you when you cannot handle a call personally at the moment. A fax machine combined with that system will save you mail and help with deadlines. Read small business publications such as *Home Office Computing, Business Start-Ups, Income Opportunities, Small Business Opportunities,* and other small business publications that regularly review the latest in office technology as well as offer important business management advice and tips.

If you are low on start-up funds, you can start small and put money back into your business as you make your first profits and buy what your business really needs.

### What Times Will You Be Open for Business?
You need to set work hours around your personal and family schedules and the times customers can reach you. If you have small children, you will probably need some coverage for a block of time to work undisturbed. Try to work regular hours, even if your business is part-time, to help establish a continuity for all concerned. It's important to schedule "off hours" so that your family will know they have your full attention then and to give yourself some free time as well. As your business grows, you can make adjustments as needed in your hours.

### What Image Do You Want Your Business to Represent?
What is your "niche"? What is special about your business? What is your philosophy? What would make someone want to use your product, service, or expertise? Does your business name clearly state what you do? Will you have a logo or trademark? Ask yourself these questions until you can describe your business, its focus, and its purpose to your business associates

and customers. This will establish your credibility and help distinguish you from your competitors as you advertise and spread the word about your venture. You want your business to be able to be easily recognized in your market.

### What Are the Legal Aspects of Your Business?

What form will your business take? For tax and legal purposes, all businesses generally fall into one of these broad categories: sole proprietorship, partnership, corporation, S corporation, and limited liability corporation (see the glossary at the back of this book for definitions). Most likely, as a home-based business owner, your business will be a sole proprietorship or partnership. Consult with an attorney or an accountant who can advise you on the tax advantages and which form is best for you.

Do not forget to check with state and local authorities for permits, restrictions, licenses, and so forth, that may be required to operate a business out of your home or to run certain types of businesses. Some other legal considerations include obtaining a federal employer identification number (EIN) (see the glossary), checking state sales tax and resale tax certifications, investigating zoning restrictions, and registering your business name (see the glossary).

### Where Do You Want Your Business to Go?

In focusing and setting goals for your business, you will be able to then define the steps necessary to get there. This is best done through your business plan. Without one, you may find your business going in too many directions at once. Read the next chapter, and use the sources listed at the end to help you in forming a plan for success.

### How Will You Finance Your Business?

Home-based and small business entrepreneurs have the reputation for being creative in financing their businesses. Some popular sources of finance are credit cards, small business loans from local banks, personal assets, moonlighting, loans from family or friends, venture capitalists, loans off insurance policies, and small business loans from state or federal government sources. Networking with other women business owners and business associations may also give you leads for financing sources. Do a careful study of the expenses of your start-up costs and expenses to run your business to get an accurate estimate of the money you will need.

### Who Will Be Those with Whom You Can Network?
Networking is one of the most important steps you can take to help your business succeed. Home-based business associations, other women business owners, Chambers of Commerce, and trade associations are just a few of the groups with whom you need to keep in contact. If no appropriate group is in your area, form one of your own with other home-based women and mothers. Networking helps market your business through referrals.

### How Will You Market Your Business?
Marketing is another important part of your business plan. As a new business owner, you will be spending a majority of time getting people to know about your business and what your business offers. Marketing is a constant with even an established business, because your competition is after your customers, too. After all, it is your customers that pay your bills! Read the marketing tips in the next chapter, take courses, and listen to what your customers are saying about your business so you can always meet their needs, even if they should change.

## Customizing a Business for Yourself

In choosing the best business (or businesses), here are four major considerations that may help you narrow the list.

*I. Self-Evaluation*
1. My work skills include _____.
2. My work experience has been _____.
3. My education has been_____.
4. My hobbies include_____.
5. I really (do or do not) _____ like working with (adult persons, elder persons, children or animals, insects, machines, plants, food, technology) _____.
6. I hate doing work that is (indoors or outdoors) _____.

## Before You Quit Your Day Job . . .

❖ Make arrangements for health insurance coverage. Find coverage with a home-based or small business association, sign up with your spouse's plan, or continue with your employer's plan through Cobra.

❖ Save six months to two years of living expenses to allow your business time to grow and make a profit. If you can, start part-time on the side and still hold your job; this approach will give you an opportunity to test your market and make sure customers exist for your venture.

❖ Establish a line of credit with your bank and credit cards for possible financial sources.

❖ Assess the skills and knowledge you have to contribute to your business. Take business management courses, or even work or volunteer in the business industry in which you will be venturing to get business management knowledge and on-the-job experience.

❖ Join trade and professional organizations (local, regional, and/or national) with which you can network, learn business tips, and begin to make contacts for referrals.

❖ Know the legal requirements for your business: apply for a federal employer identification number (EIN), state and city business licenses, state sales tax and resale tax certificates, zoning allowances, and register your business name.

7. I like (active or sedentary) _____ activities in my work.
8. I am a self-starter and have the discipline to tend to the tasks of my business's daily demands. (yes or no) _____.
9. I realistically estimate I will be able to spend _____ hours a week on my new business.

10. In _____ (number) _____(month[s], year[s])
    I hope to have my business(es) in operation.

## II. List the Business Ideas That Fit Your Abilities, Interests, Lifestyle, and Family

_____

_____

_____

_____

_____

_____

## III. Narrow the List to the Best Three Businesses, and Write Who You Think the Best Potential Customers of Each Would Be

1. Business idea 1 _____

2. Business idea 2 _____

3. Business idea 3_____

## IV. List Sources of Information for Each Business Idea So You Can Thoroughly Research It (e.g., trade industry associations and organizations, books, trade publications, other business owners, government agencies, Internet sites, etc.)

1. Business idea 1_____

_____

2. Business idea 2 _____

_____

3. Business idea 3_____

_____

## Obstacles That Hold Women Back from Entrepreneurship

❖ Financing—Women may lack funds or not know of available financing sources.
❖ Self-confidence—Women may not believe they have the business knowledge they need.
❖ Networking opportunities—A home-based business can make women feel isolated and they may not know whom to contact if they have a business-related question.
❖ Commitments—Women tend to volunteer in many outside activities, which does not leave them the time it takes to start and run a business.
❖ Unsure of what business to start
❖ Not knowing what steps to take to start a business

### Independent Contractor

Depending on what kind of business you have, your customers may be individuals, other businesses, or both. If your work involves a project and you are contracted by a business, you will be considered an independent contractor. Here are some of the items that differentiate independent contractors from employees:

Independent contractors . . .
 . . . are given or awarded projects by the company hiring their services.
 . . . bring to the company their own skills and training.
 . . . provide services not available at the company.
 . . . may do the job themselves or send another worker or subcontractor.
 . . . supply their own crew and staff if needed.
 . . . work their own hours at their own time as needed to complete the project.

. . . work at the place of their choice unless contracted to do otherwise.

. . . report to the company when the project or task is complete.

. . . pay their own expenses and liability insurance, though these may be factored in the contract fee.

. . . provide their own tools and equipment, which is part of the investment of their own businesses.

. . . work for more than one company and in the time limit designated by each contract.

The IRS is very strict with the designations of who is a company employee and who is an independent contractor. If you have any questions as an independent contractor or if you are hiring someone as such, it is best to contact a knowledgeable attorney or a certified public accountant.

## Protecting Your Product and Service

If your company or product is unique, you will want to protect these special features before you present your service or product. You can do this by obtaining a patent, trademark, or copyright, or by licensing your product or service.

A patent grants your company exclusive rights to an invention for a set period of time. It also takes considerable time and money (from $8,000 to $13,000), including attorney fees, for an uncomplicated patent grant. You have to be careful of unscrupulous companies that offer to help you obtain a patent for your idea. Write to the U.S. Patent & Trademark Office, Washington, DC 20231, for more information; call the office's introductory switchboard at (703) 308-HELP; look for patent information on the Internet at http://www.uspto.gov/web; and read the book *Patent It Yourself* by David Pressman (order it from Nolo Press, 950 Parker St., Berkeley, CA 94710; also available on CD-ROM). You can also consult with a patent attorney (see "Additional Information" at the end of this chapter).

A trademark is used to characterize the products of a company. The symbol TM next to a company or product name denotes its trademark status and may prevent other companies from selling a product similar to yours with a name that could be mistaken for your company's name. Service marks (SM) are issued to protect services. Both marks can be issued by a state or federal government.

To find out whether another company has your name, you can do an on-line search through a database such as Lexus/Nexus (check their prices) or visit one of the seventy-eight libraries in the United States designated a trademark depository institution. You can also hire a trademark agency to do the search, with prices ranging from about $85 to $1,500.

For added protection against a future dispute, you should also check each state to see whether a company has registered a name similar to yours, because many companies do not register with the federal government. This step requires searching state government records and business and telephone directories. You can also hire a paralegal or an attorney who specializes in such searches. It is also advised you look on-line to see whether there is a similar name as the one you have chosen. If not, you might want to hurry to reserve it for yourself.

In the event the name you pick has been chosen, do not be discouraged. Trademark law states that as long as you are in different businesses, you can use the same name with minor modifications or changes.

A copyright is the protection issued for specific classifications of original works. For example, books, magazines, software, and even television broadcasts can be protected by copyright. Important documents published by your business such as sales manuals, speeches, and so forth, should be marked with a copyright symbol (©), year, your business' name, and the words "All rights reserved for copyright protection." To register your copyright and for additional information and forms, contact the Register of Copyrights, Library of Congress, Washington, DC 20559.

If you have an exclusive technology such as a software program of which you own the sole rights, or if you have developed a unique product or process, licensing this product may be the best method from which you can profit. When you license your product, you grant others permission to use your concept. Before you find any licensees, though, you should consider how you will profit from licensing it and then which companies might benefit holding a license to use it. Look for an attorney who specializes in licensing (intellectual property law) by calling your local lawyers' referral service or by consulting the Martindale-Hubbell Law Directory at your public library or county law library.

## Additional Information

### Recommended Reading

*Dive Right In, the Sharks Won't Bite: The Entrepreneurial Woman's Guide to Success* by Jane Wesman (Upper Saddle River, NJ: Prentice Hall, 1997)

*Home Office Design* by Neal Zimmerman (New York: Wiley, 1996)

*Honey, I Want to Start My Own Business* by Azriela Jaffe (New York: HarperBusiness, 1997)

*How to License Your Million Dollar Idea: Everything You Need to Know to Make Money from Your New Product Idea* by Harvey Reese (New York: Wiley, 1993)

*How to Raise a Family and a Career under One Roof* by Lisa Roberts (Moontownship, PA: Bookhaven Press, 1997).

*Mompreneurs: A Practical Step-by-Step Guide to Work-at-Home Success* by Ellen H. Parlapiano and Patricia Cobe (New York: Berkley, 1996)

*Names That Sell: How to Create Great Names for Your Company, Product, or Service* by Fred Barrett (Portland, OR: Alder, 1995)

*Patent, Copyright, and Trademark: A Desk Reference to Intellectual Property Law* by Stephen Elias (Berkeley, CA: Nolo, 1996)

*Patent It Yourself*, 4th ed., by David Pressman (Berkeley, CA: Nolo, 1997); also available on CD-ROM.

*Patents, Trademarks, and Copyrights* by David G. Rosenbaum (Franklin Lakes, NJ: Career Press, 1996)

*The Stay-at-Home Mom's Guide to Making Money: How to Create the Business That's Right for You Using the Skills and Interests You Already Have* by Liz Folger (Rocklin, CA: Prima, 1997)

A *Woman's Guide to 25 Home-Based Businesses*—manual and workbook for $89.50 from Income Opportunities; to order, call (888) 836-8844.

*Working at Home While the Kids Are There, Too* by Loriann Hoff Oberlin (Franklin Lakes, NJ: Career Press, 1997)

*Your First Business*—a fill-in-the-blanks workbook and guide for $24.95; write Mainstay Company, 511 Avenue of the Americas, Suite 350, New York, NY 10011-8436.

The following items are available from the Superintendent of Documents, U.S. Printing Office, P.O., Box 371954, Pittsburgh, PA 15250 (allow 3 weeks for delivery):

Attorneys and Agents Registered to Practice before the U.S. Patent and Trademark Office—$30.

Code of Federal Regulations—$20.

General Information Concerning Patents—stock #003 004 00661 7; $2.25.

**Organizations**

U.S. Patent and Trademark Office

Department of Commerce

Washington, DC 20233

http://www.uspto.gov/

For current and proper uses of patent and copyright information.

E-Z Legal Software—offers a free (with an order) copy of the E-Z Legal Guide to Trademarks & Copyrights. Call (800) 231-9688 or visit http://www.e-zlegal.com.

Small Business Administration (SBA)—helpful booklets and videotapes (like *Business Plan for Home-Based Business* and the video *Home-Based Business: A Winning Blueprint*) for those starting a business; order by sending for the Resource Directory for Small Business Management (50¢) from the Consumer Information Catalog, Pueblo, CO 81009; http://www.pueblo.gsa.gov.

# 3

# Business Plan: A Strategy for Success

*Realize small goals to obtain big ones.*

—Norman Vincent Peale

After you have chosen an idea (or a few ideas) for a venture and evaluated it thoroughly, the next step is to prepare a business plan. A business plan is a strategic plan for your business's success. It defines your business, identifies your customers, sets your short- and long-range goals, and then maps out the strategies you need to take to reach those goals. Once it is written, it can be used as a guideline—a plan for you to review (and revise) on a regular basis to see whether your business is developing on track. A business plan is also a document that you can literally take to the bank, with the purpose of obtaining loans to finance your business.

Where can you go for help in drawing up a business plan? Books and software are available (see "Additional Information"), or you can seek help from other women business owners or contact the closest women's business development center or U.S. Small Business Development Center. The following sections describe some of the essentials of a business plan.

## Executive Summary

Your business plan should start with a title or cover page listing your company's name, address, telephone and fax numbers, and e-mail and/or Internet Web site addresses if you have them. Next is a table of contents listing the major sections of the plan and corresponding page numbers. Then comes the introduction or executive summary of your business, which can run from a couple of paragraphs to a couple pages.

The executive summary condenses the entire plan and details the important aspects of your business, the market demand for your product or services, how you will beat the competition, and the financial status and needs of your company. It gives the overview of just what your business is and where you would like it to go.

## Business Description

The business description provides your name, identifying you as the owner, and details of your experience and skills. It should also depict your business's history, give a rundown on its growth, and list the goals and objectives you have for its future and how you intend to reach them. The description should also contain the legal form you have chosen for your business—sole proprietorship (a business owned by one individual), a partnership (a business owned by two or more persons), or other legal structure (check with your accountant for more information). After the business description, you will want to provide a breakdown of the overall plan itself.

## Product or Service?

Next, you want to provide the specifics of the products or services your business offers. Define the company's parameters. If you make crafts, do you sell them retail or wholesale? If you run a service business, are your customers businesses or consumers? What makes your product or service stand out from its competitors? What benefits do your customers gain from patronizing your business? How about your prices? Where are they in relation to your competitors? Do added features justify having higher prices? Will you be able to make a profit at your current rates?

You will also want to explain how you will be able to keep up with the demand for your product or service. How are you handling the customers' demands now? Do you project growth and demand? If so, how much growth or what number of customers do you think you will be able to handle? Do you have a plan for handling customer service after your product and services are sold?

## Extra, Extra for Your Customers

Sometimes you need a few extras to bring your business's attention to new customers or to offer an incentive for old ones to return. Here are some favorite tactics:

❖ Free samples—Offer a piece of chocolate or cake at a trade show, a free tip sheet through the mail, or a free consultation to pique your customer's curiosity to want to learn more about your business.

❖ Coupons—You can join other businesses with a co-op mailing program offering discount coupons or take a display ad out in your local newspaper from which your customers can clip your coupon. Keep track of your responses to discount offers.

❖ Bonuses—Buy one, get one free; a free gift to the first fifty callers; and other little bargains help attract customers.

❖ Premiums—Giving away advertising specials such as key chains, magnets, pens, and notepads—all imprinted with your business's name and number—helps advertise your business.

## *Marketing Plan*

Your marketing plan is very important to your business plan because it identifies just who your potential customers are, being as specific as possible. Are they other home-based businesses, older adults, people with a certain income level? How large is your market? Is it growing or shrinking?

### Market Research

To answer these questions, you will have to do some market research, but how? Some companies spend thousands of dollars to hire marketing research firms. As a home-based business owner, here are some methods of market research you can do on your own for only the cost of your time:

❖ Look at the advertising sections of local newspapers and the Yellow Pages for similar businesses.

❖ Investigate such resources at a public or college library as future trend books (like *Clicking* and *Trends 2000*), market studies, census data, trade publications, and so forth.

❖ Talk to friends, relatives, and strangers for their opinions about your business concept.

❖ Talk to other women business owners in a similar venture (in a noncompeting area) to get their feedback about how they see the potential growth and expectations for their business in future years.

❖ Attend meetings and network with home-based business associations and Chambers of Commerce chapters to get some feed-back about the predicted growth of businesses like yours in the area.

❖ Ask others in your community what they like and do not like about businesses similar to yours.

After gathering this market research, describe in your business plan a summary of your results and how your business will match the competition and stand out from it.

Next, detail your advertising plans and strategy. Your business may offer an outstanding product and/or service, but unless you let your target customers know about it, it means nothing. Here are some low-cost advertising methods:

## Publicity Tips

Publicity coverage of your business can reach many potential customers. Here are some tips for getting that coverage:

* Sponsor an event—Write the story yourself and provide good-quality photos and copy for the media in case a reporter cannot attend your event.
* Invite a celebrity—One real estate business owner invites a sports star to come to his office every spring on the same Saturday as the official opening day of his town's Little League baseball season. People come in and sign a guest ledger, get a free autograph and quick photo with the celebrity, and also receive a free dogwood tree on the way out. It has become a well-known event in his community.
* Sponsor a contest and announce the winners in the local media.
* Celebrate your anniversary each year with an open house.
* Establish yourself as an expert on your business and in your industry. Write books, articles, and columns for publications, and send notices to your local papers to announce where you have been published.

* Prepare press releases to newspapers, radio stations, and cable television stations to announce your business's opening or some other special event (see the sidebar above).
* Use word-of-mouth referrals from satisfied customers. Offer a coupon or discount to your regular customers if they recommend someone else to your business.
* Post flyers on community bulletin boards.
* Create business cards. These are "billboards" for your business. With today's desktop publishing software you can design and print your own. This is good, especially in the first months of your business, because you may want to add

information to or delete information from your cards, and you only have to print up as many as you need. Make sure they contain your name, telephone and fax numbers, and e-mail and/or Web site address. Do not forget to use both sides of the card for a listing of your special services.

✤ Donate to a community auction one of your products or a coupon for a one-time visit of your service.

✤ Join a local home-based business association and pool together to have your businesses listed in a directory for distribution in the community and on the Internet.

Here are some additional methods of effective advertising, depending on your budget:

✤ Promotional and information newsletters
✤ Home shopping channels (local and national) if you have a product
✤ Classified cable television ads
✤ Trade shows and fairs
✤ Seminars and talks or speeches
✤ Weekly column in your local newspaper with tips on your topic

### Advertising Plan

In your business plan, you want to list the methods of advertising and how much your business budget will allow you to spend. Start with as many low-cost forms as you can—flyers, networking and referrals, classified ads, and so forth. Devise some method of coding or tracking the responses so you can evaluate the effectiveness of each ad. You can do this by adding letters to your address or post office box (e.g., Box 286-P—P for *Parents* magazine if you were selling children's items, or Dept. "P") or simply by asking people who inquire about your business where they heard about you.

### Calculating Expenses

Before you know how much money you will need to finance your business, you have to list your fixed costs and calculate your variable costs. As a home-based business owner, you will have fixed expenses, such as a telephone service and on-line connection fees, and variable expenses having to do with the costs of producing your products and services based on sales volume. To calculate these expenses, you have to consider various elements, described in the following sections.

### Equipment

Decide what minimum equipment you definitely need to start your business and what optional equipment you can purchase as your business begins to earn money. Almost all businesses these days will need a computer (with the peripherals of a modem, back-up disks, printer, and office suite and business-related software), if only to write your business plan and help keep records. Other important purchases are a telephone with conference calling and fax capabilities, your business promotional materials, ergonomic office furniture, and office supplies. You can start with the minimum of borrowed, used, rented, or leased equipment and purchase what your business actually needs as you run it for a while.

Ask other home-based owners what equipment they recommend, and check with the associations in your industry for recommendations of specific equipment, supplies, and software that can be extremely time- and cost-saving to your business.

### Tax Information

To prepare your business plan, you will want to know about deductions for equipment depreciation, mileage for the business use of your car, sales tax and wholesale tax, business use of your home, business tax fees, and so on, which all affect your business's expenses. That is why it is important to engage an accountant and a bookkeeper to help you set up an accounting system with which to monitor and record your income and expenditures. Make sure they are familiar with assisting home-based businesses.

Also available are a number of good software accounting programs, software for your specific industry, and reference books to help you keep records for tax purposes (see "Additional Information" at the end of this chapter).

## Financing

One of the purposes of creating a business plan is to obtain a bank loan. However, many banks are cautious about giving a loan to a start-up business or even to a home-based business that has been operating for two or three years. If you are going to approach a bank for a loan, talk to other home-based business owners to get recommendations for "friendly" banks. Make sure you have paid off any credit cards loans that you might have used to get your business running, and check to see how your own personal credit history rates. Microloans are also offered through private groups and agencies backed by the U.S. Small Business Administration (SBA).

For start-ups and small firms, the SBA's most popular program is the LowDoc Program. Qualified individuals can secure loans from a few hundred dollars to $100,000, with the money being used for start-up, expansion, working capital, or equipment or supply purposes. Contact your local SBA office or Small Business Development Center for a microloan lender in your area.

If you prefer not to go to a bank for a loan, here are some options you may want to consider:

✣ Specialty loans are now being offered by local banks in which a one-page application can land you an unsecured credit line or loan ranging from $2,500 to $50,000. Contact:
Wells Fargo/National Association of Women Business Owners (NAWBO), (800) 359-3557, extension 120
Bank of America/Women Inc., (800) 930-3993
✣ Cash awards or prize money is offered by industry organizations or groups. *Awards, Honors, and Prizes*, a library reference guide by Gale Research, lists more than twenty-thousand sources.
✣ Family, friends, and relatives help many women start businesses by lending them money. If you opt for this approach, make sure you conduct the loan like any other professional transaction and have a contract drawn up with payment terms and so forth. It can help eliminate hard feelings later on.

❖ "Angel" investors are wealthy investors seeking to invest in small businesses. Many will want some involvement with your business, however, in exchange for funding. Look for these by networking within a business or industry association.

❖ Contact your state representative's and/or senator's office to have them help steer you to your state's agencies that may handle small business support, including financing.

❖ Ask customers to prepay. Give them good reasons or some benefits for doing so.

❖ Barter with other home-based and small businesses. Through an exchange of products and/or services, you can help preserve your cash. The downside is that you will not receive any tax benefits, but check with your accountant to be sure. For more information on bartering, send a SASE to International Reciprocal Trade Association, 9513 Beach Mill Rd., Great Falls, VA 22066.

❖ Downsize your own living expenses and expenditures to save more money to invest in your business. If this method will involve family members living with you, check with them first before you embark on this strategy.

These are just a few alternative ways to obtain financing. You may brainstorm and come up with methods that work for you. Women entrepreneurs can uncover more funding options through two free resources: *The Small Business Financial Guide*, MasterCard International, (800) 821-6176; and *Access to Credit: A Guide for Lenders and Women Owners of Small Businesses*, Federal Reserve Bank of Chicago, Public Information, P.O. Box 834, Chicago, IL 60604.

## Profit and Loss Statements

Every business plan should also contain a profit and loss statement, a cash flow projection, and a balance sheet. These analyses will help you assess the minimum amount of income you'll need to operate your business and adjust your pricing to so you can begin to make a profit.

Established businesses will need a current balance sheet and income statement, tax returns for the past three years, and financial reports for the past three years.

Start-up businesses will need a balance sheet for the day the business starts and an income statement or profit and loss statement projection for two years.

## Cash Flow Projections

The start-up and established business may be asked to supply a cash flow analysis month by month for two years. To generate this, you need to calculate your break-even formula—the point where income equals outgo. Calculate the break-even point for the year by determining how many dollars in sales you must generate to make a profit. Divide this figure by twelve for a monthly breakdown. However, be aware that some allowances must be made if you have a seasonal business or typically slow sales periods during your fiscal year.

Correct pricing of your service and/or product is crucial for keeping your business "out of the red" and making a profit. Eileen Glick,* president of the Home Based Business Association of Arizona, says the key to price is to "charge what you're worth, be worth what you charge. Be proud, not embarrassed about selling something of value to others!"

## Self-Evaluation

The conclusion of your business plan should answer such questions as: When do you project your business will break even? Do you have cash reserves to cover slow periods and unforeseen expenses? Do you have a contingency strategic plan in place if the business is growing slower than expected (i.e., do you have other market avenues to explore)? The summary may also include such details as the amount of money you want to bor-

---

*Eileen Glick is coauthor of *No Apologies Pricing: How to Price Your Services and Products for Profit*. To order, send $9.95 + $1.25 shipping and handling to HBBA, P.O. 190, Phoenix, AZ 85001.

row, a payment plan for repaying it, and any other related information you believe should be included.

Even if you never take your business plan to a bank, it is a valuable tool for you to return to again and again to measure your business's current progress (or regression). You will need to refer to it often to focus on the goals you planned at the onset or to modify to find the most profitable market niche for your home-based business.

## Additional Information

### Accounting

*Software*

QuickBooks (www.intuit.com/quickbooks/), for Macintosh and Windows; (800) 446-8848.

Peachtree First Accounting (www.peachtree.com/product/pawmain.htm), for Windows 3.1; (800) 336-1420; also Peachtree Complete Accounting for Windows; (800) 247-3224.

M.Y.O.B. Accounting (www.bestware.com/product.htm), for Macintosh and Windows; (800) 322-6962.

### Advertising

*Books*

*Do It Yourself Advertising and Promotion: How to Produce Great Ads, Brochures, Catalogs, Direct Mail, Web Sites, and Much More* by Fred Hahn and Kenneth Mangun (New York: Wiley, 1996)

*Getting Business to Come to You* by Paul and Sarah Edwards (New York: Jeremy P. Tarcher/Putnam Publishing Group, 1997)

*Growing Your Home Business: A Complete Guide to Proven Sales and Marketing Strategies* by Kim T. Gordon (Upper Saddle River, NJ: Prentice Hall, 1996)

*Promoting Your Business with Free or Almost Free Publicity* by Donna G. Albrecht (Upper Saddle River, NJ: Prentice Hall, 1997)

## Obtaining Merchant Status to Accept Credit Cards

Many people today simply prefer the convenience of paying by credit card. To get their business—especially if yours is a mail-order business—you need to be able to accept credit card payments. To do this, you will have to work with a bank that will transfer the money into your account within a day or two of your sale, and then collect the money from your customer. For this service you will have to pay your bank a commission ranging from 1.5 to 5 percent for each transaction.

Monthly support or rental fees for equipment will also be an expense. Banks traditionally do not want to work with home-based business. You should ask other home-based business owners who take credit card orders with whom they have accounts, and then you should personally meet with bank personnel to discuss under what terms they will back you. Contact other banks if one turns you

*Surefire Solutions for Growing Your Home-Based Business: Win More Clients, Charge What You're Worth, Collect What You're Owed and Get the Money You Need* by David Shaefer (Chicago: Dearborn, 1997)

### Business Plan

*Books*

*Business Plan for Home-Based Business,* booklet by the SBA for $4; order from the Resource Directory for Small Business Management, SBA Publications, P.O. Box 46521, Denver, CO 80201-46521.

*Business Plans Handbook* by Gale Research (Detroit, MI: Gale Research, 1997); "a collection of actual business plans that today's entrepreneurs can modify to fit their business development needs."

down. If none will work with you, you can ask your bank to recommend an independent sales organization (ISO) that can match you with a bank that meets your needs. The disadvantage is that you will probably pay more to get the merchant status than if you opened a retail storefront.

Before you sign with any bank, though, make sure it will be worth it to you and your customers. For more information, read the following:

❖ *The Complete Guide to Getting and Keeping Visa/ MasterCard Status* by Pearl Sax and Larry Schwartz (National Association of Credit Card Merchants, updated annually); $199.95; (561) 737-8700

❖ *How to Get, Keep and Use Visa, MasterCard & American Express Credit Card Merchant Status to Earn Millions: Even If You Work at Home, Operate a Mail-Order Business or Are Just Starting a New Company* (InterWorld Corporation, 1992); $49.95; ISBN 1-880199-95-5

❖ *Master Directory of Bank Credit Card Programs* (Gordon Press, 1992); $255.95; ISBN 0-8490-5353-6

*How to Write a Successful Business Plan* by Jerre G. Lewis and Leslie D. Renn (1996); Lewis & Renn Associates, 10315 Harmony Dr., Interlochen, MI 49643; $14.95 + $3 shipping and handling.

*The Successful Business Plan: Secrets and Strategies* by Rhonda Abrams (Grants Pass, OR: Oasis, 1993). Abrams also hosts the "Idea Cafe: The Small Business Channel," http://www. ideacafe.com.

### Software
Success, Inc., by Dynamic Pathways, (714) 721-8601
Business Plan Pro, by Palo Alto Software, (541) 683-6162: www.bplans.com

The SBA Internet site, http://www.sbaonline.sba.gov, has much information for small business. One section describes in length about business start-ups and the content of a business plan.

## Financing

### Books
*ABCs of Borrowing*; SBA Publications, P.O. Box 46521, Denver, CO 80201-0030; explains what lenders look for and how entrepreneurs should prepare to borrow money for their business.

*Financial Savvy for the Self-Employed* by Grace W. Weinstein (New York: Holt, 1996)

### On-line Sources
America Business Financing Directory, http://www.business finance.com; information business financing

BankWeb, http://www.bankweb.com; a large listing of banks, state by state

FinanceHub, http://www.FinanceHub.com; range of resources and links to venture capitalists and banks. Entrepreneurs can list their business proposal for $10 and search a venture capitalist base (eleven thousand entries) for $250.

Also check the general search engines of Alta Vista, Galaxy, WebCrawler, and Yahoo! for "Small Business Information."

## Marketing

### Books
*The Market Planning Guide* by David Bangs (Chicago: Upstart, 1995)

*One-Stop Marketing: What Every Smart Business Owner Needs to Know* by Jonathan Trivers (New York: Wiley, 1996)

### Software
Marketing Plan Pro, a step-by-step guide to creating a marketing plan; check in software stores or call Palo Alto Software, Inc., at (800) 229-7526.

### Other Sources
The Home Shopping Network, 1 HSN, St. Petersburg, FL 33729

QVC/Vendor Relations, 1365 Enterprise Dr., West Chester, PA 19380

*Seminar: How to Make It Big in the Seminar Business* by Paul Karasik (New York: McGraw-Hill, 1996)

## Promotional Materials

*Books*

*Home-Based Catalog Marketing: A Success Guide for Entrepreneurs* by William J. Bond (New York: McGraw-Hill, 1993)

*The Perfect Sales Piece: A Complete Do-It-Yourself Guide to Creating Brochures, Catalogs, Fliers and Pamphlets* by Robert Bly (New York: Wiley, 1994)

*1000+ Stationery Designs: Instant Image Design Guide* by Val Cooper; Point Pacific Press, P.O. Box 4333, North Hollywood, CA 91617

*Software*

Easy Business Cards for Windows, Claris, (408) 727-8227; 290 predesigned business card styles. Works with PaperDirect papers, (201) 271-9200.

My Advanced Brochures, Mailers & More, CD for Windows; My Software Company, 1259 El Camino Real, Suite 167, Menlo Park, CA 94025-4227; http://www.mysoftware.com

## Taxes

*Book*

*How to Keep Your Hard-Earned Money: The Tax Saving Handbook for the Self-Employed* by Henry Ayim Fellman (Boulder, CO: Solutions Press, 1996)

*On-line Source*

IRS: http://www.irs.ustreas.gov

## Trade Shows

*Books*

*Trade Shows Worldwide, 1997* by Gale Research (Detroit, MI: Gale Research, 1997); check in the reference section of your public or college library.

*How to Get the Most Out of Trade Shows* by Steve Miller (Lincoln-wood, IL: NTC Contemporary Publishing, 1995)

**On-line Source**

Trade shows Web site: http://www.tscentral.com

**Other Sources**

Consultant: Trade Show Xpress, "The 'How-To' Specialists for Exhibit Marketing," 1801 South Federal Highway, Suite 214, Delray Beach, FL 33483; telephone (561) 279-4046, fax (561) 276-7322.

Trade show for entrepreneurs: *Entrepreneur* Magazine's Small Business Expo; national shows featuring business opportunities and so forth. Call (800) 421-2300 for a show location nearest you.

# Trade Show Tips

Exhibiting at a trade show can be an effective way to introduce your product to many potential customers. As a home-based business, you will want to start small, perhaps exhibiting at a small show sponsored by your local Chamber of Commerce or your local home-based business association, especially if your product or service is targeted to businesses and consumers in your area. A major or national trade show would be appropriate if you wish to reach a regional or national customer base. Whether it be a small or large show, here are some helpful tips:

❖ Try to attend the shows at which you plan to exhibit before you reserve a space to get an idea of the booth set-ups, attendees, space, and competition for your business.

❖ Look for the ideal location for a booth that would allow you to have the most people walk by.

❖ Set up a temporary booth beforehand in your home or garage so you can evaluate its appearance.

❖ Have plenty of promotional materials and/or samples for visitors to take.

❖ Do not make your booth too "crowded." You have only four to six seconds to get the attention of your prospect. Make your advertising simple and explanatory.

❖ Learn from other exhibitors, especially those who seem to attract the most people. If you have someone working with you, take some time to view the other booths, and also get some feedback from others.

❖ Have a method of getting interested people's names and addresses (a drawing, a guestbook inviting them to be on your mailing list), and follow up.

❖ Evaluate the show in respect to your business. Summarize it in writing so you can decide whether you should do the show again. Take a note of your mistakes and successes so you can learn from them.

# 4

# Who Can You Turn to for Help? Your Experts

*As a general rule, the most successful people in life are those who have the best information.*

—Benjamin Disraeli

As a home-based business owner, you will sometimes feel overwhelmed by all the jobs you have to do: record keeping, marketing, writing ad copy and planning advertising, purchasing supplies, fulfilling orders, handling customer service, and completing a multitude of other tasks, not to mention actually producing your products or providing your service! The truth is, though, you cannot do everything. This chapter will discuss some of the people and groups that can help you start and keep your business running.

## Lawyer

A lawyer can assist you in some or all of the following ways:

* Advising you about the legal structure of your business
* Helping you register a fictitious name—called doing business as (DBA)—if you do not want to use your name

❖ Advising you about methods of getting overdue accounts paid
   to you
❖ Assisting you in drawing up contracts with independent contractors and other businesses
❖ Advising you on the legalities of licensing, franchising, and
   general conduct of business

Take your time to find a lawyer with whom you feel comfortable and who has some experience with the legalities of
home-based businesses.

## Accountant or Bookkeeper

Actually, you can use the services of both an accountant and
bookkeeper for your business. If you do not have time to do your
own bookkeeping or would rather hire an independent, you will
find she can assist you in designing a record-keeping system
that is easy for you to follow. Your bookkeeper can come at
weekly, monthly, or other designated intervals. A bookkeeper
can also assist you in billing and collecting money owed to you.
She can help you have your business's records arranged so that
you can pay your quarterly estimated federal taxes (which self-
employed people must do) while making it easier for your
accountant to do your income taxes.

Your accountant will know the current tax laws affecting
home-based and small businesses and will prepare your
annual income taxes or be there to advise you. Make sure you
hire one who is familiar with deductions that can be taken for
home-based businesses.

## Insurance Agent

Insurance is very important, even with a home-based business.
You will need advice from one or more agents about the following:

❖ Business insurance—With your business, you will need
   a certificate of insurance to be hired as an independent
   contractor or to be bonded (insurance covering accidental
   breakage or damage if you work in clients' homes). Make an

appointment with your insurance agent to discuss your business operations and what type of policy she recommends.

❖ Homeowner's insurance—You may need extra coverage for any specialized equipment you buy and liability for delivery persons and customers.

❖ Health insurance—If you do not have health coverage under a spouse's health plan, then you will have to pay your own health insurance. You may want to join a local or national business association that offers group health plans such as the American Entrepreneurs Association (AEA), National Association for the Self-Employed, and others (see the "Miscellaneous Sources of Help" chapter). The IRS now allows self-employed business people to deduct 40 percent of health insurance costs.* Also talk to your agent about disability insurance, in the event you would not be able to work.

## Additional Experts

Here are additional experts whom you can hire or maybe barter with for their services if they, too, are small service business owners:

❖ Printer—You may own a quality laser printer and desktop publishing software, but printers usually have more equipment than you could afford to buy. They are important for your business because they can produce glossy brochures, postcards, copies of your newsletters, flyers, labels, advertising specialties, business stationery, and so on. They also often provide shipping and fax services. You may find, like me, that you will go to more than one printer because of their areas of specialization and prices for certain projects. You want a printer who produces professional-looking materials because those items represent your business.

❖ Desktop publisher—This expert can design your documents, manuals, business cards and stationery, and other pro-

---

*For more information on the specific IRS guidelines, request IRS Publication 533, *Self-Employment Tax,* and IRS Publication 502, *Medical and Dental Expenses,* by calling (800) 829-3676.

## Business Documents: How Long Should You Keep Them?

You are required to keep certain business documents, but do you know for how long? Here is what business experts suggest:*

❖ Three years: your business's monthly records involving credit, sales, purchases, and balances
❖ Four years: expired insurance policies, bank statements and deposit slips, and receiving and shipping records
❖ Seven years: income tax returns, checks, earning records, and independent contract records

*Consult with your accountant if you are unsure about keeping a document or record from your business.

motional materials and provide scanning for your photos and drawings.

❖ Consultants—These include business coaches, marketing consultants, business plan specialists, home-based business advisers, computer consultants, and specialists within your particular industry.

Whichever experts' services you use, develop good working relationships with them because you may need them in a business emergency!

### Networking Sources

Networking can be one of the best ways for you to get more customers for your home-based business. It is sometimes hard for someone who is on the shy side to mix with others, but you can do it in other ways than arranging face-to-face meetings. Here are a few suggestions:

❖ Internet—Business groups, business sites and links, and e-mail are all ways you can talk business without ever leaving your chair. For example, the Field of Dreams Web site (http://www.fodreams.com) lists many women's businesses around the country and their e-mail addresses so you can contact them and introduce yourself. There are many other links you can tap into as well. I network with a number of writers and business women across the country via the Internet. They not only have been valuable sources of information but have also become good friends.

♣ Associations—Business associations operate in most communities, and now more home-based associations are forming all over the country. Contact other women business owners to see which ones they feel are helpful to them. These associations and other organizations like the Chambers of Commerce offer a variety of support, programs, and speakers to help their members learn better business tips and management.

It is important, though, that you feel comfortable within your group and that you believe the time you invest is worthwhile to you. If you cannot find a business association that fits your business needs, start your own. The women home-based business owners in my tricounty area formed a group of their own. We meet only once or twice a year—and most of us do belong to at least one other business group—but we find that we can, as mothers, grandmothers, and business owners, call each other any time to ask a question, which we do often. We reserve a community room in a local bank for our biannual meetings.

♣ Small Business Development Centers (SBDCs) or Women's Business Development Centers—These groups sponsor women's entrepreneurial conferences, workshops, and seminars where you can learn about and discuss business topics as well as meet other women entrepreneurs.

♣ Business opportunity fairs, expos, and trade shows—These events are held near most large cities. Attending one will give you the opportunity to view displays and to meet other entrepreneurs who have exhibits for their businesses. Look in business publications and newsletters for dates and events.

Just remember that networking works both ways. If you wish others to send information, contacts, and customers your way, you should, in turn, reciprocate and notify your networking friends of any opportunities you hear of for them.

## Small Business Incubators

If your home business has grown to the point that you feel you should either expand or move out of your home, you might want to look into joining a business incubator. A business incubator is an association of small businesses that are usually housed in one building and share conference spaces, support staff, Internet access, delivery and mail services, and other business services that a small business could not afford on its own. Incubators also offer print and video services, expert advice by the full-time staffers who usually have business management backgrounds, and regular classes on various business topics.

Incubator facilitators not only help the business owners in learning business basics but also work with the community in which they are located to help acquaint community members with the ventures that are being nurtured. This way the community can also patronize these fledgling entrepreneurial pursuits.

The number of business incubators in the United States has grown from ten to five hundred in the last fifteen years. If you think you may want to apply to enter an incubator, visit one or two and talk to the business owners there to get some feedback. Contact the National Business Incubation Association (listed at the end of this chapter) for more information.

## Customers

Customers can be a great help to your home-based business, and not only because they pay your bills. Their feedback can help you improve your product and/or service; they can refer your business to their friends and acquaintances; and they can also pass on information to you that could be of benefit to your business. Here are some tips to keep your customers happy and loyal to your business:

✤ Offer something to your customers like a newsletter, a punch card (so many visits equals one free visit or small gift), or other special item that shows you care about them.
✤ Keep in touch by sending a birthday card offering a discount, or send them a photocopy of some information you know would be of interest to them.
✤ Give a little extra at times by providing an item or your services to a loyal customer who has an emergency.
✤ Treat all of your customers with courtesy and respect.
✤ Handle all customer complaints or concerns promptly. If one customer has repeated complaints, try to resolve the complaint satisfactorily and politely offer the names of other similar businesses that may be of better service.

### Others

✤ A business mentor can be an excellent source of information for your business start-up. If there is a professional and trade association in your business's industry, just by joining you can meet others in your type of business. Some even offer special mentoring programs. If none exist, you can join a local home-based business association or local business owners' group and link up with another woman business owner to gain experience and on-the-job training in your industry. Remember, too, when you are successful, to take the time to help other entrepreneurs or be a business mentor.
✤ Family ties can be a support system to your business. Children can be paid to do simple office duties. Spouses can help with record-keeping and bookkeeping and participate in "power meetings" or brainstorming sessions to help originate new ideas for your business. Just do not expect more than they can give, and appreciate whatever ways they do assist you.
✤ Banks and bankers can also be helpmates to your business. You should establish a relationship, however, with more than one bank. Here are some reasons why:

Different banks might offer different rates for different services.

Some may have special services for businesses and are "friendlier" to smaller businesses, with special loans and other programs.

Banks often merge and may make mistakes in information relating to your business or offer less personal customer service, or some banks close, causing a disruption that could similarly disturb your business management.

## Additional Information

### Recommended Reading

*The Buyer's Guide to Business Insurance* by Don Bury and Larry Heischman(Grants Pass, OR: Oasis, 1994).

*Collection Techniques for Small Business* by Gini Graham Scott and John J. Harrison (Grants Pass, OR: Oasis, 1996)

*Customer Service for Dummies* by Karen Leland and Keith Bailey(Foster City, CA: IDG Worldwide, 1996)

*50 Powerful Ways to Win New Customers* by Paul R. Timm (Franklin Lakes, NJ: Career Press, 1997)

*Small Business Networking for Dummies* by Dummies Technology Press (Foster City, CA: IDG Worldwide, 1997); also available as CD-ROM

*Tax Planning for the One-Person Business* by James Bucheister (Windsor, CA: Wavemaker, 1996). Ordering address: P.O. Box 1485, Windsor, CA 95492.

### On-line Source

Nolo Press—http://www.nolo.com—is known for its do-it-yourself legal books. Other legal information also is available at this site.

# How to Make Your Bank More "Friendly"

I have taken a number of articles to my bankers that quote favorable statistics about investing in women's businesses because I want them to know that women business owners are as good a risk in paying back their business loans as men. They have appreciated the information, and it helped make them aware of the women business owners in their area. Here are four tips to help make your bank more "friendly" to you and your business:

❖ Get to know a bank's personnel and management.
❖ Rather than make electronic deposits, come into the bank to meet the staff and ask a quick business question (do that during a bank's off hours). Letting them know, too, how you are involved with your community (participation in business associations, schools, local organizations, etc.) will help them to know you are committed to your area.
❖ Treat all personnel and staff as though they were your customers—with courtesy and respect. If a problem arises with your accounts, approach it with a problem-solving attitude instead of an accusatory tone.
❖ Follow the bank's procedures of listing checks, making deposits, and so forth, to lessen mistakes and to make your, and their, banking more efficient and smooth.
❖ Take the time to let the president and executives of your bank know why it is beneficial for both of you to work for entrepreneurs in your community—especially those living in your community!

# 5

# The Internet and Your Home-Based Business

*Preparing the next generation for economic literacy and empowerment is a critical element of support for women's economic development.*

—Jane Godfrey, *Independent Means*

## Does Your Business Need a Web Site?

*Small Business Success* (1997) reported a Nielsen survey of March 1997 stating that nearly one out of every four adults in the United States and Canada—or 50.6 million people—are Internet users, more than twice the number eighteen months earlier. Small businesses have been slow in the past to set up their own Web sites, but with an estimated $200 billion in Internet-related commerce projected in 2000, no large, small, or home-based business can afford not to take advantage of the Internet's potential.

How can the Internet help your business? It can reach worldwide customers and markets, advertise your business (a potential market of twenty million people—expected to double by the year 2000, according to the Cowles/Simba research firm; *Home Office Computing*, June 1997), cut your mailing costs, give you

51

# Questions to Ask Your Internet Service Provider

Before you design your own pages, you will need to pick an ISP (Internet service provider) to supply your page space on the Web. Here are some questions to ask (and do not forget to ask other home-based owners who their ISP providers are and whether they would recommend them):

❖ How much will you charge? Is it a monthly or a flat fee?
❖ Will I have direct access to my page and be able to update the pages as often as I like?
❖ Will I be able to have links to my site on the service's main page?
❖ Will I be able to have a counter for the number of "hits," or visitors, to my page?
❖ Will I be able to have image maps and data services so I can have order forms and so forth for my visitors?
❖ Can you advise me how to get my site listed on more search engines and databases?

networking opportunities via e-mail, do research, plan travel, allow you to join a trade association, and much more. But can a Web page or site help a home-based business? Definitely yes! Start-up costs for a Web site can run anywhere from $9.95 a month for a simple page to $20,000 or more for a multiframe, elaborate interactive site.

Here are some additional reasons an Internet site can benefit your business:

❖ It can display and advertise your products, twenty-four hours a day, and can be kept current with little or no expense. You can list a price list and 800 number for easy ordering.
❖ It can "personalize" your business if you provide your visitors with the history of your business, your philosophy, and daily tips that your visitors can use.

❖ You can provide links to other helpful sites (and vice versa) for your customers.

❖ Having a Web site can allow you to compete with much larger competitors—you are the same size in the eyes of the customer.

❖ It can help to improve customer service and enhance customer loyalty.

## Guidelines for Advertising on the Internet

What makes a good Web site? Here are some factors to consider before you hire a Web site developer or use one of the software programs available to create your own:

1. What do you want your Web site to accomplish (i.e., introduce people to you and your products, inform your visitors, etc.)?
2. How much time and money do you have to devote to your Web site?
3. Study effective Web sites by researching your competitors, reading publications like *Web Week, Webmaster,* and *Internet World.* Then decide how you will attract your visitors and the methods you will use to get them to react: order, sign a guestbook, send an e-mail message, request information, and so forth. You want to encourage feedback from your visitors.
4. Keep your site from becoming "stale" by regularly updating it with new content.
5. Decide if you will have your site created by a Web service, Web designer, Web company, or yourself, and then have it installed via the Internet service provider.

## Additional Information

### Recommended Reading
*Build a Web Site in a Day* by Thomas Wrona and Elisabeth Parker (Chapel Hill, NC: Ventana Communications Group, 1997)
*Build Your Own Web Site* by Louis Kahn and Laura Logan (Redmond, WA: Microsoft Press, 1996)

## On-Line Marketing Tips

❖ Put up a simple Web page or a more complex design by a Web designer.
❖ Put your e-mail address and Web site address on your business cards, business stationery, and other promotional materials you use.
❖ Get listed on as many search engines and directories as you can.
❖ Arrange links with related sites.
❖ E-mail with other business owners through association listings.
❖ Do not send unsolicited e-mail (this is known as "spam") or you may get "flamed" (receive hundreds of nasty e-mail messages in retaliation).
❖ Provide free and helpful information and/or tips on a regular basis.
❖ Have a "FAQ" section ("Frequently Asked Questions").
❖ Gather testimonials from satisfied clients, asking for permission to post them on your home page.

*Cheapskate's Guide to Building a Web Site with Windows 95/NT* by Pete Palmer (Upper Saddle River, NJ: Prentice-Hall Professional, 1998)

*Cyberpower for Business: How to Profit from the Information Superhighway* by Wally Bock and Jeff Senné (Franklin Lakes, NJ: Career Press, 1996)

*121 Internet Businesses You Can Start from Home: Plus a Beginner's Guide to Starting a Business Online* by Ron E. Gielgun (Brooklyn, NY: Actium, 1997)

### On-line Sources*

InterNIC, http://rs.internic.net, deals with domain registration and the costs for registration.

*See also "Internet Sites" in the "Miscellaneous Sources of Help" chapter.

Mecklermedia's The List, http://thelist.iworld.com, provides information about more than 3,500 Internet service providers. Submit-it, http://www.submit-it.com, is a simple way to post your Web address and twenty-word description to more than two hundred search engines and directories.

**Software**

Free Web site, with *Dun & Bradstreet's Business Solutions in a Box,* "a business builder and problem solver." Write Dun & Bradstreet, Attn: Mass Marketing Group, 3 Sylvan Way, Parsippany, NJ 07054-9947.

Microsoft Publisher 97 makes Web publishing accessible to small businesses without programming experience. Look for it at your favorite software store.

Virus protection software—you should have this installed if you plan to download information from the Internet. Check your local computer store for such software as Norton AntiVirus, WebScan, and Dr. Solomon's Anti-Virus Toolkit.

WebWise: The Cyberia Guide to Smart Web Publishing—develop Web sites without learning HTML; CD-ROM for PCs and Macs produced by McGraw-Hill, $39.95; call (800) 2-MCGRAW for ordering information.

# 6

# Franchises, Distributorships, MLMs, and Other Home Business Opportunities

*Never trust for something to turn up instead of working to turn up something.*

—Anonymous

If you would like to start a home-based business but would prefer not to start from scratch, you may want to look into investing in a franchise, a distributorship, or multilevel marketing (MLM; also called network marketing).

### Franchises

What is a franchise? With a franchise you (the franchisee) pay a company (the franchisor) for the right to sell and distribute its products and use its trademark and/or trade name. You pay an initial franchise fee, and there may or may not be ongoing royalty fees, advertising costs, or mandatory costs of purchasing the company's supplies needed to run the franchise.

According to the International Franchise Association, in 1994, franchises accounted for 40 percent of all retail sales in this country and employed seven million people. Their popularity is growing, and many new franchise opportunities will continue to open up and increase in the next century. As with any business, though, you should consider various recommendations and cautions before you invest your money. You can buy into a profitable business, or you can make the biggest financial mistake of your life! Be enthusiastic, but take the time to research these business opportunities. Be like one woman who left a corporate position to become an entrepreneur and now runs a successful food delivery franchise. It took her a year to investigate her franchise. She visited the headquarters and other franchise owners in different regions and did other research until she was satisfied this was a legitimate opportunity for her.

Here are some considerations when buying a franchise:*

+ Does this franchise have name recognition? Do people identify the franchise's name with the goods and services provided?
+ How is the franchisor going to help you gain experience and training to run this franchise? Ongoing technical support? New product development? Ongoing marketing programs?
+ Is the franchisor growth oriented with plans and support to expand the company, or does he or she just want to sell franchises?
+ How many of the franchises have closed? If 20 percent or more have shut down, that could indicate problems.
+ Has the franchisor furnished you with the legal disclosure documents as stated by law? The required Uniform Franchise Offering Circular (UFOC) should be read carefully because it provides such details about the franchisor as its corporate name, its place and date of incorporation, a basic

---

*There are a number of other concerns when purchasing a franchise. Go by the franchise associations' and FTC guidelines, and consult with a lawyer familiar with franchise contracts before you enter into any agreement.

description of the franchise being offered, as well as financial information concerning audited statements, fees to franchisors (and if any negotiated a lower fee—you can negotiate for your fees, but franchisors do not usually tell you so), and other vital information that is a must read!

❖ Will your franchise operation have an exclusive territory? You do not want another one opening two blocks away.

❖ Will you like running under the guidelines of this franchise—having to follow set regulations or buy from certain suppliers—in other words, not having as much creative leeway as you would with your own business?

### Tips for Success

❖ Know what you really want. Make sure you will enjoy running this franchise on a daily basis. Work in one for a period of time to make sure you like the operation with its products and services.

❖ Be certain you can afford the fees and expenses. Even a franchise with a recognized name will take time to attract loyal customers and thus make profits.

## Ten Hottest Franchises for Now and into the Year 2000

According to the International Franchising Association, the best franchising prospects are these:

1. Advertising services
2. Automotive repairs and services
3. Children's services/educational products
4. Hair salons
5. Health aids and services
6. Home repair/remodeling/carpet cleaning
7. Mail processing/package shipping and wrapping
8. Personnel and temporary help services
9. Printing and copying
10. Telecommunications

❧ Beware of franchisors that promise you quick riches and accept you as a franchisee too readily. A legitimate franchisor will want to make sure you will help a franchise grow.
❧ As with any new business, your own or a turnkey operation (a business already running), you may end up spending seventy to eighty hours a week getting it running.
❧ Spend the time to research the company, its financial record, how it treats it franchisees, and so on, and you may end up with a very suitable (and profitable) relationship.

### Direct Selling: Distributorships and Multilevel Marketing

Generally, a less expensive way to be affiliated with another established business is to be a distributor for it. As a distributor, you are a wholesaler who has purchased the rights to market one company's goods (not numerous companies' products as an independent sales rep would do) to customers within a given territory—though not always exclusive. With multilevel marketing (MLM; also known as network marketing), a distributor not only sells the company's products but will enlist others to sell these products or services under their supervision—called downline. You as the recruiter would then receive a percentage of the enlistees' sales.

According to the Direct Selling Association, 65 to 70 percent of direct sales are made through MLM, but these account for only 3 percent of all retail sales. Whether you sell cosmetics or baskets, thousands of distributors have made money with legitimate companies such as Mary Kay Cosmetics or Longaberger Baskets. Unfortunately, there have been many bogus network marketing programs that were nothing more than pyramid scams, and the people who were on the "bottom" of the pyramid lost all their money.

As a distributor in network marketing, you are in business for yourself and set your own hours. Generally, you purchase the starter kit with order forms, samples, and supplies that you sell directly to the consumer. Here are some questions to consider concerning network marketing:

❧ Do you like or use the products or services you will be selling?

## When Checking the Background of a Networking Marketing Opportunity, Ask . . .

. . . the Direct Marketing Association and the Multi-Level Marketing Association whether they have information on the company about which you are seeking information.

. . . your Better Business Bureau, state's attorney general's office, and/or state's department of consumer affairs whether they have on record any complaints about the company.

. . . the Federal Trade Commission (FTC) ([202] 326-2222) whether any formal complaints have been registered.

. . . the company itself a set of questions, and request referrals from a number of others who have invested in this company's business opportunity. Then call those owners to get their opinions.

✤ Do you like the persons with whom you will be dealing? Do your instincts say to trust them?

✤ How long has this company been in business? Can you talk to a number of other distributors with this company?

✤ Is the company product oriented rather than recruitment oriented?

The Direct Selling Association alerts you to avoid the following:

✤ Salespeople who deprecate other products, firms, or salespersons.

✤ Firms that take advantage of your lack of experience.

✤ Companies that falsely announce that you have won a contest or that they are taking a survey.

✤ Companies that charge an entry fee much more than the cost of a sales kit.

❖ Firms that pressure you to purchase a large number of supplies and products but will not repurchase them if you decide to withdraw from the business.

❖ Companies that sell few or no products to customers.

If you work with a legitimate company and feel confident to handle the decisions required as a distributor and network marketer, you can be a success at this home-based, money-making, alternative business venture.

## Home Business Opportunities

Besides franchises, distributorships, and MLMs, many other home business opportunities are advertised in magazines and newspapers and on radio and television. As with the previously discussed business ventures, approach any opportunity with a skeptical attitude before signing any checks. Here are several important questions to consider:

❖ As an owner of this business opportunity, what will your daily business activities involve?

❖ How much money do you want to earn?

❖ How much time do you have to give to this new venture?

❖ What is the asking price of the opportunity, and is it negotiable?

❖ Can you pay by credit card (much less of a danger of losing your money than if you pay by cash or check)?

❖ Can you talk to other buyers of the business opportunity?

You can look into home business opportunities that interest you, but be skeptical of ones that promise big bucks and little work. There is no substitute for business success via hard work and persistence—other than someone giving you a ready-made business complete with manager and employees. It is much more thrilling to succeed through your own efforts, but be educated and know from all angles into what you are venturing!

For more information about business opportunities, send a legal-sized SASE to the American Business Opportunity Institute, Inc. (address cited in "Additional Information").

## Additional Information

### Recommended Reading

*Direct Selling: From Door to Door to Network Marketing* by Richard Berry (Newton, MA: Butterworth-Heineman, 1997)

*The Franchise Fraud: How to Protect Yourself Before and After You Invest* by Robert L. Purvin, American Association of Franchisees and Dealers (New York: Wiley, 1994)

*Home Businesses You Can Buy: The Definitive Guide to Exploring Franchises, Multi-Level Marketing, and Business Opportunities Plus: How to Avoid Scams,* by Paul and Sarah Edwards and Walter Zovi (New York: Putnam, 1997)

*Income Opportunities Guide: Buying a Profitable Franchise;* $39.95 + $5 shipping and handling. Call (800) 858-4783 for information and credit card orders.

*Multilevel Marketing: The Definitive Guide to America's Top MLM Companies,* 2nd ed., by Will Marks (Arlington, TX: Summit Publishing Group, 1997)

*The Selling-from-Home Sourcebook: A Guide to Home-Based Business Opportunities in the Selling Industry* by Kathryn Caputo (Cincinnati: F & W, 1996)

*Start Your Own Network Marketing Company: Build Your Business with a Proven System* by Angela L. More (Rocklin, CA: Prima, 1998)

*Top Franchises: Get the Inside Data: Success Magazine's Guide to Selecting a Franchise* by Jeffrey E. Kolton (1997). To order, call (212) 883-7100.

Series of franchise business books: *Evaluating and Buying a Franchise: 1998 Directory of Franchising Organizations* (revised annually), *How to Franchise Your Business,* and *Understanding Franchise Contracts.* Write for a catalog to Pilot Books, 127 Sterling Ave., P.O. Box 2102, Greenport, NY 11944-2102; (800) 79-PILOT; http://www.pilotbooks.com.

### Organizations

American Association of Franchisees and Dealers (AAFD)
P.O. Box 81887
San Diego, CA 92138-1887

http://www.aafd.org/
A nonprofit trade association; supports and promotes AAFD Fair Franchising Standards. Membership benefits include consultations with attorneys and accountants, newsletter subscription, and more.

The Women's Franchise Network
International Franchise Association
1350 New York Ave., Suite 900
Washington, DC 20005
Helps women understand the diverse opportunities that franchising offers them. World's oldest and largest trade association, representing franchisors and franchisees. Offers a number of helpful publications about franchising. Write for a free copy of the IFA Publications Catalog or IFA's Franchise Opportunities Guide.

Public Reference Branch
Federal Trade Commission
Washington, DC 20580
http://www.ftc.gov/index.html—"Facts for Consumers"
Provides a package of information about the "FTC Franchise and Business Opportunity Rule" free of charge.

American Business Opportunity Institute, Inc.
c/o Andrew A. Caffey
3 Bethesda Metro Center, #700
Bethesda, MD 20814
Send a legal-sized SASE for information about its publications, programs, and services.

Direct Selling Association (DSA)
1666 K St., NW, Suite 1010
Washington, DC 20006

Multi-Level Marketing International Association (MLMIA)
1101 Dove St., #170
Newport Beach, CA 92660
Membership comprises companies as well as distributors that are involved in the MLM aspect of direct selling.

# 7

# Home-Based and Work-at-Home Business Scams

*The secret of managing money is to live as economically the day after payday as you did the day before.*

—Anonymous

Unfortunately, with the growth of home-based businesses, so too has the number of fraudulent money-making schemes or scams increased. The Federal Trade Commission (FTC) says persons hopeful in looking for entrepreneurial opportunities lose more than $100 million a year to prepackaged businesses that promise big riches with little effort. Look on the Internet, pick up a newspaper or small business publication, and you can find many classified and display advertisements that offer such work-at-home opportunities as reading books for money, assembling crafts, sewing baby items, stuffing envelopes, and so on.

Some advertise home opportunities with the complete business package, including the computer, software, and manual. One older couple in my community thought one such business was the opportunity for their retirement. They took out a second mortgage on their home for $15,000. The couple ended up with a computer and software that was out-of-date and did not receive the support that the company had promised. The couple also had no business experience, nor had they researched their community to see whether the business package they had purchased would have a customer base.

For only a small investment of time, they could have saved their money and used that $15,000 toward a small business start-up—doing something in which they may have already have had experience and with a market. The company that swindled them has now been ordered to repay its customers the money they invested. The trouble is that the company declared bankruptcy, and the victims, who had invested an average of $9,000 each, will be lucky if they receive even a small percentage of their money.

Here are some tips to avoid becoming the victim of a money-making scam. Avoid any business opportunity that does the following:

❖ Promises you huge profits as you run the business in your spare time
❖ Does not name the money-making opportunity and wants you to send money for details
❖ Asks for money before it sends you any business information
❖ Refuses to give you the names of others who have invested in this business opportunity
❖ Refuses to send you literature about its company's services and products
❖ Is readily willing to negotiate the price of its business opportunity if you say you cannot afford its price

Do not be impulsive and too anxious to spend your money for the promises of riches. Give yourself time to consider, reflect, and, above all, conduct research and more research before you embark on any business venture. Trust your instincts, and if the opportunity sounds too good to be true, it probably is!

## Final Tip

If you believe you have been the victim of a scam—even for a small amount of money—do not be ashamed. People of all ages and backgrounds have fallen to scams. What is very important is that you report the scam and file a complaint. Scam artists are literally banking (with your and others' money) that you will not report them. That is how they make their money: reeling people in, shutting down, and starting up another scam somewhere else.

To add insult to injury, if you have been victim of a scam, your name may have been sold to other scam artists. Some will even pose as representatives of government officials who offer to get your money back—for a fee! Learn from your mistake, and get wise to protect yourself from any future frauds.

## Additional Information

### Organizations
Federal Trade Commission (FTC)
Washington, DC 20580
(202) 326-2222
The Federal Trade Commission cannot help resolve individual disputes, but it can take action if there is evidence of a pattern of deceptive or unfair practices. To register a complaint, write or call the FTC.

National Fraud Information Center (NFIC)
P.O. Box 65868
Washington, DC 20035
(800) 876-7060
Write or call to get updates on the latest frauds and scams; to report a fraud of which you have been a victim; or to report a practice you suspect is a fraud.

### On-line Sources
http://www.ftc.gov/WWW/opa/9611/misdfort.htm—FTC listing of samples of phony get-rich-quick self-employment schemes, including work-at-home scams, pyramid schemes

on the Internet, prepackaged business opportunities, and
so forth
http://www.ftc.gov/index.html—FTC's "Facts for Consumers"
section
http://www.fraud.org/—NFIC's Web site

**Other Sources**
The Call for Action Hotline: (301) 652-HELP
Your consumer protection office, usually located in your county
seat
The Better Business Bureau's office nearest you
Your local postmaster—the U.S. Postal Service investigates
fraudulent mail practices.
The State Attorney General's Office in your state or the state of
the company in question

# Part II

# 101 Home-Based Businesses

# Explanation of Each Business Feature

*To business that we love we rise betime, and go t't with delight.*
—William Shakespeare

Each business idea profiled in this book will contain most of the following details, depending on what information was available, which varied for each business idea. More sources are available for each business, but I could not possibly have listed them all. My goal is to give you a variety of sources to help get you started in one or more of the businesses featured—a "jump start" to save you time in your research.

* **Description**—an overview of the activities involved in conducting the business featured.
* **Estimated start-up costs**—the estimated costs to purchase the basic equipment needed. Most businesses will use a computer for bookkeeping and running business-related software.
* **Pricing guidelines**—an idea about what to charge for your products or services. Look in the resources I have listed in chapter 3, "Business Plan," about how to set your prices, and

also go by guidelines recommended by your industry, your competitors' rates, and what you need to make a profit.

❖ **Marketing and advertising methods and tips**—suggestions for informing potential customers about your business and ways to get them to patronize your business.

❖ **Essential equipment**—industries' and related sources' recommendations for the basic tools and supplies you will need to start up your business. Most entrepreneurs use the basic tools and then invest in ones more to their liking or more appropriate to their business after they have been running the business for a time. It saves them unnecessary start-up expenses until they see what is really needed.

❖ **Recommended training, experience, or needed skills**—the knowledge, background, and/or training needed as well as tips for gaining experience. Some businesses require a degree, certification, or license by the owner to operate.

❖ **Income potential**—the possible earnings for the business featured (hourly, annually). Variations of income are not uncommon because your experience, your customer base, and the demand for your business's products and service can vary depending on your area and business acumen.

❖ **Best customers**—suggestions as to who would be the most likely persons to purchase your goods and/or services.

❖ **Success tips**—advice from the business's industry and entrepreneurs to help you succeed.

❖ **Franchises, distributorships, and licenses**—listing of home business franchises and opportunities related to this particular business. It is not an endorsement for any enterprise. Please investigate and research any such operation before you invest any funds (see chapter 6 for more guidelines).

❖ **Additional information**—where available, lists of related trade and/or nonprofit associations, books and publications, home study courses, business start-up guides, software, Web sites, and other helpful resources pertaining to each business idea. Please note: Many associations do not have start-up business information but rather exist for membership networking opportunities and sharing of industry-related information. Where requested, please send a business-size (long), self-addressed stamped envelope (designated in this book as LSASE) to ensure a reply to any information requests you may make. Many associations are nonprofit and staffed by volunteers, and they cannot be expected to handle all requests.

❖ **Additional business ideas**—suggestions for related business ventures.

I have attempted to provide you with the best possible and most reliable resources for each venture, but I ask you to forgive any sources that are inaccessible or incorrect as telephone numbers, addresses, Internet sites, and other information are all subject to change owing to unforeseeable circumstances. If you encounter any difficulties with a particular source or cannot find the specific information you are seeking, please contact me (Priscilla Huff, Box 286, Sellersville, PA 18960), and I will be happy to assist you.

Remember, part of the entrepreneur's character is to persist to find the information she needs. Someone, somewhere will have the information necessary to start and run your home business. Do not give up until you find the answers to your questions. I wish you 101 more best wishes for your entrepreneurial ventures.

# Pet and Animal
# Businesses

*Animals make the best therapists: They listen to your complaints and
never give you their opinions.*

—Anonymous

If you love animals and want to have a part- or full-time business, combining both may be a profitable venture for you. With
over fifty-three million pet-owning households existing in the
United States, the market for pet services and products is rapidly
growing, as attested to the nearly $20 billion spent by Ameri-
cans in 1996 on pet products and services. Many women all
across the nation are involved with pets and livestock businesses. Women often have a "gentle touch" when it comes to
handling animals, to which all species of animals seem to respond. This section describes just a few of the animal-related
business ideas that are possible.

## Additional Information
### Recommended Reading
Storey's How-To Books for Country Living, Schoolhouse Road,
Pownal, VT 05261; books on raising various kinds of

animals. Write for a current catalog or visit http://www. StoreyBooks.com.

**Organizations**
Pet Industry Joint Advisory Council
1220 19th St., NW, Suite 400
Washington, DC 20036
http://petsforum.com/PIJAC/
PIJAC is the largest trade association representing all divisions of the pet industry. Its purpose includes education and advocacy. It maintains an information center.

American Pet Association
P.O. Box 725065
Atlanta, GA 31139-9065
(800) APA-PETS
http://www.apapets.com
e-mail: apa@apapets.com

**On-line Source**
Pet Products and Pet Information—one of 1,250 "shopping centers of the Mallpark" on the Internet at http://www. mallpark.com.

≈ 1 ≈
# SPECIALTY ANIMAL BREEDING: BISON

With the quest for healthier eating, bison (the correct name, not buffalo) meat is fast becoming a meat in demand. Compared with beef, it is lower in fat, cholesterol, and calories; higher in protein and iron; tastes similar; but costs twice as much because of its relative scarcity. Bison are fed primarily on grass and not subjected to drugs, chemicals, or hormones. If you have access to land and facilities and are familiar with livestock care, you may want to investigate this growing new meat market. You can raise bison just for breeding purposes if you prefer not to get involved with selling them for eating.

Sam Albrecht, executive director of the National Bison Association, says one of the ranch managers of a large herd of bison whom he knows prefers women to work his bison. The manager says that women tend to be more patient and quiet than the men who have been working cattle all of their lives and that the bison work better with the women.

### Estimated Start-up Costs
$20,000 to $30,000, depending on the facilities and land you have available

### Pricing Guidelines
❖ Adults (fully grown) sell for about $3,500.
❖ Weaned heifer (female) calves sell for about $2,000 (they are currently worth more as breeding stock than meat), bull calves sell for around $700 apiece.
❖ Meat prices: $5 to $6/pound for ground bison meat; $15 to $20/pound for prime steak cuts.

### Marketing and Advertising Methods and Tips
❖ Network with others who raise bison through national, state, and regional associations, which can recommend the markets in your area.
❖ Offer tours of your ranch/farm to the public and hand out fact sheets about the pros of bison meat.
❖ Contact gourmet restaurants and specialized caterers.

### Essential Equipment
❖ Facilities and grazing needs are similar to those of raising beef cattle (land and shelter). Arid areas will need more grazing acreage than those areas with sufficient rain to produce more-productive grazing fields. Adult bison and lactating bison eat more than young bison.
❖ Strong fences (6 feet and higher), shelter, and pens. Bison are naturally hardy and generally need less housing and veterinary care than cattle.

### Recommended Training, Experience, or Needed Skills
Experience with working and raising cattle, livestock, and/or bison. If possible, work with these animals before you go into this business, so you understand their nature. Bison should be handled more slowly and calmly than domesticated livestock.

### Income Potential
$40,000 + (depending on the size of your herd)

### Type of Business
$2/3$ home business, $1/3$ marketing and taking care of other business demands

### Best Customers
❖ Others interested in purchasing breeding stock to establish their own herds
❖ Health-conscious markets and restaurants specializing in unusual cuisine

### Success Tips
❖ Join the National Bison Association (see "Additional Information") for networking and gathering valuable information. Talk and visit with other bison producers in your area to determine fencing and health concerns and possibly to work first on a bison ranch/farm.
❖ Albrecht says, "Start slowly, with weaned calves so that you can learn about bison as they mature." He also reports that many ranchers have an "Absentee Owner" program where a person can buy an animal, let someone else take care of it while you visit your bison to learn from the manager on care, and also help out during handling. According to Albrecht, "It works great!"

### Additional Information
**Organization**
   National Bison Association
   4701 Marion St., Suite 100
   Denver, CO 80216

"Membership in the National Bison Association is the best way to learn more about the bison industry." Has an information packet for $12.00 + $3 shipping and handling that includes 170 pages of information on bison production; a copy of the trade publication *Bison World*; brochures; a copy of their newsletter; sales data; fact sheets; publications' order form; information on fencing, handling, and so forth; and a listing of state and regional associations.

### Additional Business Ideas
❖ Selling bison-related gifts (jewelry, note cards, and so forth)
❖ Touring school assemblies to present programs about the American bison—past and present

## ❧ 2 ☙
# PET DAY CARE
With so many people having to work, pets are often left alone all day and longer until an owner is able to get home to attend to them. From loneliness and boredom, many pets do damage to their homes and/or develop behavior problems. Owners want their pets to have exercise, companionship, and loving care while they are at work or away. Thus, boarding kennels, which were once used primarily for vacationing owners, are now being used as "day care" for cats, dogs, and other pets.

### Estimated Start-up Costs
$15,000 to $50,000 (small to full-service business)

### Pricing Guidelines
$10 to $18 a day

### Marketing and Advertising Methods and Tips
❖ Flyers at supermarkets, veterinarian offices, pet food stores, animal shelters, and bulletin boards in businesses' lounges

❖ Press releases to announce a "Day Care for Animals." Send to local media—newspapers, cable TV, radio.
❖ Talks to animal groups and clubs

### Essential Equipment
Runs, pens, and crates; harnesses and leashes; food and water bowls; animal toys; beds and blankets; grooming brushes and equipment

### Recommended Training, Experience, or Needed Skills
❖ Experience with the type and breed of animals coming to your day care
❖ Training courses, work experience in kennels and facilities that care for pets
❖ A love and knack for working with animals

### Income Potential
$40,000 to $60,000

### Type of Business
Most of time spent at home-based facility

### Best Customers
Working individuals and couples, persons going on extended travel

### Success Tips
❖ You should let pet owners know you will treat their pets as if they were your own and that you love animals (you should not be in this business if you do not!).
❖ Look for something unique you can offer with your day care (i.e., trips to the vet, specialized training, special activities, etc.).
❖ Your facilities should smell good, be adequately disinfected to ensure the health of the pets in your care, and have at least one veterinarian on call.

❖ Make sure you have the zoning permits you need to have such facilities in addition to the proper licenses and adequate liability insurance to cover your business.

## Additional Information
### Recommended Reading
*Career Success with Pets: How to Get Started, Get Going, Get Ahead* by Kim Barber (New York: Macmillan, 1996).

*CATNIP*, P.O. Box 420012, Palm Coast, FL 32142-9779; $20/ twelve issues; a monthly newsletter with information on the health and well-being of cats published by Tufts University School of Veterinary Medicine.

*Groom and Board*, H. H. Backer Associates, Inc., 20 E. Jackson Blvd., Suite 200, Chicago, IL 60604; trade publication published nine times a year. Write for subscription information.

### Organization
American Pet Boarding Association
P.O. Box 931
Wheeling, IL 60090
Defines criteria for the humane boarding care of companion animals and recognition of boarding facilities that meet those criteria.

### Home Study
International Correspondence Schools
"Animal Care Specialist"
925 Oak St,
Scranton, PA 18540-9888

## Additional Business Ideas
❖ Offer special training and pet-related products at your facilities.
❖ Animal yard clean-up at $25 an hour.

## ∞ 3 ∞
## PET ID AND REGISTRATION SERVICES

Having a pet missing or lost can be a traumatic experience for an individual or family. With this pet business, you can offer photo and information registering services put into a database in the event a pet becomes lost or stolen. ID photos, tattoos, tags, and electronic ID products (some of which must be inserted by veterinarians) are just some of the devices that can be sold with this business. You can offer distribution of flyers, contacts with local animal agencies, and insertion of classified ads into local newspapers as part of your services.

### Estimated Start-up Costs
$3,000 for computer and office set-up; $500 to $1,200 if you already own a computer

### Pricing Guidelines
$5 to $10 per license; $45 per registration package

### Marketing and Advertising Methods and Tips
❖ Flyers at veterinarian offices, animal shelters (i.e., Humane Society, Society for the Prevention of Cruelty to Animals), grooming and boarding businesses, and pet supply stores
❖ Talks at animal clubs and pet clinics
❖ Press releases to local newspapers, pet publications, radio and TV stations
❖ Sponsor a pet show at a local school.

### Essential Equipment
❖ Tags, dog licenses (check with your county and local authorities about requirements to sell the licenses)
❖ Electronic ID devices
❖ Computer with database of customers and pet information
❖ Business cards, business phone
❖ Camera for photos of registered pets

*Recommended Training, Experience, or Needed Skills*
❖ Love and working knowledge of various kinds of pets
❖ Knowledge of latest pet ID devices
❖ Good sales skills combined with an understanding of owners' concerns for their pets

*Income Potential*
$5,000 to $10, 000 part-time; $15,000 to $35,000 full-time (depends on the population in your area of pets and people)

*Type of Business*
$3/4$ at home, $1/4$ marketing

*Best Customers*
Pet owners, owners of valuable show animals

*Success Tips*
❖ Most lucrative to combine with another pet-related business (see "Pet Detective")
❖ Keep up-to-date with the latest electronic devices and other ID devices.

*Additional Information*
**Organization**
  Electronic ID, Inc.
  131 E. Exchange Ave., Suite 116
  Fort Worth, TX 76106
Manufacturer of electronic ID devices; write for the distributor nearest you.

*Additional Business Ideas*
❖ Sell custom-designed pet tags at dog shows, pet supply stores, and to mail-order pet catalogs.
❖ Work with electronic fencing companies.

## ᴁ 4 ᴂ
# PET DETECTIVE

This business works well with the previous one in that after you have registered a pet, you do the actual searching for a lost or stolen pet, using both your ID devices and your neighborhood and community networking sources.

### Estimated Start-up Costs
❖ $500 for flyers and basic office supplies
❖ $2,000 to $3,000 for computer and accessories as well as a scanner to scan in photos of lost pets

### Pricing Guidelines
❖ $50 to $65 a day to search for pets
❖ $45 for setting a humane trap with the animal's favorite food or toys
❖ One week's daily search and media contacts (radio, newspaper, flyers in eating establishments, retail stores) for $150 to $200

### Marketing and Advertising Methods and Tips
❖ Flyers in veterinarian offices, police stations, animal shelters, kennels, grooming centers, and pet supply and feed stores
❖ Press release of opening business, substantial awards offered by owners of lost pets, and "happy ending" stories
❖ Photos of lost pets on cable channels
❖ Host or sponsor outdoor pet clinics
❖ Classified ads in pet publications, classified-ad newspapers

### Essential Equipment
❖ Phone with answering system
❖ Pager and/or mobile telephone
❖ Computer, scanner, photocopier, and color printer for flyers
❖ Assorted animal leashes, humane traps and crates, and nets
❖ Business cards and licenses

### Recommended Training, Experience, or Needed Skills

❖ Knowledge of how to handle different kinds and breeds of dogs, cats, and other popular pets
❖ A good reputation for doing thorough searches and genuinely caring for lost pets
❖ A good network of sources to help you quickly find lost pets

### Income Potential

$3,000 part-time; $25,000 to $35,000 full-time

### Type of Business

$1/4$ at home keeping a database and running the business, $3/4$ marketing and actually searching for lost pets

### Best Customers

Pet owners, owners of show animals and livestock

### Success Tips

❖ Be sincere in your sympathy and understanding to a pet owner's distress over losing a pet.
❖ Develop a reputation for tenacity and persistence in finding the lost pets.
❖ Be able to mobilize quickly your sources and contacts as soon as you are notified about a lost pet. The quicker you get the word out to the public, the more likely you will find a lost pet.

### Additional Information

#### Organizations

American Society for the Prevention of Cruelty to Animals
424 E. 92nd St.
New York, NY 10128
(212) 876-7700

The ASPCA is the oldest humane organization in America. It has over 350,000 members and donors in the United States. Call for more information; the extension number 4357 can answer any questions concerning general animal behavior. The Web site is http://www.aspca.org.

### Additional Business Idea

Give talks and programs of basic animal care, including demonstrations and tips on how to keep your pet from getting lost or stolen, to schools and community groups.

### ᵥ᷄᷄ 5 ᷄᷄

# ANIMAL BEHAVIORAL CONSULTANT

In this business, you would specialize in one species' behaviors. Consultations could cover issues ranging from housebreaking the animals to teaching the owners how to understand the nature of their animal and how to control its destructiveness to property and so on. Most animal behaviorists have a gift for working with troublesome animals and almost instinctively know how to approach the animals with which they work. If you have the background, knowledge, and experience to help owners, this may be an ideal business for you.

Many times these animals are expensive show dogs, race horses, or just beloved pets whose behavior has become so extreme that the owner's next step will be to get rid of or destroy the animal. Your expertise will help the owner and animal live in harmony together.

### Estimated Start-up Costs

✤ Expenses for animal training and psychology courses if you feel you need additional knowledge and or training
✤ $500 to $1,500 (add $2,500 to $3,000 if you do not have a computer)

### Pricing Guidelines

Depends on your training, qualifications, experience, and reputation, but roughly $25 to $75 per consultation or house call

## Marketing and Advertising Methods and Tips
❖ Notices in veterinary offices, pet stores, grooming businesses
❖ Direct mail to animal associations and clubs about the animal in which you specialize
❖ Internet site
❖ Ads in pet or specific animal breed publications
❖ Paid animal advice column in trade or pet journals and publications
❖ Promotional materials (brochures, business cards)
❖ Ads in business sections of your telephone directory

## Essential Equipment
❖ Animal-related equipment necessary for the behavior modification needed
❖ Home office equipment

## Recommended Training, Experience, or Needed Skills
❖ Degree and/or training in veterinary science or animal psychology
❖ Experience with the breeds and animals with which you will be working

## Income Potential
❖ $30 to $80 an hour
❖ $45,000 to $80,000 a year full-time, depending on your success rate and reputation for helping resolve your clients' animal problems

## Type of Business
$1/4$ in home handling business operations, $3/4$ out of home marketing and working with animals

## Best Customers
❖ Devoted (especially higher-income) individual pet owners
❖ Owners of show or expensive animals (dogs, horses, cats)

## Success Tips

✣ Be confident in your ability to work with the animals you handle.

✣ If your success rate in solving the animals' or owners' problems are good, your services will be in demand.

✣ Approach each situation in a caring and systematic manner.

✣ Have a network of other animal coaches or behaviorists with which to exchange ideas and problem-solving ideas.

## Additional Information

### Recommended Reading

*Do Dogs Need Shrinks?* by Peter Neville (Seacacus, NJ: Citadel, 1992)

*101 Training Tips for Your Cat* by Carin Smith (New York: Dell, 1994)

*101 Training Tips for Your Dog* by Kate Delano and Condax Decker (New York: Dell, 1994)

*Volunteering with Your Pet: How to Get in Animal-Assisted Therapy with Any Kind of Pet* by Mary R. Burch, (New York: Macmillan, 1996)

### Home Study

Professional Career Development Institute
3597 Parkway Lane, Suite 100
Norcross, GA 30092
Write for a current catalog, requesting "Animal Care" information.

## Additional Business Ideas

✣ Pet therapist—using animals to help people with various mental disabilities

✣ Pet talent agent—matching suitable animals with entertainment establishments

## ❧ 6 ❧
# PET SPECIALTY ITEMS

If you already have a pet-related business, have extensive experience with an animal (or bird, reptile, etc.) or with varied animals, or have originated a new pet product, you may want to either add to your business or concentrate solely on selling pet specialty products.

Several women in my area have taken their animal-related hobbies and begun selling animal products. One woman invented a special net mask her horses could wear over their heads so flies would not get to their eyes and cause irritations. Another raises Angora rabbits and sells their wool as well as beautiful hats, gloves, and sweaters she knits from the fur.

You can sell your items to pet catalogs (see the "FAQs" chapter), pet stores, at pet and specific-breed animal shows and conventions; start your own mail-order catalog of pet products; and/or sell your products from a commercial Web site.

### Estimated Start-up Costs
$5,000 to $25,000 for product development, catalog design, and production

### Pricing Guidelines
Will be based on market research, demand for your product, and the profit margin you need to make

### Marketing and Advertising Methods and Tips
❖ Press releases and advertisements in pet and animal publications (in the pet product trade and pet owner journals, newsletters, and magazines)
❖ Direct mail with brochures, samples, and on-site demonstrations
❖ Booths at pet industry trade shows to showcase your items or to pick up items from other companies to sell
❖ Internet Web site

## Essential Equipment
+ Home office: computer, software for sales, promotional materials, photocopier, fax, and telephone and answering system
+ Supplies and materials if you produce the items yourself

## Recommended Training, Experience, or Needed Skills
+ Knowledge of the animals so you can design or carry the items they need
+ Sales experience
+ Knowledge of mail-order basics and basic business management

## Income Potential
From $1,000 a month in the beginning to $25,000 to $50,000 + a year as your line of items grows

## Type of Business
$1/2$ in home doing business management, production, order fulfillment, research; $1/2$ out of home marketing and traveling to stores and businesses

## Best Customers
+ Pet and animal owners
+ Pet stores and grooming centers
+ Specific dog, horse, cat, and other animal clubs and associations
+ Boarding kennels

## Success Tips
+ Research what products are out there and see where you can find a niche market that is not being met (e.g., items for only large-breed dogs; chemical-free and natural pet snacks, etc.).

❖ Start with a small number of products and add to your line as you can afford to.

❖ Keep up with the pet industry trade news to know what the "hottest"-selling and predicted items will be.

## Additional Information
### Recommended Reading
*Home-Based Mail Order: A Successful Guide for Entrepreneurs* by William J. Bond (Blue Ridge Summit, PA: Tab, 1990)

*How to Profit through Catalog Marketing*, 3rd ed., by Katie Muldoon (Lincolnwood, IL: NTC, 1995)

*Online Marketing Handbook: How to Promote, Advertise, and Sell Your Products and Services on the Internet*, 2nd ed., by Daniel S. Janal (New York: Van Nostrand Reinhold, 1997)

*Pet News*—quarterly newsletter of the World Wide Pet Supply Association, 406 South First Ave., Arcadia, CA 91006-3829.

### Organizations
National Mail Order Association
2807 Polk St. NE
Minneapolis, MN 55418-2924
Excellent for small mail-order businesses; publishes monthly newsletter *Mail Order Digest*.

Pet Industry Distributors Association
5024-R Campbell Blvd.
Baltimore, MD 21236

American Pet Products Manufacturers Association
255 Glenville Rd.
Greenwich, CT 06831

World Wide Pet Supply Association
406 South First Ave.
Arcadia, CA 91006-3829

Pet Industry Joint Advisory Council
1220 19th St., NW, Suite 400
Washington, DC 20036
http://petsforum.com/PIJAC/

### Additional Business Ideas

❖ Licensing your own specialty product

❖ Selling your best-selling product on a home shopping channel

❖ Building unique pet houses—see *Making Pet Palaces: Princely Homes and Furnishings to Pamper Your Pets* by Leslie Dierks (New York: Sterling, 1996)

❦ ● ❧

## MISCELLANEOUS PET BUSINESSES

❖ Pet health insurance—check for state licensing requirements and necessary training in the insurance industry.

❖ Pet matching service—matching people and the pets best suited to their likes and lifestyles

❖ Horse business—see *Starting and Running Your Own Horse Business* by Mary Asby McDonald (1996); order from Storey's How-To Books for County Living (see address on page 73).

# Business-to-Business Services

*Being in your own business is working eighty hours a week so you can avoid working forty hours a week for someone else.*
—Ramona E. F. Arnett

As big businesses continue to downsize, cut benefits, use more part-time workers, and make other economizing moves, they will still need those business services that were performed by original employees. Often a former worker-turned-entrepreneur will contract her services back to a former employer (which is why you should not tell your boss off before you leave a company). Networking with and patronizing other small and home-based businesses will also help you boost your profits (as well as theirs). Here are two sources of information that offer a good overview of this career choice:

❖ *Business Information Sources* by Lorna M. Daniells (Los Angeles: University of California Press, 1993)
❖ *Journal of Business-to-Business Marketing,* The Hawthorn Press, Inc., 10 Alice St., Binghamton, NY 13904-1580; P.O. Box E-0821, 17 Lexington Ave., New York, NY 10010 (editor contact).

## ॐ 7 ॐ
# ADMINISTRATION BUSINESS (OVERFLOW) SERVICE

As an owner of an administration business (overflow) service, you will do tasks for small businesses that have periodic busy times and need to contract out the work they cannot handle. This would involve tasks like professional word processing, data entry, reports, general office overflow assistance, correspondence, reminder services, mass mailings, bookkeeping, creating business forms, graphs, charts, newsletters, brochures, flyers, and other forms of desktop publishing.

### Estimated Start-up Costs
$5,000 to $15,000

### Pricing Guidelines
$35 to $40 + an hour; charge by the job (see industry standards suggested by the National Association of Secretarial Services).

### Marketing and Advertising Methods and Tips
+ Letters to smaller companies experiencing growth and/or regular fluctuations of work loads
+ Yellow Pages under "Business Services"
+ Networking with local and home-based business associations
+ Referrals from satisfied customers
+ Direct mail to new area businesses (postcards, brochures) (hint: read the legal notices in your local papers for announcements of business name filing)
+ Notices to churches, associations, and nonprofit organizations

### Essential Equipment
+ Computer and related software; printer; fax, photocopier, scanner, business number and answering system, and ergonomic office chair
+ Business stationery, stamps, and business cards

### Recommended Training, Experience, or Needed Skills

✤ Secretarial, office manager, computer and word processing and desktop publishing skills, experience, and training

✤ Ability to be customer oriented and offer fast and professional services

### Income Potential

$25,000 to $40,000

### Type of Business

$2/_3$ in home office, $1/_3$ marketing and meeting new and present clients; sometimes you may work on site at a time convenient to both yourself and your client.

### Best Customers

✤ New businesses in your community and those looking for "office support" employees

✤ Associations, schools, and nonprofit organizations

✤ College and university students

### Success Tips

✤ You must be able to produce professional-looking work in a short amount of time.

✤ Do not be discouraged when you begin, as there may be other more-established business services in your area. Find your niche or a customer need that is not being fulfilled, and offer this to your customers.

✤ Keep up with technology and trends in this industry by joining an association.

### Franchises, Distributorships, and Licenses

General Business Services (GBS)
1020 N. University Parks Dr.
P.O. Box 3146
Waco, TX 76707

Offers its clients business, tax, financial, and management counseling as well as accounting services, products, and personnel services. Write for details and investment costs.

### Additional Information
**Recommended Reading**
*How to Start a Secretarial and Business Service;* order from Pilot Books, 127 Sterling Ave., P.O. Box 2102, Greenport, NY 11944-2102; write or call for catalog and information:(800) 79-PILOT.

### Organization
Association of Business Support Services International, Inc.
22875 Sovi Ranch Parkway, Suite H
Yorba Linda, CA 92887

### Home Study
McGraw-Hill Continuing Education Center
4401 Connecticut Ave., NW
Washington, DC 20008
Courses in desktop publishing and word processing; write for current catalog.

Lifetime Career Schools
101 Harrison St.
Archbald, PA 18403
Courses in "secretarial" office procedures, typing, communication, and phone skills.

### Additional Business Ideas
Business referral service

### ᔑ 8 ᕐ
# ADVERTISING AGENCY
Very few businesses can survive without some sort of advertising, so advertising expertise is sought by almost every company, no matter its size. However, this is a very competitive business, so you will need to find your specialty niche of the businesses for

which you will work and then convince them that your advertising expertise will be of value to their company. Your best assets in this business are your creativity and knowledge of the industry of your customers.

### Estimated Start-up Costs
$5,000 to $17,000

### Pricing Guidelines
$35 to $80 an hour; or work on a monthly retainer or per-project basis.

### Marketing and Advertising Methods and Tips
* Networking with other small and home-based businesses by joining trade associations, local business associations, and clubs, and by attending women's entrepreneurial conferences
* Referrals from satisfied clients
* Conducting seminars or classes at local schools and colleges
* Advertising for clients in trade and association publications
* Business ads in your telephone directory's business section
* Direct mail to target customers
* Internet Web site

### Essential Equipment
* Home office: computer with on-line access, scanner, photo software, fax, business line and answering service, desktop publishing software, photocopier, and laser printer
* Promotional materials: letterhead, business cards, and brochures

### Recommended Training, Experience, or Needed Skills
* Degree and/or experience working in an advertising agency
* Need to be highly creative and competitive
* Have to be aware of the current market and be better than your competition
* Knowledge in the business or hobby field of your clients

✤ Must instill confidence in your clients that your advertising campaigns and skills can help their company get more business

✤ Skill at writing ad copy and doing design and layout

### Income Potential
$30,000 to $75,000 +

### Type of Business
$1/2$ working on ad campaigns and your own marketing, $1/2$ working onsite at your clients' businesses

### Best Customers
Home-based and small companies in your area of hobby, business, or organization

### Success Tips
✤ You have to be energetic and motivated to get clients, and then keep them with good ad results.

✤ You must be able to communicate well with your clients to understand their business, what makes it unique, and what can attract customers.

### Franchises, Distributorships, and Licenses
There are a number of home-based business advertising services ranging from advertising specialties to elevator billboard advertising. See small business publications like *Business Start-Ups Magazine* (September 1997) for their features of home-based business opportunities.

### Additional Information
**Recommended Reading**
*Advertising Age;* Subscriber Services, 965 East Jefferson Ave., Detroit, MI 48207

*The Advertising Agency Business: The Complete Manual for Management and Operations*, 3rd ed., by Eugene J. Hameroff and Herbert S. Gardner, Jr. (Lincolnwood, IL: NTC, 1997)

*Entrepreneur's Small Business Development Catalog*, "Advertising Agency"—call (800) 421-2300; $69.50 + shipping and handling

*How to Start and Manage an Advertising Agency* by Jerre G. Lewis and Leslie D. Renn (1996); Lewis & Renn Associates, Inc., 10315 Harmony Dr., Interlochen, MI 49643

*Standard Directory of Advertising Agencies*; 3004 Glenview Rd., Wilmette, IL 60091

**Organizations**

American Advertising Federation
1101 Vermont Ave., NW, Suite 500
Washington, DC 20005

American Association of Advertising Agencies (AAAA)
666 3rd Ave., 13th Floor
New York, NY 10174-1801

Publishes *Agency Magazine* quarterly, free to members. Send an LSASE for membership information.

*Additional Business Ideas*

Ad copywriter for advertising agencies and direct-mail companies

## ≪ 9 ≫
# BUSINESS ORGANIZER

As businesses strive to cut costs and increase their profits, many business owners do not have the time, inclination, or know-how to organize their company's daily procedures and operations, which must be done correctly to save dollars and time. If you have the experience and efficiency knowledge to help businesses become better organized, your services will be in demand. You can offer this expertise to companies through presenting workshops, seminars, and on-site training, and by writing a manual of procedures.

### Estimated Start-up Costs
$3,000 to $9,000

### Pricing Guidelines
$35 to $150 an hour, or set fees for specific jobs or work on a retainer basis for periodic visits. Follow industry guidelines.

### Marketing and Advertising Methods and Tips
❖ Determine your target companies and business owners, and then send promotional materials followed up with a personal visit. You will need to educate your clients as far as what your services are and how you can increase their profits.
❖ Referrals and recommendations from satisfied clients
❖ Ads in trade publications
❖ Industry trade shows

### Essential Equipment
❖ Computer and related business software (business management, time management, desktop publishing software)
❖ Pager or cellular phone
❖ Promotional materials: business cards, brochures, and introduction portfolio
❖ Workshop and training materials: manuals, workbooks in which you describe guidelines that executives and employees can follow

### Recommended Training, Experience, or Needed Skills
❖ Have work experience in the industry and businesses that you will seek as clients.
❖ Volunteer for nonprofit organizations and friends' businesses.
❖ Exchange information with other organizers.
❖ Read books on the topic and enroll in workshops.
❖ Have good people skills.

✤ Be knowledgeable in business efficiency management, business software, and other technology that can help organize a company.

### Income Potential
$20,000 to $50,000; realize, though, it will take time to build a client base and thus your profits. Marketing your service will take most of your start-up hours and at least half of your business operation.

### Type of Business
$^1/_4$ for home office business management, $^3/_4$ with clients or holding your training sessions, seminars, and so forth.

### Best Customers
❖ Find your niche customers in your market research and from actually conducting your business.
❖ Small and other home-based businesses that do not have the staff to handle all the daily activities of running a business need help with all the tasks they have to do.

### Success Tips
❖ You have to be confident in your presentations to convince businesses that they need your services.
❖ Network with other business owners for business and referrals.
❖ Keep current with the professional organizer industry.
❖ Use questionnaires and evaluations from both management and their employees to get an overall picture of the organizational needs of the companies.
❖ Be professional and flexible to give each company the recommendations easiest for them to implement and follow.

### Franchises, Distributorships, and Licenses
The Wright Track (to Small Business Success)
P.O. Box 3416
Oak Park, IL 60303

Advisory services for small businesses, small business coaches, business and marketing plans.

## Additional Information
### Recommended Reading
*Business Systems Engineering: Managing Breakthrough Changes for Productivity and Profit* by Gregory, H. Watson (New York: Wiley, 1994)

*Changing the Way We Work* by R. Meredith Belbin (Newton, MA: Butterworth-Heinemann, 1997)

*Entrepreneur's Small Business Development Catalog,* "Professional Organizer"; (800) 421-2300; $69.50 + shipping and handling

*How to Make a Thousand Mistakes in Business and Still Succeed* by Hal Wright (Oak Park, IL: The Wright Track, 1995); $14.95 + shipping and handling; to order contact The Wright Track, P.O. Box 3416, Oak Park, IL 60303.

*Organizing Your Work Space: A Guide to Personal Productivity* by Odette Pollar (Menlo Park, CA: Crisp, 1992).

### Organization
National Association of Professional Organizers
1033 La Pasada Dr. #220
Austin, TX 78752-3880
Write for details about conferences, its newsletter, and local chapters.

### Home Study
"Small Business Management"
International Correspondence Schools
925 Oak St.
Scranton, PA 18515

## Additional Business Ideas
❖ Specialize in just one area of business organization, such as software, customer relations and databases, and so on.
❖ Create and sell efficiency management videos.

## ᨆ 10 ᨆ

# CLIENT PROSPECTING SPECIALIST

With this venture, you will help businesses find their best niche or targeted markets. You will search for the clients—local, regional, state, national, or international—in the databases that exist and also among your networking sources. With this business, you can start by helping other home-based businesses get clients and expand to include larger businesses as you gain experience.

### Estimated Start-up Costs
$1,000 to $6,000

### Pricing Guidelines
* Your rates can be based on fees per client that actually signs up with your customer or on a per-project fee involving the research and reports on the best customers that you have found for your client, or use a combination of both.
* $50 to $75 an hour, depending on your experience and the companies who are your clients

### Marketing and Advertising Methods and Tips
* Networking with business owners through association memberships
* Word-of-mouth referrals
* Advertisements and articles about business prospecting in trade publications
* Direct mail of your promotional materials and personal visits
* Talks to business groups and associations

### Essential Equipment
* Home office: computer with hard disk and modem or laptop computer, fax machine, laser printer, suite software, database access software, on-line access to Internet, and subscriptions to business databases

❖ Promotional materials: business portfolio (business cards, brochures, referral letters)

### Recommended Training, Experience, or Needed Skills
❖ Computer skills for accessing information
❖ Presentation skills
❖ Management and work experience/training/education in the field(s) in which you are specializing to establish yourself as an expert
❖ Persistence and ability to find clients that are ideally suited to your companies

### Income Potential
$30,000 to $50,000, depending on the time you have to build your business and the size of the businesses for whom you are working

### Type of Business
$\frac{1}{2}$ searching for clients for your customers and compiling the information, $\frac{1}{2}$ interacting with your customers and their potential clients

### Best Customers
❖ Those in the industry and trade with which you have expertise and knowledge
❖ New businesses that are looking for clients

### Success Tips
❖ Thoroughly understand the needs of the companies that are your customers so you can give them the best match of clients.
❖ Network with business centers, business incubators, other home businesses, and associations for new clients for both your customers and yourself.

## Additional Information
### Recommended Reading
*Effective Communication with Customers and Clients* by Fred Gwyn (Cincinnati: South Western, 1993)

*50 Ways to Win New Customers: Fast, Simple, Inexpensive, Profitable and Proven Ideas You Can Use Starting Today!* by Paul R. Timm (Franklin Lakes, NJ: Career Press, 1993)

*Getting New Clients*, 2nd ed. by Dick Connor, Jeff Davidson, and Richard A. Connor (New York: Wiley, 1993)

*138 Quick Ideas to Get More Clients* by Howard L. Shenson and Jerry R. Wilson (New York: Wiley, 1993)

### Software
Business ConnX—helps you select potential customers using detailed marketing and credit information on more than eleven million U.S. businesses. Contact Serious Business Software, 701 Experian Parkway, Allen, TX 75013; (813) 288-8548; http://www.seriousbusiness.com/sbs.html.

### Other Source
D&B MarketPlace—business-to-business search with a database of more than ten million companies stored on a CD-ROM; (800) 999-9497; http://www.imarketinc.com.

## Additional Business Ideas
✤ Marketing research—conducting continual surveys of consumers' and/or businesses' needs and selling these findings to the related businesses that would be interested

✤ A newsletter about marketing and business topics

## ꙮ 11 ꙮ
# CUSTOMER RELATIONS DATABASE
With this business, you keep a database of your clients' customers with such information as their addresses, birthdays, products they purchased, and so forth. Then you will send

birthday cards, postcard notices, personalized notices, and special sales promotions for selected clients to help promote customer loyalty and relations with the company. Many people complain today about being treated with little respect, as if they were a "number," so this service can be a valuable asset.

## Estimated Start-up Costs
$3,000 to $8,000

## Pricing Guidelines
❖ $55 to $65 to enter each customer's name on your database
❖ $2.50 per sheet of thirty mailing labels
❖ $50 to $60 for 100 full-color, imprinted birthday cards

## Marketing and Advertising Methods and Tips
❖ Direct-mail promotional pieces followed by calls for presentations
❖ Word-of-mouth referrals
❖ Networking at local Chambers of Commerce, home-based business associations, and women's business clubs
❖ Yellow Pages advertising
❖ Internet Web site for local advertisers
❖ Talks to business groups about improving customer services

## Essential Equipment
❖ Home office: computer with database and organizing software, printer (color ink jet), labels, cards, postcards, and publishing software
❖ Promotional materials: brochures and business cards

## Recommended Training, Experience, or Needed Skills
❖ Background, training, or education in customer service, human resources, sales and marketing
❖ Experience with handling customer relations
❖ Good writing skills

## Income Potential
$5,000 to $10,000 part-time, $25,000 to $35,000 full-time, depending on the number of businesses to which you provide your service

## Type of Business
$2/_3$ in-house managing your databases and mailing the promotional materials, $1/_3$ marketing and visiting your customers for updates

## Best Customers
Small retail businesses that depend on repeat customers from their community (e.g., automobile salespeople and dealers, jewelers, appliance and furniture stores and salespeople, real estate agents)

## Success Tips
❖ Emphasize the "personal touch" with your business.
❖ Work closely with the companies to coordinate and design the items you send their customers in the mail.
❖ Periodically survey the customers of the companies for feedback on your mailings and the companies' services.

## Additional Information
### Recommended Reading
*The Complete Database Marketer: Second Generation Strategies and Techniques for Tapping the Power of Your Customer Database* by Arthur M. Hughes (Chicago: Probus, 1995)

*Strategic Database Marketing: The Master Plan for Starting and Managing a Profitable, Customer-Based Marketing Program* by Arthur M. Huges (Chicago: Probus, 1994)

*Valuing Your Customers: Quality Database Marketing* by Angus Jenkinson (New York: McGraw-Hill, 1995)

**Organization**
International Customer Service Association (ICSA)
401 North Michigan Ave.
Chicago, IL 60611

**Software**
Day-Time Organizer 2.1 by Day-Timer Technologies; (800) 859-6954; http://www.daytimer.com.
Act! 3.0 for Windows 95 and Windows 3.1 by Symantec; http://www.symantec.com

*Additional Business Ideas*
❖ Create your own line of courtesy cards and literature to sell to businesses for their customers.
❖ Customer service consultant—see *Customer Service for the New Millennium: Winning and Keeping Value-Driven Buyers* by Robert B. Tucker (Franklin Lakes, NJ: Career Press, 1997)

## ❧ 12 ❧
# COUPON ADVERTISING AND MAILING SERVICE

With this service, you will group promotional coupons from local small businesses and mail them in one envelope to the designated customers. You coordinate, print, and distribute targeted direct-mail coupon advertising campaigns for local businesses. Your business helps these smaller businesses afford direct mail by sharing the costs of advertising. Some community-based coupon businesses will sell these coupon books as fund-raising events for nonprofit organizations.

*Estimated Start-up Costs*
$7,000 to $16,000

*Pricing Guidelines*
Charge each company a rate for each mailing to x number of addresses; $300 + per thousand.

## Marketing and Advertising Methods and Tips
* Direct mail to targeted small and home-based businesses and follow-up telephone calls to make an appointment for a presentation
* Yellow Pages ad
* Word-of-mouth referrals
* Join local business associations for networking and making business contacts.

## Essential Equipment
* Home office: computer with mailing software, desktop publishing software, color printer, fax, telephone and answering capabilities, and photocopier
* Promotional materials: business cards and brochures

## Recommended Training, Experience, or Needed Skills
* Work, training, or experience in advertising, marketing, direct mailing, and co-op (coupon) mailing services
* Knowledge of mailing software and postal regulations

## Income Potential
$20,000 to $35,000, depending on the number of mailings you do per year.

## Type of Business
$2/3$ conducting business and mailings, $1/3$ marketing and meeting with your clients

## Best Customers
* Local, small, and home-based businesses that have limited advertising budgets
* Businesses that provide services and products to consumers

## Success Tips
* Have a good management system and pay attention to deadlines.

✤ Regularly evaluate the responses of the consumers to see whether they are using your client's coupons and why.

### Franchises, Distributorships, and Licenses
SuperSaver Coupons
80 Eighth Ave., #315
New York, NY 10011
(212) 243-6800
Offers coupon books for $5,000 to $15,000.

### Additional Information
**Recommended Reading**
*Direct-Marketing Coupon Designs: Designer Clip Art: 300 Creative Copyright-Free Camera-Ready Professional Layouts/Clip-Art Resource Book* (New York: McGraw-Hill, 1990)
*Entrepreneur's Small Business Development Catalog,* "Co-Op (Coupon) Mailing Service"; (800) 421-2300; $69.50 + shipping and handling

### Software
My Professional Mail Manager for Windows 95 and 3.1, by My Software Co.; (415) 473-3600; http://www.mymailist.com
ZP416 for Macintosh by Semaphone; (408) 688-9200; http://www.semaphorecorp.com/cgi/order.html

### Additional Business Ideas
Desktop publishing service—designing coupons, postcards, and mailings for businesses

### ↝ 13 ↜
## EXECUTIVE DIRECTOR SERVICES
An executive director service is also called an association management service. If this is your business, you are a specialist in handling many or all (if you are the founder) of the operations of

a trade or consumer association or organization. These groups are often run by volunteers who simply do not have the time or resources to carry on the many facets of operation that need to be performed. Services could include keeping a database of members, fundraising, producing a newsletter, marketing, and performing other essential activities.

These groups are formed for the purpose of promoting their trade, hobby, or special interest. If you have a unique interest, occupation, or pastime, you may want to start your own association. Look in the *Encyclopedia of Associations* (Gale Research) in the reference section of your library to see whether any exist for your idea or to make contacts with those already established. These groups can be established to be nonprofit or for profit.

### Estimated Start-up Costs
$3,000 to $10,000

### Pricing Guidelines
❖ $2,500 to $4,500 per month, depending on the tasks you perform and the association's budget
❖ Most executive directors are paid on a monthly or yearly retainer basis.

### Marketing and Advertising Methods and Tips
❖ Contact and network with trade, professional, and nonprofit organizations.
❖ Advertise in trade journals and newsletters.
❖ Attend trade conferences and conventions to make personal contacts.

### Essential Equipment
❖ Computer and home office equipment: fax, telephone with answering system, and on-line service for research and e-mail
❖ Promotional materials: business cards, stationery with letterhead, and brochures

### *Recommended Training, Experience, or Needed Skills*
❖ Degree and/or experience in human resources, office management, communications, financial management, fundraising, and administrative duties
❖ Working in volunteer capacities in one or more associations to get an idea of their operations and also to help you make contacts for personal referrals
❖ Good people skills

### *Income Potential*
❖ $1,000 to $4,000 + a month is an average payment as a retainer fee.
❖ $20,000 to $50,000 for directing an association or associations. You may specialize in a certain field such as fundraising and work for more than one organization.
❖ $18,000 to $50,000 + if you establish your own association, depending on your members; the dues you charge; whether you sponsor seminars, training, and conferences; and so forth.

### *Type of Business*
$1/2$ at home conducting business, $1/2$ attending meetings and traveling

### *Best Customers*
Professional and trade groups, hobbyists, religious institutions, nonprofit organizations

### *Success Tips*
❖ You will have more success at your position if you have had some experience or training related to the association you are assisting or managing.
❖ You should have marketing knowledge to increase the membership and increase your association's recognition.

## Additional Information
### Recommended Reading
*Associations and the Global Marketplace: Profiles of Success* by Kimberly A. Svero-Ciani (Washington, DC: American Society of Association Executives, 1995)

*Encyclopedia of Associations* (Detroit: Gale Research); available in the reference section of most libraries. Published annually and features over twenty-three nonprofit U.S. organizations.

*Principles of Association Management: A Professional's Handbook,* 2nd ed., by Henry Ernsthal and Vivian Jefferson (eds.) (Washington, DC: American Society of Association Executives, 1988)

### Organizations
American Society of Association Executives
1575 I Street, NW
Washington, DC 20005
Leading organization of nearly twenty-five thousand association executives who manage trade associations, individual membership societies, voluntary organizations, and other nonprofit U.S. and foreign associations. Also serves associate members who provide products and services to the association community. Support, meetings, trade shows; publishes *AMC Connection Newsletter,* quarterly.

Society for Nonprofit Organizations
6134 Odana Rd., Suite 1
Madison, WI 53719
"A nonprofit membership organization that provides information and resources to the nonprofit sector." Publishes *Nonprofit World Journal: The National Nonprofit Leadership and Management Journal.*

## Additional Business Ideas
❖ Web site designer for associations
❖ Volunteer specialist—finding volunteers to help staff associations

## ∽ 14 ∾
# HUMAN RESOURCES CONSULTANT

Human resources is a term covering many issues involving employees in the workplace. You can specialize in one area that you market to many companies or help small companies set up human resource departments to handle their own employee issues. With the many complex issues facing employers, your business should be in demand.

### Estimated Start-up Costs
$5,000 to $10,000

### Pricing Guidelines
* $35 to $75 an hour
* $1,000 to $2,000 per workshop or seminar

### Marketing and Advertising Methods and Tips
* Referrals
* Ads in trade publications
* Membership in local business associations
* Direct mail to companies followed up with a presentation
* Newsletter on human resource topics mailed to present and prospective clients

### Essential Equipment
* Home office: computer, printer, suite software, modem, fax, telephone, and answering system
* Promotional materials: brochures and business cards
* Human resource manuals and workshop materials

### Recommended Training, Experience, or Needed Skills
* Degree, training, and experience in human resources, psychology, and business management
* If possible, work in human management departments in several companies to get a broader outlook on business trends.

❖ Should be able to communicate and interact well with people
❖ Sales ability

### Income Potential
$35,000 to $70,000; start part-time while you build a client base and decide whether you want to specialize in one area.

### Type of Business
¹/₃ managing your business and preparing your materials; ²/₃ marketing and conducting classes, training workshops, and analyses at your clients' workplaces

### Best Customers
❖ Companies without human resource departments
❖ Companies with steady growth and that are increasing their work forces. (If the company is downsizing, you can help set up counseling and job referral programs.)

### Success Tips
❖ Take time to research this field thoroughly and study how human resource departments are run in different companies, in different industries.
❖ Your own experiences, and training will help determine your area of concentration.
❖ Try to be a "problem solver" for your clients, and be able to implement strategies so companies can enable their employees and personnel to be satisfied and productive.
❖ Take the time to develop your programs, so that you can offer more than one seminar, workshop, manual, and so forth, to companies.

### Franchises, Distributorships, and Licenses
Resource Associates Corporation
31 Hickory Rd.
Mohnton, PA 19540
Human resources training/consulting; write for information.

### Additional Information

**Recommended Reading**

*Barron's Business Library: Human Resources* by Richard G. Renchkley (Hauppage, NY: Barron's Educational Series, 1997)

*Care Packages for the Workplace: Little Things You Can Do to Regenerate Spirit at Work* by Barbara A. Glanz (New York: McGraw-Hill, 1996)

*Driving Fear Out of the Workplace: How to Overcome Invisible Barriers to Quality, Productivity, and Innovation* by Kathleen D. Ryan and Daniel K. Oestreich (San Francisco: Jossey-Bass, 1993)

### Additional Business Idea

Conduct seminars for businesses' employees on sexual harassment and discrimination issues.

## ࿖ 15 ࿖

# TIME MANAGEMENT SPECIALIST

As a time management specialist, you will be assisting your clients in streamlining their tasks and operating procedures for better productivity. You will also help the businesses' employees work more cooperatively and efficiently. If it is a sole proprietorship, you will analyze present operating procedures and business management and make or demonstrate which duties can be performed in a timely fashion and which may be better handled by another business.

### Estimated Start-up Costs

$2,500 to $7,000

### Pricing Guidelines

✤ $50 to $75 an hour
✤ $2,000 + for workshop

### Marketing and Advertising Methods and Tips

✤ Press releases
✤ Ads in local and regional trade and business publications

❖ Produce a newsletter covering time management and send to present and prospective business clients.
❖ Talks and seminars to business groups
❖ Direct mail with promotional materials to prospective clients
❖ Memberships in business associations

### Essential Equipment

❖ Home office: computer, printer, fax, modem, photocopier, telephone with answering system, and time management software
❖ Promotional materials: brochures and business cards
❖ Workshop and training manuals and handout materials

### Recommended Training, Experience, or Needed Skills

❖ Business and time management courses, training, education, and work experience
❖ Ability to communicate and teach time management skills
❖ Skill at evaluating and analyzing and coming up with practical solutions that a business can implement easily and at low cost

### Income Potential

$20,000 to $40,000

### Type of Business

$1/3$ in home office managing your business and preparing course and materials; $2/3$ marketing and conducting on-site conducting training and workshops

### Best Customers

❖ Small companies experiencing growth
❖ Sole proprietorships and partnerships that are trying to handle a multitude of business tasks as their business grows

### Success Tips

❖ Companies and businesses will be looking for you to give them practical steps, goals, action plans, scheduling tips, and new systems to help them run their businesses more efficiently and profitably.

❖ Offer an initial analysis price and then different programs with relevant prices to help the companies improve their use of time.

### Additional Information
#### Recommended Reading

*Beyond Time Management: Business with a Purpose* by Robert J. Wright (Newton, MA: Butterworth-Heinemann, 1996)

*Cycle Time Management: The Fast Track to Time-Based Productivity Improvement* by Patrick Northey and Nigel Southway (Portland, OR: Productivity Press, 1994)

*Do It Right the Second Time: Benchmaking Best Practices in the Quality Change Process* by Peter Merrill (Portland, OR: Productivity Press, 1997)

*Time Management for Dummies* by Jeffrey J. May (Foster City, CA: IDG Books Worldwide, 1997)

### Additional Business Idea
Time management software designer for specific industries

◦ ● ◦

# MISCELLANEOUS BUSINESS SERVICES

❖ Independent contractor agent
❖ Incorporation services for businesses
❖ Manufacturing consultant

# Children's Businesses

*Children are my favorite people.*

—Anonymous

With many parents working and the increase of single-parent households, there is barely enough time to do even routine chores. However, most parents want to give their children opportunities to participate in school, sports, music, dance, art, and other varied experiences to develop backgrounds and skills. Because of the demand, business experts foresee growth in such children-related businesses as recreation, play and entertainment, early childhood and supplemental education, computer skills, creative activities, and fitness programs. Other children-related ventures predicted to be profitable are child safety services, nanny services, child care, postpartum care, and children's transportation.

The criteria—first and foremost—in a child-related business is to love and understand children and to have staff that share your philosophy about children. If you want to feel "forever young," start a child-related business!

## ⊸ 16 ⊷
# EDUCATIONAL CONSULTANT

Many parents want the best education for their children. Several adults' lives are in transition: divorce, death of a spouse, loss of a job, desire to get more education and/or training for a new career, and so forth. Homeschooling is rapidly growing around the country. Students need to find the best college that meets their goals and educational spending budgets. How to find financing for one's education can be a time-consuming and frustrating experience (did you ever fill out a form to borrow money?). Coaching high school and college graduates to take entrance exams and educational tests required for admittance to colleges or graduate schools (including medical and law schools) is a big business in many communities. These are just a few of the reasons an educational consultant can have a successful business. You can specialize in one (or more) of these areas and help people of all ages get the education they desire.

### Estimated Start-up Costs
$7,000 to $10,000

### Pricing Guidelines
$30 to $50 an hour, or fees $500 to $1,000 for a course (SAT, etc.) held for a given number of weeks

### Marketing and Advertising Methods and Tips
❖ Promotional literature to school counselors, advisers, county human services departments, colleges and universities, and tutoring services
❖ Yellow Pages advertising
❖ Classified ads in local newspapers and parenting publications
❖ Ads on local cable TV channels
❖ Word-of-mouth referrals from satisfied parents and clients

### Essential Equipment
❖ Home office: computer and educational-related software, printer, fax and telephone answering system, and cellular phone

❖ Promotional materials: business cards, brochures, handouts on study tips and other educational tips that you can give out at talks to parents groups (have your contact information on these sheets)

❖ Books and manuals in your subject or area of expertise

### Recommended Training, Experience, or Needed Skills

❖ Degree in your area of specialization

❖ Training in psychology or counseling also helpful

❖ Experience and knowledge about college admission procedures, policies, tests, and so forth

❖ Keep up with the latest rules and changes in educational requirements in the area of your specialization.

❖ Good teaching skills and communications skills

### Income Potential

$15,000 to $100,000

### Type of Business

$1/2$ in home office (most of your time will be spent in your home office if it is set up for you to meet with clients in your home), $1/2$ meeting with clients in their homes or in rooms rented for larger classes

### Best Customers

❖ Parents of college-bound children

❖ Adults desiring to get more education and/or training for a new career

❖ Parents who homeschool their children

❖ Students searching for the best college that fits their goals and budgets

❖ People searching for educational financing

❖ Students looking for courses to help prepare them for the entrance exams

❖ Parents of children and adults with special needs

### Success Tips

❖ With education costs rising, your customers will depend on your expertise and knowledge to help prepare and guide them to the best institutions that will meet their aspirations.

❖ Keep a database of your customers to keep in touch with them as they go on toward more education.

## Franchises, Distributorships, and Licenses
Hope Career Centers
2735 S. Newton St.
Denver, CO 80236
(303) 934-1018
Educational information and financial aid services; write or call for information.

## Additional Information
### Recommended Reading
*The Educational Consultant,* 3rd ed. (Austin, TX: Pro-Ed, 1993)
*Educational Consulting: A Guidebook for Practitioners* by Fenwick W. English and Betty Steffy (Englewood Cliffs, NJ: Educational Technical Publications, 1994)

### Organization
Independent Educational Consultants Association (IEC)
4085 Chain Bridge Rd., Suite 401
Fairfax, VA 22030
Publishes annual directory; holds conferences, workshops, and seminars. Send a LSASE for membership information.

## Additional Business Ideas
❖ Consider educational product development—creating materials, books, software, and products based on your own educational experience and expertise.
❖ If you have a special education or social services degree, you can help parents find the best community programs they need for their child's mental or physical disabilities.

## ◁ 17 ▷
# DOULA SERVICES

*Doula* is a Greek word that pertains to a woman who supports and sustains new mothers and their families—"one who mothers the mother." It is based on an old custom of mothers helping mothers adjust to their lives that have changed due to the birth of a baby. The practice of some health plans allowing the release of new mothers from the hospital within one or two days of birth has increased the demands for such services.

Some doulas are also midwives and experienced labor companions. They will give constant support through the labor and birth process as well as later during the period of adjustment at home with the family. Some areas of the country (and some physicians) are more receptive to this personal service business than others.

### Estimated Start-up Costs
$3,000 to $5,000

### Pricing Guidelines
❖ $350 to $600 per client; depends on the amount of time you will spend—some clients need longer assistance, depending on their circumstances
❖ $400 for five days of care

### Marketing and Advertising Methods and Tips
❖ Contact midwives and childbirth instructors.
❖ Word-of-mouth referrals will be one of the best methods of marketing your services.
❖ Doctor's offices; some doctors will give referrals and others will not, depending on their acceptance of the role of doulas.
❖ Place ads in parenting publications.
❖ Talk to parents' and mothers' support groups.

### Essential Equipment
❖ Telephone with answering service
❖ Cellular phone and pager

❖ Dependable transportation
❖ Brochures and business cards

### Recommended Training, Experience, or Needed Skills
❖ Forty hours of certification coursework (see "Organization" on page 123)
❖ Education in postpartum conditions, breast-feeding, and first aid
❖ Experience and/or training in obstetric nursing and counseling
❖ Ability to function at times with little sleep
❖ Ability to present information to mothers and respect their decisions concerning themselves and their infants

### Income Potential
$20,000 for $35,000 for an individual; $50,000 + if you have others working for you

### Type of Business
Most of your time will be spent out-of-home in clients' homes, though you will have a home office for your base and for conducting business matters.

### Best Customers
Expectant and new mothers

### Success Tips
❖ Make sure you are qualified and certified to help new mothers either during or after the birth (or both).
❖ You may need to educate persons in your community about exactly what a doula does.
❖ You may work with nursing entrepreneurs to help women having home births.
❖ You must enjoy working with new mothers and their babies and helping their families.
❖ This business can involve longer hours than you would like.

### Additional Information
#### Recommended Reading
*The A to Z of Pregnancy and Childcare: A Concise Encyclopedia* by
Nancy Evans (Alemeda, CA: Hunter House, 1993)

*Mothering the Mother: How a Doula Can Help You Have a Shorter,
Easier and Healthier Birth* by Marshal H. Klaus, John H. Kennell,
and Phyllis H. Klaus (Reading, MA: Addison-Wesley, 1993)

*Natural Baby Care: Pure and Soothing Recipes and Techniques for
Mothers and Babies* by Colleen K. Dodt. Order from Storey's
How-To Books for Country Living, Schoolhouse Road, Pownal,
VT 05261; http://www.StoreyBooks.com.

#### Organization
Doulas of North America (DONA)
1100 23rd Ave. East
Seattle, WA 98112
Send a LSASE or visit http://www.dona.com/

### Additional Business Idea
Create "care" baskets for new mothers with such items as prepared meals; soothing bath oils and natural, handmade soaps;
and small gift Items for the babies.

### ⨳ 18 ⨳
# MAKING CHILDREN'S FURNITURE

Children are just delighted when they find furniture "just their
size." Children's furniture would include rockers, desks, high
chairs, ladder-back chairs, beds, youth chairs, training chairs,
stools, rocking cradles, standing cradles, clothes trees, hat racks,
sports equipment holders, book shelves, and wall shelves. You
could also scale down this furniture to doll size or to miniature
and reach two other markets for your work. If you already have
skills in woodworking or you think you might like to do this kind
of work (with your own creative touch), this could be a profitable
and fun venture for you.

### Estimated Start-up Costs
$5,000 to $7,000 for basic woodworking equipment, tools, and courses

### Pricing Guidelines
Shop rate between $30 and $45 or more an hour

### Marketing and Advertising Methods and Tips
* In most cases, you will be selling your furniture directly to the public. You may get some children's retail stores to carry some of your pieces.
* Advertise with classified ads and on cable TV.
* Send press releases to local media.
* Word-of-mouth referrals from satisfied customers

### Essential Equipment
* Buy as you make your profits. Look for good, used equipment at sales and in the classified ads. Tip: Take a person along with you who is knowledgeable about woodworking equipment if you are unsure about a new or used piece of equipment.
* Woodworking books and drawing board to design your own furniture style
* Table saw (one of the first pieces of equipment you should buy), scroll, band saw, table sander, drill press, cordless and/or electric drills, and screwdrivers; other hand tools
* Lumber, painting and drawing materials

### Recommended Training, Experience, or Needed Skills
* Woodworking courses at local vo-tech schools and/or apprenticeship or work with experienced woodworkers
* Knowledge of basic carpentry and furniture-making skills
* Knowledge of paints and finishes
* Artistic and creative flair for designing your own style of furniture

### Income Potential
$30,000 to $40,000

## Type of Business
$^1/_2$ at home designing, making, and producing your items; $^1/_2$ marketing and showing your furniture to prospective buyers

## Best Customers
Parents and grandparents, collectors, craft and children's retail stores

## Success Tips
❖ Do not use someone else's design, pattern, or famous figure (like the Disney characters) without first obtaining permission and a licensing agreement. If you originate a design, you can copyright your work. To register your unique designs, write to the U.S. Copyright Office, Library of Congress, Washington, DC 20559, for required forms and fees; ask for the form to register visual arts.

❖ Make sure your furniture (or any that you may refinish) is safe, and use nontoxic paints and finishes.

❖ If someone requests a custom-made piece, require that at least 50 percent of the price be paid before you make it.

## Additional Information
### Recommended Reading
*Art and Craft of Making Children's Furniture: A Practical Guide with Step-by-Step Instructions* by Chris Simpson (Philadelphia: Running Press, 1995)

*Checklists and Operating Forms for Small Businesses* by John C. Wisdom (New York: John Wiley and Sons, 1996)

*Creative Paint Finishes for Furniture* by Phillip C. Myer (Cincinnati: North Light Books, 1996)

*Decorative Painting Sourcebook* by Sandra Carpenter (Cincinnati: North Light Books, 1997)

*Juvenile Merchandising*, 2125 Center Ave., Suite 305, Fort Lee, NJ 07024-9791; $36/twelve issues.

*The Law (in Plain English) for Craftspeople*, 3rd ed., by Leonard D. Duboff (Loveland, CO: Interweave Press, 1993)

*Painted Furniture* (Quick & Easy Series) by Richard Wiles (New York: Sterling, 1997)

*The Woodworker's Guide to Pricing Your Work* by Dan Ramsey
  (Cincinnati: Betterway Books, 1995)

### Additional Business Ideas
Clean, refinish, and sell good, previously used children's furniture. Sell through classified ads, children's consignment shops, or weekly flea markets.

### ⊰ 19 ⊱
# NURSERY DECORATING SERVICE
With rising birthrates, many new parents will be looking to set up their first baby nurseries. If you have a talent for decorating, have created your own nursery, and have received many compliments on that nursery, you may want to consider this creative service business. You will need to know the latest in baby furniture, styles, products, as well as safety concerns. You may or may not need a license to operate, depending on your service—an interior designer generally has more technical training (and needs appropriate licenses) than an interior decorator who advises on furnishings, furniture, and wall coverings.

### Estimated Start-up Costs
$3,000 to $5000

### Pricing Guidelines
$30 to $50 an hour or a flat fee per room, which can range from $65 for a small room to $275 for a large room. Your fees could also include you getting the furnishings for the rooms you decorate.

### Marketing and Advertising Methods and Tips
❖ Newsletters and newspaper targeting parents
❖ Flyers in pediatrician's and obstetrician's offices; day care centers

❖ Keep a portfolio of photographs of nurseries you have designed for prospective customers to view.
❖ Word-of-mouth referrals from satisfied customers
❖ Referrals from baby furniture and supply stores
❖ Have a "Decorating for Baby's Room Night" at a decorator and paint store or a local baby good's store.
❖ Booth at a baby goods trade show
❖ Direct mail to day care centers and nursery schools

### Essential Equipment
❖ Home office: computer, design-related software, inkjet printer, photocopier, telephone and answering system, and drawing table
❖ Promotional materials: photo portfolio, brochures, and business cards
❖ Swatches, samples, and books showing different styles of furniture and babies' room accessories

### Recommended Training, Experience, or Needed Skills
❖ Training or education in interior design or interior decorating
❖ Artistic talent and creativity
❖ Good communication and business management skills

### Income Potential
$25,000 to $60,000

### Type of Business
$1/2$ at home planning and coordinating the rooms for your customers, $1/2$ decorating your client's rooms, shopping (if that is included in your fee) for the items, and coordinating any other people who are doing the decorating

### Best Customers
❖ New parents
❖ Day care centers and corporations that have on-site day cares

❖ Professional offices that cater to children
❖ Retailers that sell baby goods
❖ Nurseries and preschools

## Success Tips
❖ Join parenting associations and local business groups to network and promote your business.
❖ Decide whether you want to do just the decorating design; do the actual decorating (painting, sewing, arranging of furniture and fixtures) yourself or subcontract others to do it; and/or purchase and set up the furniture, and so forth, that the parents select.
❖ Develop a good relationship with retail and decorating supply stores.

## Additional Information
### Recommended Reading
*Babies' and Children's Rooms (for Your Home)* by Candie Frankel (New York: Friedman/Fairfax, 1997)

*Better Homes & Gardens Designing Kids' Rooms* by Meredith Books (Des Moines, IA: Better Homes & Gardens, 1997)

*Entrepreneur's Small Business Development Catalog*, "Interior Designer"; (800) 421-2300; $69.50 plus shipping and handling

*How to Start a Home-Based Interior Design Business* by Suzanne Dewalt (Old Saybrook, CT: Globe Pequot, 1997)

*Laura Ashley Decorating Children's Rooms: Creating Fun, Practical, and Safe Surroundings* by Joanna Copestick (New York: Crown, 1996)

### Home Study
Professional Career Development Institute
3597 Parkway Lane, Suite 100
Norcross, GA 30092
Write for a listing of courses.

### On-line Source
http://www.concentric.net/ ~ casals/decor.shtml
General decorating information.

## Additional Business Ideas

❖ If you are an artist, specialize in murals and scenes for nurseries and children's rooms.

❖ Decorator designer referral service—for a flat fee ($100 + ), show customers videos and photo portfolios of various designers and decorators that the parents can choose to create the look they want.

## ⊸ 20 ⊱

# PARENTING SPECIALIST

Often new parents do not live near immediate family members who can help them with child-rearing problems or give advice when a minor (or major) crisis happens to one of their children. As a parenting specialist, you will work with these parents in solving their child-rearing dilemmas or refer them to other specialists who are qualified in areas that you are not.

You can go to their homes to help with a newborn baby, address sleeping or eating problems and behavior habits, or even plan a sleep-over, party, or outing. You may be called on at odd hours if a parent is panicking or unable to handle a problem. You could offer "drug-free" behavior modification techniques if you have a degree in psychology or counseling.

## Estimated Start-up Costs

$1,000 to $4,000 +

## Pricing Guidelines

❖ $25 to $55 an hour

❖ Fee for a certain number of visits and phone calls

## Marketing and Advertising Methods and Tips

❖ Yellow Pages

❖ Referrals from other parents

❖ Direct mail to nursery schools, daycare centers, hospitals, pediatricians, and play groups

❖ Ads in parenting publications

* Cable TV classified ads
* Flyers on community bulletin boards in banks, grocery stores, and other businesses
* Talks to parent and community groups on raising and dealing with children
* Offer courses at hospitals, schools, and day care centers.

## Essential Equipment
* Home office: computer with modem and Internet access for research, laser or inkjet printer, and business phone with answering service (panicky parents will want to talk to a person)
* Cellular phone and pager
* Child development books, tapes, and other resources

## Recommended Training, Experience, or Needed Skills
* Degree or training in child psychology, early childhood education, special education, education, and/or counseling
* Experience working with all ages of children
* Helpful if you are a parent yourself

## Income Potential
$4,000 to $45,000 +

## Type of Business
$1/2$ at home with phone consultations or meeting with parents in your office, $1/2$ in parents' homes

## Best Customers
* Parents, grandparents, guardians, and primary caregivers of children and teenagers
* If you have a degree child psychology, education, or special education, you may be contracted as a consultant for schools, mental health centers, group homes, and drug rehabilitation centers.

## Success Tips

❖ Be able to analyze a situation with children, and give practical steps parents or caregivers can understand and follow.
❖ Be creative in your solutions and tailor them to each child.
❖ Be caring, calm, and supportive to harried parents.
❖ If the children are old enough, involve them in the solutions.
❖ Keep a sense of humor and have lots of patience.

## Additional Information

### Recommended Reading

*The ABC's of Parenting: A Guide to Help Parents and Caretakers Handle Child-Rearing Problems* by Joan Barbuto (Saratoga, CA: R & E, 1994).

*1,2,3, The Toddler Years: A Practical Guide for Parents and Caregivers* by Irene Van De Zande (Santa Cruz, CA: Santa Cruz Toddler Care Center, 1995)

*13 to 19: A Parent's Guide to Understanding the Teenage Years* by Wendy Grant (New York: Element, 1996)

*25 of the Best Parenting Techniques Ever* by Meg F. Schneider and Judi Craig (ed.) (New York: St. Martin's, 1997)

## Additional Business Ideas

❖ Publish a parents' newsletter.
❖ Start a parents' association.

## ~ 21 ~
## PARTIES-IN-A-BAG

With busy parents working and having little time to get party decorations for their children's parties, you can help them with your "Parties-in-a-Bag" service. You provide bags that contain special party decorations, balloons, candles, paper products, favors, and so forth, according to the themes you offer. This service's niche is that these party bags are ready to go at a moment's notice from a customer. You can be as creative as your imagination will allow.

## Estimated Start-up Costs
$500 to $2,000 for home office equipment and party supplies

## Pricing Guidelines
* Standard party bags: for party of eight with decorations and paper products—$34.95
* Theme bags (movies, characters, heroes, dinosaurs, dolls, etc.): for party of eight, theme-related decorations, paper products plus party favors—$47.50
* Deluxe theme bag with more elaborate decorations and favors—$60 to $100

## Marketing and Advertising Methods and Tips
* Flyers on community bulletin boards
* Referrals from event planners, party-related businesses, party equipment rentals, and cake decorators
* Referrals from satisfied parents; from friends and acquaintances for adult parties (birthdays, retirements, anniversaries, etc.)
* Have magnets advertising specialty party favors and print your business name on any party bag that will be sent home with party attendees.
* Ads in parenting magazines
* Deliver balloon bouquets with your business card attached.
* Donate some of your party bags to charity auctions or as door prizes and merchant drawings.

## Essential Equipment
* Scheduling software
* Party supplies, decorations, and favors
* Vehicle for deliveries
* Bags you create yourself or buy and decorate
* Promotional materials: balloons, advertising specialties, flyers, and business cards

## Recommended Training, Experience, or Needed Skills
* Read party idea books.

❖ Volunteer or assist in friends' and relatives' parties to get a working knowledge of the supply needs and operations of a child's party and an adult's party.

## Income Potential
$30,000 to $60,000, depending on the number of party requests

## Type of Business
$1/2$ in home putting together the bags and conducting business, $1/2$ out purchasing supplies and delivering party bags and balloon bouquets

## Best Customers
❖ Parents of children celebrating birthdays will be your main customers.
❖ Office workers who are holding birthday, retirement, and baby shower parties for coworkers

## Success Tips
❖ Offer delivery service with your party bags.
❖ Supply a sheet or booklets with suggested (and appropriate) party games and activities.
❖ Do market research in your community to see what the competition is offering, so you can make yours competitive and special.
❖ Keep up with the news, trends, and themes appropriate to both children and adults.
❖ Offer holiday theme party bags for celebrations for all ages.

## Additional Information
### Recommended Reading
*Child Magazine's Book of Children's Parties* by Angela Wilkes (New York: Dorling-Kindersley, *Child* Magazine, 1996)
*Children's Party Business* (booklet) by Priscilla Y. Huff (1997); Little House Writing & Publishing, Box 286, Sellersville, PA 18960; $6.95 (PA residents, $7.43) + $1 shipping and handling

*Decorating Gift Baskets, Boxes, and Bags* by Amanda Knight (New York: Sterling, 1996)
*Great Ideas for Gift Baskets, Bags and Boxes* by Kathy Lamancusa (Blue Ridge Summit, PA: Tab Books, 1992)
*It's Party Time: How to Start and Operate Your Own Home-Based Party Planning Business* by M. L. Hine (New York: Carlton, 1996)

**Organization**
M & M International Inc.
13860 W. Laurel Dr.
Lake Forest, IL 60045
Extensive party and celebration supplies. Write or call for a catalog: (847) 680-4700.

*Additional Business Idea*
Party decorating service

## ⋘ 22 ⋙
## SPECIAL CHILD (AND ELDER) DAY CARE

"Entrepreneurs with a love of children and a head for management can find a sure-bet business in opening an at-home child (or elder care) business," says Patricia C. Gallagher. The author of *Start Your Own At-Home Child Care Business* (and mother of four) also says, "With careful planning and an earnest desire to provide a safe and loving environment, the day care business can be very satisfying."

Because the U.S. population is also aging—especially with the baby boomers now in their fifties (shortly after the year 2020, there will be more Americans over age sixty-five than under age thirteen; *Newsweek*, January 27, 1997)—there is and will continue to be a need for in-home and elder day care services. Thus, with the young and old needing care, a business related to either of these populations' needs should prove profitable. The niches being highlighted in this section are the special day and elder care services that are needed: sick, evening, and drop-in child and elder care services. Parents of young children and adult children of mature adults will need your services. You can provide these in your home or in your clients' homes.

### Estimated Start-up Costs
$3,000 to $5,000

### Pricing Guidelines
Weekly charges: $40 per child, $50 per adult

### Marketing and Advertising Methods and Tips
**For Children's Day Care**
- ❖ Yellow Pages
- ❖ Flyers on community bulletin boards, pediatrician's offices, and school bulletin boards
- ❖ Ads in classified and parenting newspapers
- ❖ Word-of-mouth referrals from satisfied parents
- ❖ Talks to parents' groups on child development

**For Elders' Care**
- ❖ Flyers at senior adult centers
- ❖ Mailings to doctor's offices specializing in gerontology
- ❖ Advertisements in newsletters and publications that target mature adults
- ❖ Referrals from health agencies and satisfied customers

### Essential Equipment
- ❖ Home office: computer, business-related software, telephone and answering system/voice mail, printer, fax, pager, and cellular phone
- ❖ Child care: quality furniture (can be bought used), learning toys (check for safety), cribs, high chairs, changing table, playpens, first aid supplies, craft supplies, educational materials, videos, art and craft supplies, games, children's books; outdoor area (fenced)
- ❖ Elder care: craft and hobby materials; radios, televisions, cassette or CD players; outdoor sitting and activity area; books;

desks. Facilities will have to be accessible to persons with disabilities.

### Recommended Training, Experience, or Needed Skills

**Child Care**

- ✤ Licensing and training, education in early childhood education, psychology, and child development
- ✤ Nursing degree (for handling ill children or children with special needs)
- ✤ Experience working in one or more child care centers
- ✤ First aid and child CPR training
- ✤ Love of children

**Elder Care**

- ✤ Licensing and training, education in gerontology topics and psychology; first aid, CPR, and health training—preferably nursing
- ✤ Love of seniors

### Income Potential

At-home care: $20,000 to $40,000, depending on the number of persons and what you are permitted by your local and state regulations

### Type of Business

$3/4$ at home taking care of your attendees, $1/4$ marketing and getting supplies

### Best Customers

- ✤ Parents who are going to night school, work the night shift, have temporary job assignments, have appointments, or cannot miss work (for your sick-child care)
- ✤ Elder parents whose children attend night school, work the night shift, go on trips, or need temporary care of their loved one

## Success Tips

❖ For your special care services—evening care, sick-child care, drop-in day care—you should have brochures and information printed to hand out so the primary caregivers of the children and seniors will know your hours, the extent and limits of your care, the charges, and any other information you feel is important.

❖ Make sure you have the adequate and necessary insurance (liability, etc.) that your business requires.

❖ Make sure you have the mandatory licenses and qualifications needed to run your care services.

❖ Allow yourself at least a year to research critical issues such as state regulations, required inspections, zoning issues, restrictive ordinances, and insurance concerns.

❖ Visit and work in facilities that serve the ages of people whom you will be serving.

❖ Recognize that operating your care service requires not only a caring and loving personality but also financial and management knowledge.

❖ Do market research in your community to see whether such services are needed.

## Franchises, Distributorships, and Licenses

Family Child Care Success System
3901 Dartmouth Dr.
Minnetonka, MN 55345
Materials to prepare you for a family child care business. Send a LSASE for more information.

## Additional Information
### Recommended Reading

*Elder Practice: A Multidisciplinary Approach to Working with Older Adults in the Community* by Terry Tirrito, Ilene Nathanson, and Nieli Lange (Columbia, SC: University of South Carolina Press, 1996)

*Entrepreneur's Small Business Development Catalog,* "Child Services" and "Day Care Services"; (800) 421-2300; $69.50 each plus shipping and handling

*Families in Flux: New Approaches to Meeting Workforce Challenges for Child, Elder, and Health Care in the 1990s* by Sara A. Levitan and Elizabeth Conwey (London: Bureau of National Affairs, 1990)

*National Business Library's 1998 Small Business Catalog,* "Child Care" and "Daycare for Seniors"; (800) 947-7724; $49.95 each plus shipping and handling

*Start Your Own At-Home Child Care Business,* revised and expanded ed., by Patricia C. Gallagher (St. Louis, MO: Mosby-Year Book, 1994)

*Start Your Own Childcare Business* by Dawn Kilgore (ed.) (Upper Saddle River, NJ: Prentice Hall, 1996)


## Organizations

National Association for Home Care
519 C St. NE
Washington, DC 20002-5809
Send a SASE for information.

National Home Caring Council (division of the Foundation for Hospice and Homecare)
519 C St., NE
Washington, DC 20002

National Association for Family Child Care
1313-A Pennsylvania Ave., NW, Suite 348
Washington, DC 20004
Offers accreditation to day care providers who meet their states' requirements. Send a LSASE for membership and other information.

Friend of the Family
880 Holcomb Bridge Rd., #1608
Roswell, GA 30075
Makes personnel referrals for child and elder care.

**Home Study**
International Correspondence Schools
925 Oak St.
Scranton, PA 18515
Offers many courses, including "Child Day Care" and "Home
Health Aide."

### Additional Business Ideas
❖ Create materials for day care and elder care facilities.
❖ Subcontract your services to schools for before- and after-
school care programs.
❖ Start a referral service for elder and child care.

## ∝ 23 ∽
# SPECIAL SUBJECTS
# INDEPENDENT CONTRACTOR
With education costs burgeoning, many public and private
schools are cutting out "special" subjects such as art, music,
dance, adapted physical education, programs for gifted students,
and other unique studies. If you are a certified teacher or trainer
in these areas, you can contract your services to public, charter, and private schools; day care and creative learning centers;
tutoring centers; and/or home schooling groups.

### Estimated Start-up Costs
$500 to $3,000

### Pricing Guidelines
$35 to $50+ an hour, or a fee designated in a mutual agreement
and contract for a certain length of time and number of days

### Marketing and Advertising Methods and Tips
❖ Direct mail and presentations to school administrators and
school boards in your areas

❖ Referrals from previous employers, parents, and students
❖ Ads in educational trade and day care publications and homeschooling newsletters
❖ Hospital recreational programs
❖ Centers sponsoring group homes for persons with physical and mental disabilities

### Essential Equipment
❖ Materials and equipment related to your subject
❖ Contracts
❖ Filing systems
❖ Business phone and answering system, cellular phone, and pager
❖ Optional: van that you can equip to carry your equipment and supplies

### Recommended Training, Experience, or Needed Skills
❖ Business management courses
❖ Teaching certifications in your area of expertise
❖ Creativity in devising challenging lessons

### Income Potential
$20,000 to $40,000

### Type of Business
$1/4$ at home for planning lessons (unless your students come to your home), $3/4$ teaching on-site

### Best Customers
❖ Schools that are eliminating or cutting back on enrichment programs
❖ Hospitals with recreational therapy programs
❖ Centers and foundations that direct group homes for persons with mental and physical disabilities
❖ Senior citizen centers

❖ Day care programs (children, elder persons) and nursery schools
❖ Homeschooling groups

*Success Tips*
❖ Make sure you have all necessary licenses, degrees, and certifications in your area of specialization.
❖ Develop good communications with the schools and centers for which you work.
❖ Welcome observations, and give thorough evaluations of students' progress if required.
❖ Have a culminating program at the end of your contracted period (i.e., concert, art show, gym show, recital, etc.) for families.
❖ Check to make sure you have adequate insurance coverage, and with a lawyer if you have questions concerning any contracts.

*Additional Business Ideas*
Sponsor summer creative programs at your home (if your facilities permit it), or contract to day camps, Bible school programs, and community park programs.

# MISCELLANEOUS CHILDREN'S BUSINESSES

❖ Children's sports consultant—sponsor clinics to teach sports skills, offer coaching clinics for new coaches, and present sports safety clinics; invite athletic trainers and sports medicine specialists.
❖ Infant and children's swimming school—in individual's home pools, teach swimming and pool safety; contact Infant Swimming Research, P.O. Box 5857, Winter Park, FL 32793-5857; and read *We Are All Water Babies* by Jessica Johnson and Michel Odent (Berkeley, CA: Ten Speed Press, 1995).

❖ Children's regional resource guides—publish resource directories of information about local or regional areas for parents

❖ Playgroup—see *Starting and Operating a Playgroup for Profit;* order from Pilot Books, 127 Sterling Ave, P.O. Box 2102, Greenport, NY 11944-2102; $3.95; or call (800) 79-PILOT.

# Computer and
# Internet Businesses

*Where we go and what we do advertises what we are.*

—Anonymous

Just as the telephone became a mainstay of almost every business's communications, so too has the computer. It has forced many of us—often kicking and screaming all the way—to learn its operations, software, and programs to conduct business, keep up with the competition, and now to take our ventures onto the Internet and the World Wide Web. Computer Industry Almanac, Inc., shows computers per capita are increasing at a current annual rate of 3.5 units per 100 people in the United States. As of January 1, 1996, there were only twenty-four U.S. Internet service businesses. One year later, 2,298 were operating (*American Business Information*).

The Web permits communication within the Internet through the use of hypertext links that are highlighted key words, also known as "hot text." By clicking on these hypertext words, the user is instantly transported to a connecting computer through a labyrinth of tens of thousands of computer networks.

Businesses are rushing to set up Web sites to advertise their businesses with projections that Internet advertising will grow by 20 to 30 percent (or more) a year for the next five years. Prices, however, to advertise your business on the Internet can run as low as $59.95 a month to $50,000 a year. Businesses can be linked to a host computer costing thousands of dollars or use the more affordable rates to connect through a local on-line services provider that supplies Internet access at a flat rate, similar to basic phone service.

Advertising (not "spamming"—see the glossary) takes place through a business's Web site, which is created by a Web site designer, or you can learn to do it yourself with the software programs now available. The advertising possibilities when you have your own Web site are unlimited as to the customers you can reach, but the downside is that your site will be just one of millions that exist and can literally get "lost" in cyberspace. The goals are first to get potential customers to visit your site; second, to keep them there long enough to read what your business is offering; and third, to give them a reason to return on a regular basis.

One woman entrepreneur in my county owns a business called The Chocolate Factory. She pays a commercial service to design her Web page and update it periodically. She says she does not have time to design it herself since she also produces the chocolate candies. However, the expense has been worth it to her sales as the site has enabled her to sell chocolate to customers as far away as Japan! Thus, as with any advertising form, you have to research what works for your business, so you should take the time to talk to other home-based business owners with Web sites, read books and articles on this topic, and decide whether this advertising venue will increase your profits. To ignore this rapidly growing source of advertising, though, may leave your business far behind the competition.

Even small towns' local business associations are joining together for Web sites. Local customers can browse through the sites of businesses only a few miles away but may not have the time to visit the stores. Women entrepreneurs I know use the Internet for its research capabilities to gain business information, network via e-mail with other women business owners and support associations throughout the country and the world, and look for new markets they never would have imagined before.

## Recommended Reading

*Advertising on the Internet* by Robbin Zeff and Bradley Aronson (New York: Wiley, 1977)

*The Complete Idiot's Guide to Creating an HTML Web Page* by Paul McFedries (Indianapolis: Que Corporation, 1996)

*CompuFax Monthly*—"a computer tips newsletter designed specifically for computer consultants to redistribute as their own"; $39.95/year via e-mail (http://www.pwgroup. com/compufax/); $49.95/year on diskette via U.S. mail

*Creating Killer Web Sites: The Art of Third Generation Site Design* by David Siegel (Indianapolis: Hayden, 1996)

*Enterprise One to One: Tools for Competing in the Interactive Age* by Don Peppers and Martha Rogers (New York: Bantam, Doubleday, Dell, 1997)

*Entrepreneur's Small Business Development Catalog*, "The Internet Entrepreneur"; $69 + $7.95 for shipping and handling; send order to 638 Lindero Canyon Rd., Agoura Hills, CA 91301-5464; or for credit card orders, call (800) 421-2300

*Home Office Computing*, P.O. Box 53543, Boulder, CO 80323-3543; $16.97/twelve issues

*HomePC*, P.O. Box 420212, Palm Coast, FL 32142-9468; $12.97/ twelve issues

*How to Earn More Than $25,000 a Year with Your Home Computer: Over 140 Income-Producing Projects* (Secaucus, NJ: Citadel, 1997)

*Income Opportunities'* "The Internet: A World of Home Business Opportunities"; $79.50 + postage and handling; call (888) 836-8844 to order; http://www.incomeops.com

*Internet World*, P.O. Box 7462, Red Oak, IA 51591-2462; $14.97/ twelve issues

*Laura Lemay's Web Workshop: Creating Commercial Web Pages* by Laura Lemay and Brian K. Murphy (Indianapolis: Sams.net, $39.99)

*Making Money with Your Computer at Home: The Inside Information You Need to Know to Select and Operate a Full-Time, Part-Time, or Add-On Business* by Paul and Sarah Edwards (New York: Putnam, 1997)

*101 Businesses You Can Start on the Internet* by Daniel S. Janal (New York: Van Nostrand Reinhold, 1997)

*Secrets of Successful Web Sites* by David Siegel (Indianapolis: Hayden, 1997)

*Smart Computing,* P.O. Box 85380, Lincoln, NE 68501-9807; $29/ twelve issues

*The Web and Media Pricing Guide* by J. P. Frenza and Michelle Szabo (Hayden, 1997)

*Web Developer,* P.O. BOX 7463, Red Oak, IA 51591-2463; $19.97/ six issues

*The Web Magazine,* Subscription Dept., P.O. Box 56943, Boulder, CO 80323-6943; $12/twelve issues

*Webonomics: Nine Essential Principles for Growing Your Business on the World Wide Web* by Evan I. Schwartz (New York: Broadway, 1997)

*Web Publishing Unleashed: Professional Reference* by William R. Stanek, book and CD-ROM (Indianapolis: Sams.net, 1997)

Books on computer programs and related topics can also be found at Microsoft Press's Web site: mspress.microsoft.com.

### Book Clubs
Small Computer Book Club
A Newbridge Book Club
P.O. Box 6021
Delran, NJ 08075

Many computer and Internet books from which to choose. Write for membership information.

### Organizations
International Association of Computer Professionals (IACP)
c/o C.E.S. Business Consultants
4133 E. Freedom Circle
Ooltewah, TN 37363
http://www.computerexperts.com/iacp/members/benefits.html

Offers books and newsletters; orders for the following publications can be sent to the address given here or, for Visa/MasterCard shoppers, by calling (800) 524-2307:

*How to Get and Keep Customers for Your Computer-Based Business*—"secret marketing formula" for five computer-based businesses: desktop publishing, software consulting, hardware consulting, database programming, and computer training; promotional materials and diskette; $29.95 + $4 priority mail shipping and handling; http://www.computerexperts. com/ces/getkeep.html

*How to Run a Successful Computer Training Business from Home*—step-by-step guide, diskette with flyers, brochures, and so forth; $21.95 + $4 U.S. priority mail shipping and handling; http:www.computerexperts.com/ces/cesshowt. html

*Keeping Your Sanity in a Home Business*—tips and marketing information; $14.95 + $4 U.S. priority mail shipping and handling; http://www.computerexperts.com/ceskeep.html

International Internet Association
23623 N. Scottsdale Rd., D-31252
Scottsdale, AZ 85255

Women in Computers
41 Sutter St., Suite 10006
San Francisco, CA 94104
http://www.awc-hq.org
Association for women in computing; monthly newsletter, annual conference. Send a LSASE for membership information.

**Home Study**
NRI Schools
4001 Connecticut Ave., NW
Washington, DC 20078-3543
Offers such courses as "Webmaster," "Multimedia Programming," "Desktop Publishing with PageMaker," and "Networking with Windows NT."

## Software
Included here are just a few of many software programs available—check with a local computer consult if you need help in selecting.

Business Internet Suite, by Peachtree Software, Norcross, GA; $129; (800) 247-3224

My Internet Business Page, My Software Company, 129 El Camino Real, Suite 167, Menlo Park, CA 94025-4227; (800) 391-6060; http://www.mysoftware.com

## Supplies
Surplus Direct
Box 2000
Hood River, OR 97031-2000

Computers, accessories, and software. Write for a current catalog.

Most of the ventures featured in this section are on-line businesses you can start. They are just a few of the many that are and will be on-line. Some are traditional businesses, others exist because of the Internet and World Wide Web, and still others have yet to be created. You may come up with a computer-related and/or on-line business that is completely new! The possibilities are endless.

Take your time and learn all you can about computers and Internet businesses. It may take as long as a year to finally open your doors (or Web site), but it is better to follow your business plan step by step and know what you are doing than to rush headlong into business failure.

For most of the Internet businesses, the start-up information is similar in the following areas.

### Estimated Start-up Costs
✤ Average $5,000 to $7,000
✤ Start-up costs can range from just a few hundred dollars to $25,000 and up.
✤ $2,500 for computer equipment and $2,000 to $3,000 for

Web creation (large ad agencies could charge from $5,000 to $25,000 and up)

❖ An information business will cost much less than a business with inventory to sell via mail order.

❖ You also have several options (and prices) to connect your business to the Internet. Prodigy and America Online offer low-cost options—you design your own home page for about $9 to $19.95 a month, and they maintain all the security, software, and hardware for it. You cannot take orders, though. Call for more information: America Online: (800) 827-6364; Prodigy: (800) 776-3449.

❖ Digital Mall—hosts your site, provides the equipment and telephone lines, maintains security and maintenance. Charges for other services. Monthly rental prices range from several hundred to several thousand dollars.

❖ Direct connection—your computer would be hooked up through your Internet service provider directly to the major telephone carriers. This would cost at least $25,000 to purchase the computers, modems, software, and telephone line. Large companies will use this type of connection more than small businesses.

## Marketing and Advertising Methods and Tips

❖ Register with the most popular search engine directories such as Yahoo, Web Crawler, Lycos, HotBot, Infoseek, Alta Vista, and others.

❖ Link with other businesses sites.

❖ Announce your site opening by sending press releases.

❖ Create a signature—an electronic business card—at the end of each e-mail. Include your name, business, e-mail address, Web site address, telephone number, and any other information that describes your business.

❖ Do not engage in spamming—unwanted solicitations to news groups or mailing lists.

❖ List your Web site and e-mail addresses on all your business stationery and promotional materials.

❖ Advertise in trade, hobby, and business publications.

## Essential Equipment
Computer with modem (14.4 kbps, 28.8 kbps preferred or faster), CD-ROM drive, telephone line, "browser" software (allows you to use the Web; Netscape Navigator and Microsoft Explorer are two of the most popular), printer

## Tips for a Successful Web Site
❖ Have your Web site present your products or services in an attractive format.
❖ Make it easy for customers to access the information they want.
❖ Know your reasons for why your business is on-line: to reach worldwide customers? To give out information? Other?
❖ Update your site regularly with useful information so your customers will want to come back to your site and be customers for life.

## ∾ 24 ∾
# CLASSIFIED ADS (INTERNET BUSINESS)
In this Internet business, you create a home page of advertisements that can list a variety of items for sale or use classified ads as another service for your site—for example, a vintage car page with classified ads for parts, cars, restoration services, and so forth. Sellers and buyers like the convenience and can reach a much larger audience than with a newspaper classified.

## Pricing Guidelines
❖ Charge for listing an item or service for sale.
❖ Sell banner ads to local merchants.
❖ Run a blind response box (the buyer does not know who is selling the item).
❖ Charge fees for handling inquiries and forwarding mail.

## Recommended Training, Experience, or Needed Skills
Be good at writing copy if the customer wants you to write the classified ads.

**Best Customers**
People wanting to buy, sell, or trade items

**Success Tips**
* Visit other classified sites for some ideas how you want yours to be set up.
* Automate your placing of ads and customer billing to free up more of your time.

**Additional Information**
**Recommended Reading**
*The Art Business Encyclopedia* by Leonard Duboff (New York: Allworth, 1997)
*Buying and Selling Antiques and Collectibles for Fun and Profit* by Don and Joan Bingham (Boston: Tuttle, 1994)

## ⤳ 25 ⤴
# COLLECTORS' SITE (INTERNET BUSINESS)

When a friend gave her husband a hand-carved carousel horse she had found in an antique shop, she wanted to find out how much it was worth. To help her out, I searched on the Internet and found a Web site just for carousel collectors. It listed people and businesses that had carousel figures for sale along with color photos, gave the association's address, featured a magazine devoted to this topic, and listed present-day carvers of carousel animals. I was able to find a man who gave appraisals for carousel animals for a $10 fee and a photo. Her horses (she ended up purchasing another one), by the way, were not from original American carousels (and would have been possibly worth thousands of dollars if they were an original Denzel or Mueller carving), but she did find out that they are worth about twice the amount she paid for them.

If you have a hobby and special interest and knowledge in this endeavor, you could host your own site for others with similar interests around the world. The more information you provide on a regular basis, the more visitors you will have to your site.

## Pricing Guidelines
❖ Sell pieces from your own collections and related gift items.
❖ Charge fees to other collectors for selling their things on your site.
❖ Charge fees to businesses that purchase advertising space to sell items to this target market of particular collectors.

## Marketing and Advertising Methods and Tips
❖ Ads in hobbyist publications and newsletters
❖ Booths at hobby shows

## Recommended Training, Experience, or Needed Skills
❖ Knowledge and contacts in your hobby industry
❖ Helps to be an "expert" in your field. Tip: Often if you write a book or two on your hobby, this will help establish you as an "expert" in your field. If you cannot find a publisher, publish it yourself and sell from your Web site (see "Sourcebook Writer" and "Self-Publisher" in the "Word Businesses" section for more information on self-publishing).

## Best Customers
❖ Other hobbyists looking to buy or sell their collector's items
❖ Advertisers wanting to reach this market

## Success Tip
People love to know how much their collector's items are worth. Periodically, invite other experts in this field to write topics on appraising a sample piece or the background and history of it.

## Additional Information
### Recommended Reading
*The Complete Idiot's Guide to Buying and Selling Collectibles* by Laurie E. Rozakis (New York: Alpha, 1997)

*Kovels' Antiques and Collectibles,* 30th ed., Price List (1998) by
Ralph and Terry Kovel (New York: Crown Publisher)
*Price Guide to Flea Market Treasures,* 4th ed., by Harry L. Riner, Jr.
(Radnor, PA: Wallace-Homestead, 1997)
*The Where-to-Sell-It Directory;* order from Pilot Books, 127 Ster-
ling Ave., P.O. Box 2102, Greenport, NY; (800) 79-PILOT.

## ❦ 26 ❧
# COMPUTER CLEANING
# (COMPUTER BUSINESS)

This is a technological cleaning business in which you set up
regular visits to home-based and small (or large) businesses to
clean their PCs and their peripherals—an office equipment
cleaning services business. Your services could include cleaning,
removing paper dust, providing antistatic coating, refilling toner,
and so forth.

### Estimated Start-up Costs
* ❖ $3,000 to $12,000
* ❖ Cost of training for computer maintenance courses

### Pricing Guidelines
* ❖ $35 to $60 an hour or contract fee decided on the number of
  visits and units you clean and maintain
* ❖ $1 to $3 per telephone unit; $3.50 to $8 per computer
* ❖ $25 to $45 per student if conducting a workshop for employees or new computer owners

### Marketing and Advertising Methods and Tips
* ❖ Direct mail to businesses, followed by appointments to give
  free estimates of your service
* ❖ Articles in business publications
* ❖ Join local business associations to network your service.
* ❖ Yellow Pages
* ❖ Launch a press release campaign on how your business can
  save computer users money in increased efficiency, longevity,
  and use of their technical equipment.

## Essential Equipment

❖ Computer and specific cleaning equipment and solutions
❖ Promotional materials: regularly send out professional-looking brochures and flyers about the value of your business.

## Recommended Training, Experience, or Needed Skills

❖ Some technical knowledge of the workings of computers
❖ Good communications skills and ability to help customers deal with computer "crises"
❖ See whether you can take training courses sponsored by the manufacturers of the equipment that you will be cleaning and maintaining. They can instruct you in the specifics of handling their equipment as well as the recommended solutions to use and other guidelines.

## Income Potential

$45,000 to $60,000

## Type of Business

$1/4$ at home conducting your business and marketing plans, $3/4$ on the site of your customers' businesses

## Best Customers

❖ Any business to which the operations of their computers and equipment is essential
❖ Computer retailers—you can contract with them to give service to new customers or conduct weekly seminars on computer maintenance and operations.
❖ Computer consulting businesses

## Success Tips

❖ Be knowledgeable with each of the systems you maintain.
❖ If possible, arrange servicing times that will not interfere with your customer's daily business operations.

❖ It may be inconvenient, but be available for emergency calls. Have a network of computer repair persons, troubleshooters, consultants, and the like, also on call to help your clients if they have computer technical problems.

❖ Make sure you are adequately insured and bonded so that if you inadvertently damage any equipment, you will be covered by insurance.

### Franchises, Distributorships, and Licenses
Scott Direct
2501 22nd Ave. N, #1002
St. Petersburg, FL 33713
(813) 528-2677
Computer cleaning and repair; write or call for more information.

### Additional Information
Supplies
Perfect Data Corporation
110 W. Easy St.
Simi Valley, CA 93065
http://www.perfectdata.com/catalog/toc.htm
Producers of maintenance products for computers and office peripherals. Write for a catalog or visit the Web site.

### Additional Business Idea
Create your own video about cleaning and maintenance techniques to sell to businesses and corporations. Advertise in trade publications and on the Internet. For tips, see *Videomaker's Comprehensive Guide to Making Videos* by Video Magazine Editors (New York: Butterworth-Heinemann, 1996) and *Marketing with Video: How to Create a Winning Video for Your Small Business or Non-Profit Organization* (book and video), by Hal Linden, from Oak Tree Press, 256 Guinea Hill Rd., Slate Hill, NY 10973; (914) 355-1400.

∞ 27 ∞

# DESKTOP VIDEO PRODUCTION COMPANY (COMPUTER BUSINESS)

With this business, you create graphics, special effects, audio production, and educational materials for business clients.

### Estimated Start-up Costs

From $2,500 (using rented equipment) to $40,000 to $50,000 purchasing your own equipment

### Pricing Guidelines

- ❖ $50 an hour and up.
- ❖ Fee per project can run several thousand dollars. It is recommended to ask for 50 percent down on the project, with the rest paid on delivery.
- ❖ Check video industry standards.
- ❖ Compare your rates with those of other similar services.

### Marketing and Advertising Methods and Tips

- ❖ Press releases to newspaper, radio, and TV (major stations as well as local cable stations)
- ❖ Word-of-mouth referrals
- ❖ Send out demo reels and business brochures, and follow up with an appointment to specific targeted markets.
- ❖ Telemarketing to targeted markets
- ❖ Sponsor a free seminar for businesses at a local college.

### Essential Equipment

- ❖ Promotional materials: demo tapes, brochures, and business cards
- ❖ Production: computer with desktop publishing and graphics software
- ❖ Graphics workstation (can cost $40,000 + )
- ❖ Diagnostic equipment and furniture

### Recommended Experience, Training, or Needed Skills
✤ Knowledge of computer graphics equipment and software
✤ Hands-on experience working on projects (volunteer or work at a cable TV studio). An apprenticeship would be ideal.
✤ See whether animation seminars or courses are offered at schools near you.
✤ Ability to "visualize" an idea as it can be imputed to your computer
✤ Be creative but also a problem solver in what you design.

### Income Potential
$45,000 to $100,000 +

### Type of Business
$3/4$ in your home office/studio, $1/4$ marketing and consulting with your customers

### Best Customers
Businesses, institutions, and others that need computer animation and video graphics for advertising, audiovisual, and/or educational materials

### Success Tips
✤ Read trade and local business journals and publications to identify your customers' needs.
✤ Determine who your target customers are, and approach them with ideas about how you can help their organizations grow and profit.

### Additional Information
#### Recommended Reading
*Digital Character Animation* (book and CD-ROM) by George Maestri (Indianapolis: New Riders, 1996)
*3D Graphics and Animation from Starting Up to Starting Out* (book and CD-ROM) by Mark Ciambruno (Indianapolis: New Riders, 1997)

*3 D Graphics: Tips, Tricks, and Techniques* by David J. Kalwich (San Diego: AP Professional, 1996)

### Additional Business Idea
Video-editing service—freelance, off-line editing of videotapes

## ◈ 28 ◈
# INTERNET MARKETING SPECIALIST (INTERNET BUSINESS)

With this business, you will be creating the marketing advances for each of your client's businesses. You must be able to ascertain from your customer what she expects out of her commercial Web site and then design a basic business strategy that will sell the company's products and/or services.

### Pricing Guidelines
$35 to $75 + an hour

### Marketing and Advertising Methods and Tips
❖ You can specialize in marketing in one industry or handle a variety of businesses.
❖ Web site

### Recommended Training, Experience, or Needed Skills
❖ Marketing experience or degree
❖ Ability to create effective Internet communications
❖ Knowledge of the industry in which you are specializing

### Income Potential
$25,000 to $45,000

### Success Tips
❖ Network constantly to broaden your contacts.
❖ Find your niche and focus on it.

❖ Locate your customer's best marketing avenues through customer surveys and feedback.

❖ Be able to analyze the components of your customer's Web site and make recommendations to increase customer responses.

### Franchises, Distributorships, and Licenses
RMS Internet Marketing Group
27 Haverhill
Chester, NH 03036
Information on Internet Yellow Pages advertising; write for information.

### Additional Information
### Recommended Reading
*Cybermarketing: Your Interactive Marketing Consultant* by Regina Brady (Lincolnwood, IL: NTC Business Books, 1997)

*The Internet Marketing Plan: A Practical Handbook for Creating, Implementing, and Assessing Your Online Presence* (book and CD-ROM) by Kim M. Bayne (New York: Wiley, 1997)

See also the book offered by IACP, *How to Get and Keep Customers for Your Computer-Based Business,* listed at the beginning of this chapter.

### Additional Business Idea
Internet market research—searching for the best markets for your customers

❦ 29 ❧

# INFORMATION TECHNOLOGY CONSULTANT (COMPUTER BUSINESS)
*Income Opportunities* magazine (March 1997) quotes Pete Collins, director of entrepreneurial advisory services for Coopers & Lybrand in New York, as saying, "People who are in the business of training people to become more efficient in information

technology, or people who are providing temporary information-technology [services] will do a very, very significant business."

In this business you will use your technical expertise and ability to explain complex technical language into understandable terms and operations to other business owners and employees.

*Estimated Start-up Costs*
$10,000 to $15,000

*Pricing Guidelines*
$30 to $75

*Marketing and Advertising Methods and Tips*
❖ Direct marketing to targeted customers in your particular industry, followed by an appointment and visit
❖ Ads in trade publications
❖ Network with other businesses in trade and business groups.
❖ Referrals from business customers
❖ Speak at regional conferences and seminars.
❖ Write articles or columns for publications in the industry from which you want to get customers.

*Essential Equipment*
Computer, printer, fax, laser printer, cellular phone, and training materials

*Recommended Training, Experience, or Needed Skills*
❖ Degree or working knowledge of computer software, sales and marketing, training, and implementation
❖ Ability to teach, communicate, and relate to people
❖ Work experience in the industry to which you want to sell your services

*Income Potential*
$25,000 to $100,000 +

## Type of Business
$1/3$ in home office conducting your business and planning your materials, $2/3$ on site conducting analysis and training customers

## Best Customers
❖ Small businesses that need to get the best technology for their money
❖ Businesses that are rapidly expanding their staff or want to update their technology to be more productive

## Success Tips
❖ You have to stay visible to your clients through creative marketing—with an Internet site or a one-page trade newsletter sent to current and prospective customers.
❖ Get customer feedback about your recommendations to see how effective your advice has been.
❖ Be knowledgeable about the trends and movements in technology and the trade in which you are specializing.

## Additional Information
### Recommended Reading
*Analyzing Outsourcing: Reengineering Information and Communication Systems* by Daniel Minoli (New York: McGraw-Hill, 1994)
*The Business Plan Guide for Consultants* by Herman Holtz (New York: Wiley, 1994)
*Business Re-engineering with Information Technology: Sustaining Your Business Advantage: An Implementation Guide* by John J. Donovan (Upper Saddle River, NJ: Prentice Hall, 1994)
*Byte-Magazine;* Princeton-Hightstown Rd., Box 555, Hightstown, NJ 08520-1450; (800) 232-2983; $24.95/year
*The Complete Guide to Consulting Contracts* by Herman Holtz (Chicago: Dearborn Trade, 1997)
*Computing Strategies for Reengineering Your Organization* by Cheryl Currid (Rocklin, CA: Prima, 1997)

**Organization**
APC Administrator
Association of Professional Consultants
2785 Bluebird Circle
Costa Mesa, CA 92626
http://www.consultapc.org
"Full membership requires a minimum of two years of full-time consulting experience where that experience was the major source of income." Full membership is $225; write for other requirements for membership, on your business stationery.

Business Technologies Association
12411 Wornall Rd.
Kansas City, MO 94145
Holds a semiannual trade show and publishes *Business Technology Solutions,* monthly.

Professional and Technical Consultants Association (PATCA)
P.O. Box 4143
Mountainview, CA 94040
Send LSASE for membership criteria and information.

*Additional Business Ideas*
Provide temporary information-technology services for businesses that are just beginning to expand but cannot yet afford to hire full-time, trained employees.

꧁ ● ꧂

# MISCELLANEOUS COMPUTER AND INTERNET BUSINESSES

❖ Web site designer/HTML programmer—contact the Association of Internet Professionals at http://www.association.org.
❖ Personal images—with your computer and scanner, photos, designs, or video images are scanned into a computer scanner where they can be transferred onto T-shirts, mugs, plates, and so forth. You will also need a computer thermal-transfer printer, heat-transfer paper, and heat-transfer presses.

# Creative Businesses

*If I didn't start painting, I would have raised chickens.*
—Grandma Moses

One craftsperson told me that she believes people become more creative as they grow older. Whether or not you agree with that statement, creativity is listed as one of the essential characteristics of an entrepreneur of any age. Thus, if you create original objects, products, works of art, or all of the above, you already have the makings of a businessperson.

Many craftspeople work part-time, while others work full-time at their craft. Some have no formal training; others have master's degrees in fine arts. Some sell at local craft shows and community gatherings, and others at prestigious events that permit only juried items to be exhibited. According to the Hobby Industry Association, at least 15 percent of U.S. households include someone trying to turn their crafts hobby into a business (*Income Opportunities*, May 1997).

No matter, though, if you sell your creations—many items or one-of-a-kind items—you are in business (see the section on "FAQs" about a hobby versus a business) and will have to follow all or most of the business start-up guidelines featured in the opening chapters of this book. If you prefer to keep your art or craft as a hobby, then do not quit your day job.

It is difficult to earn a living solely with your arts and/or crafts. If you do dream of earning money with your creations, then study the specific recommendations of the professionals, associations, and publications of your industry. Find your niche in the industry, your market, and what sells best and works for you. To succeed you must manage your creative venture, and you *must keep up with industry trends!* If you persist, you can reach the goal of being a professional artist and/or craftsperson, working and earning money with your hands to create products that are like no others in the world.

## *Helpful Sources for Professional Artists and Craftspersons*
### Recommended Reading
#### *Books*

*The Artist's Resource Handbook* by Daniel Grant (New York: Allworth, 1997)

*The Art of Teaching Craft* by Joyce Spencer and Deborah Kneen (out of print, but check you local library's listing of craft books)

*Arts and the Internet: A Guide to the Revolution* by V. A. Shiva (New York: Allworth, 1996)

*The Basic Guide to Selling Arts and Crafts* by James Dillehay (Torreon, NM: Warm Snow Publishers, 1997)

*The Business of Being an Artist* by Daniel Grant (New York: Allworth, 1996)

*The Business of Crafts: The Complete Directory of Resources for Artisans* by the Crafts Center (New York: Watson-Guptill, 1996)

*The Crafter's Guide to Pricing Your Work* by Dan Ramsey (Cincinnati, OH: Betterway Publications, 1997)

*Crafting for Dollars: Turn Your Hobby into Serious Cash* by Sylvia Landman (Rocklin, CA: Prima, 1996)

*Handmade for Profit: Hundreds of Secrets to Success in Selling Arts and Crafts* by Barbara Brabec (New York: Evans, 1996)

*How to Produce a Successful Crafts Show* by Kathryn Caputo (Harrisburg, PA: Stackpole Books, 1997)

*How to Show and Sell Your Crafts* by Kathryn Caputo (Cincinnati, OH: Betterway Publications, 1997)

*How to Start a Home-Based Crafts Business,* 2nd ed., by Kenn Ober-
recht (Old Saybrook, CT: Globe Pequot, 1997)

*Pricing Your Craftwork* by James Dillehay (Torreon, NM: Warm
Snow Publishers, 1997)

*Profitable Crafting* by Priscilla Y. Huff (booklet) (1997); Little
House Writing and Publishing, Box 286, Sellersville, PA 18960;
$6.95 + $1 for postage and handling (PA residents add 6 percent sales tax)

### Business Guides

*Entrepreneur's Small Business Development Catalog,* "Craft Business," $69 + shipping and handling; call for catalog or credit
card orders, (800) 421-2300.

*National Business Library's Small Business Catalog,* "Make Money
with Crafts," $39.95 + shipping and handling. Call for cata-
log or credit card orders, (800) 947-7724.

### Publications

*ArtNetwork,* P.O. Box 1268; Penn Valley, CA 95946; resource publications for fine artists including *ArtWorld Hotline, ArtNetwork
Yellow Pages,* and *ArtSource Quarterly,* to help them advance
their careers.

*The Crafts Report: The Business Journal for the Crafts Industry,* P.O.
Box 1992, Wilmington, DE 19899; http://www.craftsreport.
com; twelve issues for $29 a year; lists art and handcraft com-
petitions, conferences and symposia, exhibitions, workshops,
and seminars. An *essential* publication for the professional
artists and craftsperson.

If your market is the interior design industry, see "Resources for Craftspeople," in the February 1997 *Crafts Report,*
which lists trade and consumer publications in this industry.

### Show Guides

*The ArtFair Sourcebook,* 2003 NE 11th Ave., Portland, OR 97212;
listings, ratings, and tracking system (software, calendar)
of the nation's top five hundred fine art and craft events.;
$150 for initial subscription, $75 for consecutive yearly
renewals.

*Arts 'n Crafts Showguide,* ACN Publications, P.O. Box 104628-Q, Jefferson City, MO 65110-4628; write for subscription information.

*A Step Ahead, Ltd.,* Ronay Guides, 2950 Pangborn Rd., P.O. Box 33462, Decatur, GA 33462; lists arts and craft shows, fairs, festivals, competitions, exhibits, and so forth, in *separate guides* for Georgia, Florida, Alabama, Tennessee, North Carolina, South Carolina, and Virginia. Write (include an LSASE) for current prices.

*Sunshine Artist* magazine, Palm House Publishing, 2600 Temple Dr., Winter Park, FL 32789; $29.95/12 issues.

### Mail-Order Companies

Chester Book Company
4 Maple St.
Chester, CT 06412
Books by fine artists and handcrafters. Write for catalog.

Dover Publications, Inc.
31 E. 2nd St.
Mineral, NY 11501
A wide selection of books in all fields including arts and crafts, copyright-free design books, and copyright-free business clip art. Write for catalog (takes three to four weeks to arrive).

The Front Room Publishers
P.O. Box 1541
Clifton, NJ 07015-1541
http://www.intac.com/~rjp
(973) 773-4215 for credit card orders
Write for a copy of the *Learning Extension Catalog,* which carries directories, books on crafts, and crafts marketing; *Promotionals That Work . . . on a Budget (for Craft Shops/Galleries & Other Craft Retailers),* $4; and *Directory of Craft Malls and Rent-A-Space Shops,* 2nd ed., $16.45 postage paid.

Lark Books
50 College St.
Asheville, NC 28801
Many books, kits, and supplies for crafts; write for a catalog.

Success Publications
3419 Dunham, Box 263
Warsaw, NY 14569
Send a LSASE for listing of publications including *How to Sell Your Homemade Creations*, $15; *How to Sell to Catalog Houses*, $10; *Making Money at Arts and Crafts Shows*, $10; and *How to Run a Home Craft Boutique*, $10.

### Book Clubs

Crafter's Choice with Better Homes and Gardens Craft Club
P.O. Box 8823
Camp Hill, PA 17012-8823
Many how-to books on all types of crafts including *Crafts Market Place* by Argie Minolis (ed.)—over 560 places in North America to sell crafts.

*The Crafts Report (TCR)* Book Club
P.O. Box 1992
Wilmington, DE 19899
http://www.craftsreport.com
Selections such as *Business Forms and Contracts (in Plain English) for Craftspeople* by Leonard Duboff; *Directory of Wholesale Reps for Craft Professionals* by Sharon Olson; *The Law (In Plain English) for Crafts People*, rev. ed., by Leonard Duboff; and *Photographing Your Craftwork* by Steve Meltzer.

For more craft book selections or to order, call (800) 777-7098 or (302) 656-2209.

Leaflets for Less
Leisure Arts
P.O. Box 420235
Palm Coast, FL 32142-0235
Cross-stitch, knit and crochet, plastic canvas, and other crafts project leaflets from the bimonthly *Home Shopper*.

North Light Book Club
1507 Dana Ave.
Cincinnati, OH 45207
Books and videos for artists.

**Organizations**
American Craft Association
21 S. Eltings Corner Rd.
Highland, NY 12528
A division of the American Craft Council, this group gives its members access to health benefits, a credit card program, discounts, and so forth. Membership includes a subscription to the newsletter *The Voice*.

American Craft Council (ACC)
72 Spring St.
New York, NY 10012-4019
Membership, $40 per year, includes a subscription to *American Craft* magazine, free admission to juried craft fairs, access to library, discounts, and more.

Association of Crafts and Creative Industries
P.O. Box 2188
Zanesville, OH 43702-2188

Volunteer Lawyers for the Arts
1 E. 53rd St.
New York, NY 10022
Helps advise artists, craftspeople, writers, and so forth. Write for information.

**On-line Source**
http://www.procrafter.com—information, tips, and listings for professional craftspersons

**Supplies**
*The Crafts Supply Sourcebook: A Comprehensive Shop-by-Mail Guide*, 4th ed., by Margaret Boyd (Cincinnati: Betterway Books, 1997)
*Designer Source Listing*, 1997-98 ed., by Maryanne Burgess (ed.) (Carikean Publishing, P.O. Box 1171, Chicago, IL 60640); has twenty-one categories, from "Beads" to "Workshops," of sources for sewers and crafters. Send a LSASE for current price.
Dick Blick Art Materials, P.O. Box 1267, Galesburg, IL 61402-1267; write or call for catalog, (800) 828-4548.

## Art and Craft Inventory Tips

Sometimes the hardest fact of being an artist or crafts-person is that you have to also know the basics of (product) business management (i.e., marketing, sales, legal ramifications, and record keeping). If you do not keep good records of your expenses, income, and inventory, you will never know whether you are making money and from where it is coming! Use business software to help you or your own manual system (whatever works best for you). Here are some inventory tips:

* Keep a record of how many items are being made and sold in each of your product categories.
* Keep a record of the customers (name, address of consumers and businesses) who are buying each of your items, how much they are buying, and if they are paying. Develop direct-mail strategies to let them know of your future items and/or places you will be exhibiting.
* Study the markets and industry to try to predict which directions your sales may take so you can be prepared to expand in those new directions.
* Evaluate all these items and your business plan periodically—monthly, every six months, yearly.

The Jerry's Catalog: The Encyclopedia of Artist Materials, P.O. Box 58638, Raleigh, NC 27658; http://www.jerryscatalog. com; write or call for catalog, (800) 827-8478; in NC, (919) 878-6782.

### ∽ 30 ∾
# BASKETS

Basketry is the oldest-known craft and has been called the "mother of pottery." Unfortunately, few cultures saved baskets unless it was for burial or ceremonial occasions. Most of the traditional weaves and techniques are still used in basketry today. What makes the differences in basketry are the colors used and the kinds of materials available to the basket makers.

Today you can buy the materials to make the type of baskets that interest you, or you can study what materials in your area could be used. Many baskets are still being made from whatever bark, split wood, twigs, reeds, bamboo, canes, and grasses that can be gathered or bought.

If this craft interests you, look for local basket makers, crafts guilds, or courses to get instructions in basketry basics. Follow traditional patterns or originate your own.

### Estimated Start-up Costs
$500 to $1,000

### Pricing Guidelines
Read *The Weaver's Friendly Handbook for Pricing and Selling Handmade Baskets,* which helps the basket weaver place a value on her labor and account for other costs. Also included in this seventy-six-page booklet are suggested mediums to sell one's baskets as well as price worksheets. To order, send $5.95 + $2 shipping and handling (payable to Grace Davis) at 118 Mills Circle, Fort Huachuca, AZ 85613.

### Marketing and Advertising Methods and Tips
❖ Craft fairs and shows
❖ Fine art galleries (depending on your skill and reputation)
❖ Craft co-ops
❖ Courses you teach
❖ Word-of-mouth referrals
❖ Advertising at nature centers and in art publications
❖ Displays at libraries, banks, and other businesses
❖ Tags that describe you and your craft

### Essential Equipment
Sharp utility knife, scissors, and awl; clamps or clothespins; needles; crochet hooks; assorted pliers; reeds, grasses, and other weaving materials

### Recommended Training, Experience, or Needed Skills

"Desire to learn and use your creativity. It only takes a little time to master the basic techniques," says Tina Barrows, basket instructor, maker, and collector. With courses, it should only take a few hours to learn the basics. Master the traditional techniques so well that you do not even have to think about them when you craft your baskets.

### Income Potential

$5,000 to $10,000

### Type of Business

$3/4$ in home, $1/4$ marketing and teaching courses

### Best Customers

- ❖ Consumers attending craft shows
- ❖ Gift basket vendors who specialize in country baskets
- ❖ "Country-style" gift stores
- ❖ Antique stores that carry traditional crafts
- ❖ Mail-order customers
- ❖ Local (or national) cable television stations
- ❖ Craft home party businesses
- ❖ Catalogs (see the "FAQs" chapter and the beginning of this chapter)

### Success Tips

- ❖ Develop your style. Try to find your niche market. Do not let others talk you into something that is not right for you. A tremendous satisfaction can be gained from pursuing your own version of any craft. The variations are limitless!
- ❖ You have to decide whether you are going to make many items or one-of-a-kind artwork.

### Franchises, Distributorships, and Licenses

The Basket Connection
20959 S. Springwater Rd.
Estacada, OR 97023
Decorative baskets. Write for information.

## *Additional Information*
### Recommended Reading
*Basketry Bits,* P.O. Box 8, Loudonville, OH 44842; $16/four
   issues
*Baskets from Nature's Bounty* by Elizabeth Jensen (Loveland, CO:
   Interweave Press, 1991)
*Contemporary Wicker Basketry* by Flo Hoppe (Asheville, NC: Lark
   Books, 1996)
*The Idea Magazine for Basketmakers,* 2417 Hancock St., Port
   Huron, MI 48060; $17/one year
*Interwoven News,* P.O. Box 580, Ranier, OR 97048; $8/four issues
*Natural Baskets* by Maryanne Gillooly, ed. (Pownal, VT: Storey
   Communications, 1992)

### Classes
Look for classes at local folk museums, community centers, craft
centers, and elsewhere.

   Brookfield Craft Center
   P.O. Box 122, Rt. 25
   Brookfield, CT 06804-0122

### Conferences
   The Basketry School, Conferences
   P.O. Box 15457
   Seattle, WA 98115-0457
   (800) 87-WEAVE

### Supplies
   August Moon Basketry
   Rt. 4, Box 135
   Pageland, SC 29728

   C & D Baskets
   15 Maple St.
   Livermore Falls, ME 04254
E-mail for price list: cdbasket@megalink.net

### Videos

*Traditional New England Basketmaking* by John McGuire, ninety
minutes, $39.95 + $3.50 shipping and handling; Brookfield
Craft Center, Box 122, Brookfield, CT 06804

*Willow Basket Making Video* by Tom Butts; explains how to make
a willow basket; $29.95 plus $4 postage and handling; to
order, e-mail tbutts@initco.net.

### Additional Business Idea

Broom making—see *101 Best Small Businesses for Women* by
Priscilla Y. Huff (Rocklin, CA: Prima, 1996)

❧ 31 ❧

# CERAMIC CRAFTS

Ceramics comes from the Greek word *keramos*, which means
"potter's earth." It is often associated with pottery but includes
such products as brick, glass, porcelain, and enamels that are
used in a variety of art and commercial objects. Different clay
formulas, firings, and heat settings create the different kinds of
ceramics products.

You can create and sell your own products and/or have a
commercial studio where you instruct students. You can specialize in ceramic pieces (cups, bowls, frames, etc.), pottery,
and/or decorative tiles.

### Estimated Start-up Costs

$5,000 to $10,000

### Pricing Guidelines

❖ Individual pieces: your prices are determined by what your
   market will bear and whether you are selling one-of-a-kind
   pieces or many (wholesale). Go by suggested industry guidelines (see also *Pricing Your Craftwork* on page 165).

❖ "Do-it-yourself" studios: sell unpainted pieces that your customers choose, from $2 to $45 (varies with the pieces you

offer your customers) + $7/hour for colors, materials, glazing, and firing; and $4.50/hour for children twelve years and under.

## Marketing and Advertising Methods and Tips
- Flyers on community bulletin boards
- Yellow Pages
- Classified ads in "free" newspapers and parent-targeted, local publications
- Networking with local and state craft clubs, associations, and guilds
- Art and craft shows and fairs
- Direct mail to flower and artists' gift shops

## Essential Equipment
- Kiln or access to one
- Shop for your work and customers' work if you have a commercial studio
- Playroom for children if you want parents of young children to attend
- Home office computer with billing and inventory software
- Promotional materials: brochures and flyers
- Ceramic coffee mugs, picture frames, bowls, figures, and other assorted items for your customers to paint and design
- Commercial molds to make the greenware (unfired clay items)
- Storage space for molds and your own pieces

## Recommended Training, Experience, or Needed Skills
Take courses at ceramic stores, studios, craft centers, folk art centers, and colleges

## Income Potential
$5,000 to $30,000

## Type of Business
$3/4$ at in-home studio, $1/4$ marketing

## Best Customers
* Patrons at craft shows and fairs for individual pieces
* Galleries, gift and craft shops
* Studio: mature adults who want to learn a new hobby or skill
* Children for after-school lessons or homeschooled children
* Creative birthday parties for children

## Success Tips
* Study your market and competitors to see how your products compare (and differ).
* "Test-market" your items to see what sells best.
* For your studio, offer a variety of classes to fit the busy schedules of people today.
* You may be able to market classes to local private or public schools who do not have budgets for art classes.

## Additional Information
### Recommended Reading
*The Big Book of Ceramics: A Guide to History, Materials, Equipment and Techniques of Hand-Building, Molding, Theory, Kiln-Firing, and Glazing* by Joaquin Chavarria (New York: Watson-Guptill, 1994)

*Entrepreneur's Small Business Development Catalog,* "Ceramic Pottery Studio," $69 + $7.95 for shipping and handling; call (800) 421-2300 for a catalog or credit card orders.

*Handbuilt Ceramics* by Kathy Triplett (Asheville, NC: Lark Books, 1997)

*Handmade Tiles: Designing, Making and Decorating* by Frank Giorgini (Asheville, NC: Lark Books, 1994)

*Studio Potter* and *Studio Potter Network Newsletter,* Box 70 Goffs-town, NH 03045; $30/one year (for both)

## Supplies
A.R.T. Studio Clay Co., 1555 Louis Ave., Elk Grove Village, IL 6007-2383; glazes, kilns, tools, potters wheels, books, and so forth; http://www.artclay.com

*Additional Business Idea*
Mosaics—*Making Mosaics* by Leslie Dierks (New York: Sterling, 1997)

## ᴈ 32 ᴇ
# CRAFT AND SEWING SUPPLIES
# (Mail Order)

With this business, you can sell craft and/or sewing supplies through the mail. You can carry supplies that cater to a special market or general materials. You will need to have a resale tax number from your state, familiarize yourself with mail-order laws and guidelines, and understand postal regulations.

*Estimated Start-up Costs*
$10,000 to $25,000

*Pricing Guidelines*
15 to 25 percent (or higher) mark-up/commission

*Marketing and Advertising Methods and Tips*
* Classified ads in sewing magazines, how-to craft magazines, and women's publications
* Press releases to these publications to announce your business and/or to announce unique products you carry
* Direct mail to readers of these publications (buy mailing lists)
* Direct mail to you own list of customers
* Internet retail site (see chapter on Computer and Internet Businesses)

*Essential Equipment*
* High-end computer and software for mailings, entering orders, doing invoicing and inventory control, and so forth
* Telephone system for taking orders

❖ Toll-free numbers
❖ Catalog—create simple catalogs using desktop publishing software and then expand as you get more orders.

### Recommended Training, Experience, and Needed Skills
❖ Take courses from the Direct Marketing Association (see address on page 178).
❖ If possible, work or network with other home-based mail-order businesses (with a noncompeting business).
❖ Read books and manuals about mail-order marketing and selling.
❖ Have knowledge of the craft and sewing industry and experience and background in making crafts, or have sewing skills.
❖ Be skilled in writing good copy for your ads.

### Income Potential
$20,000 to $40,000 +, depending on the size of your business

### Type of Business
$3/4$ at home taking orders, fulfilling them, and so on; $1/4$ attending trade shows and doing marketing research

### Best Customers
Hobbyists, sewers, crafters, your specific market niche

### Success Tips
❖ Find quality products and the best markets for them.
❖ Evaluate the mail-order catalogs and their products and see what you can offer that is "special" to your customers.
❖ Work up your own mailing list of good customers and give them "extras"—special discounts, bargains, informational tip sheets, and newsletters.
❖ Be patient and persistent.
❖ Know mail-order laws and postal regulations.

## Additional Information
### Recommended Reading

*Entrepreneur's Small Business Development Catalog*, "Mail Order Business"; $69 + $7.95 for shipping and handling. Call (800) 421-2300 for a catalog or credit card orders.

*Home-Based Catalog Marketing: A Success Guide for Entrepreneurs* by William J. Bond (New York: McGraw-Hill, 1993)

*Home-Based Mail Order: A Success Guide for Entrepreneurs* by William J. Bond (Blue Ridge Summit, PA: Tab Books, 1990)

*How to Create Catalogs That Sell* by Research Education Staff (Piscataway, NJ: Research Education Association, 1995)

*How to Start a Home-Based Mail-Order Business* by Georganne Fiumara (Old Saybrook, CT: Globe Pequot, 1996)

Lewis & Renn Business Books, *How to Start and Manage a Mail Order Business* (1996); $14.95 + $3 for shipping and handling, to Lewis & Renn Associates, 10315 Harmony Dr., Interlochen, MI 49643

National Business Library, *Small Business Catalog*, "Mail Order," $39.95 + $6.50 for shipping and handling. Call (800) 947-7724 for catalog or credit card orders.

*101 Tips for More Profitable Catalogs* by Maxwell Sroge (Lincolnwood, IL: NTC, 1995)

*Strategies for Getting Charge Card Merchant Status at Your Bank (Even If You Are Running a Home-Based or Mail Order Business)* by John Cali (Reston, VA: Great Western Publishing Co., 1991)


### Organizations

Direct Marketing Association
1120 Avenue of the Americas
New York, NY 10036
http://www.the-dma.org
Seminars, library and information services, conferences, and exhibitions

National Mail Order Association
2807 Polk St. NE
Minneapolis, MN 55418-2954
Excellent information for small mail-order businesses; publishes monthly newsletter, *Mail Order Digest*.

## Mailing Lists

Compilersplus
466 Main St.
New Rochelle, NY 10801

The Polk Company
1155 Brewery Park Blvd.
Detroit, MI 48207-2697

## Software

Mail Order Wizard, Haven Corp., 802 Madison St., Evanston, IL 60202-2207; write for information and prices.

Mailer's Software, 970 Calle Negocio, San Clemente, CA 92673-6201

Mail Tools, MySoftware Company, (800) 607-4848; http://www.proventure.com

## Other Sources

*Crafts Supply Sourcebook*, 4th ed., by Margaret Boyd (Betterway Books, 1507 Dana Ave., Cincinnati, OH 45207, 1997)

*Designer Source Listing* (sewing and needle arts source book) by Maryanne Burgess (Carikean Publishing, P.O. Box 11771, Chicago, IL 60611-0771); (773) 728-6118

### ∽ 33 ∾
# DECORATIVE SCREENS

This craft is a combination of art, craft, and practicality. Decorative screens can be used almost anywhere in the home or business. They provide a separation of space in a creative and decorative style. You can build the screen frame out of wood and then "fill" the spaces with fabric, leather, punched tin, yarn, dyed and painted fabric, and so on. You can design your own to sell and/or take custom orders.

## Estimated Start-up Costs
$5,000

## Pricing Guidelines
❖ Prices will vary according to the demand and market for your screens.
❖ Fireplace screen—average size (38" x 33"), from $100 to $300 +
❖ Standing screen—average size (72" x 66"), from $500 to $650 +

## Marketing and Advertising Methods and Tips
❖ Prepare color brochures or album with photos of how screens could be used in the home and/or office decor.
❖ Have a display at a bank or community room.
❖ Take samples to home furnishing shops, furniture stores, institutions, professionals' offices, and businesses that use dividers.
❖ Rent space at craft malls and take orders from your samples.
❖ Exhibit at craft and home party shows.
❖ Take a table at a home trade show.
❖ Display ads in home furnishing publications.

## Essential Equipment
❖ Basic woodworking tools: saws, clamps, finishing nails, stains, and finishes
❖ Wood for frames
❖ Fabric, string, metal, wood, or other materials to have on the screens

## Recommended Training, Experience, or Needed Skills
❖ Need basic woodworking skills (or subcontract someone who can build the frames for you); take courses at local vo-tech schools.
❖ Painting and artistic skills

## Income Potential
$5,000 to $20,000, depending on your production and markets

## Type of Business
$^3/_4$ at home in your workshop, $^1/_4$ out of home marketing

## Best Customers
* Consumers for decorative screens for rooms, home offices, and fireplaces
* Craft shops
* Professional offices and businesses
* Museums and art centers

## Success Tips
* Develop your own style and niche.
* Study the kinds of screens that are being created.
* Constantly market your product.

## Additional Information
### Recommended Reading
*Screen Works: Practical and Inspirational Ideas for Making and Using Screens in the Home* by Marion Elliot (Dayton, OH: Lorenz, 1997)

## Additional Business Ideas
Make standing and folding display stands for craftspersons to exhibit at fairs.

## ❧ 34 ☙
# HOME-BASED ART GALLERY
If you have an avid interest in fine art and a downstairs area in your home, an attached building, or a garage, in an area that gets a moderate amount of traffic, you may want to open a fine arts home gallery. If your borough or township requires permits and parking space, you should check to see whether you will be allowed to open your gallery.

What is the difference between a crafts (home) shop and a fine arts and handcraft gallery? One gallery owner says, "A [fine arts and handcraft] gallery features original and one-of-a-kind pieces that are priced as such." A craft (home) shop usually has items that are less expensive, can be reproduced, and often have a theme such as Victorian, Country, or Southwest.

### Estimated Start-up Costs
$7,000 to $20,000

### Pricing Guidelines
20 to 40 percent commission on each piece sold

### Marketing and Advertising Methods and Tips
- Yellow Pages
- Internet Web site
- Local and tourist publication ads
- Direct mail to former customers (postcards, brochures of featured guest artists' exhibits)
- Ads in local newspapers and on cable TV and radio
- Press releases of upcoming events and contests
- Network with other galleries or artist guilds.
- Advertising may also involve educating your community as to the nature of an art gallery. Regularly submit announcements to local and regional newspapers of scheduled exhibitions, courses you offer, and your gallery's hours.

### Essential Equipment
- Several rooms with ample wall space
- Parking space (street or lot)
- Computer and software for galleries for inventory, billing, and other business management
- Cash register and credit card–processing equipment
- Shelves, easels, and partitions for displaying art

### Recommended Training, Experience, or Needed Skills
Training and knowledge in fine art and work experience in an art gallery or museum

## Income Potential
$10,000 to $25,000, depending on patrons and other art-related events you sponsor

## Type of Business
$3/4$ in home running the gallery during opening hours, $1/4$ out marketing and looking for new exhibitors

## Best Customers
* People of all ages who have an interest in art
* Craftspeople and artists who need a venue to display and sell their work

## Success Tips
* Make sure you can devote the time you need to run a gallery along with all the other responsibilities in your life.
* Offer lessons, art day camps, or workshops for both children and adults to earn extra money.
* It helps to have worked in a gallery before.
* Ask yourself how much money you have to invest and how long you can run your gallery until you begin making a profit.
* Research your location. If other museums and galleries are in your area, more people will come to your gallery.
* Make sure you have insurance coverage.
* Advertise in trade publications for artists.
* Planning is essential, and persistence will pay off.
* Have contracts signed for consignments detailing your commissions, length of time displayed, damages responsibility, orders, and so forth (check with a lawyer familiar with such agreements and contracts).

## Additional Information
### Recommended Reading
*The Gallery Management Manual* by Zella Jackson (New York: Consultant Press, 1995)

### Additional Business Ideas

❖ Custom framing services

❖ Craft shop (home)

❖ Craft boutique—see *How to Run a Home Craft Boutique;* $10 (Success Publications; see the address on page 167).

⤏ 35 ⤎

## INVENTOR'S CONSULTANT

As an inventor's consultant, you should be familiar, of course, with the patent process. For a fee, you can help give your clients legitimate sources from which to choose to help get their idea to product—if it is a feasible idea. With ideas that have potential, you will do your research and evaluation and present the results in a written report along with a list of the experts who can assist your client in taking the next steps with her ideas.

### Estimated Start-up Costs

$2,500 to $5,000

### Pricing Guidelines

❖ $55 to $65 an hour, or $200 to $500 + upfront fee (depending on the time involved) for an overall analysis of the inventor's idea

❖ Offer a free telephone or in-person consultation to discern whether the person should go forward with getting her idea patented. If it is, your fee for services would involve listing the inventors' associations, patent search information methods, reputable patent attorneys, and manufacturers.

### Marketing and Advertising Methods and Tips

❖ Advertise to inventors' groups. You will have to prove a success rate with your clients along with their names and addresses so they know you are a legitimate consultant (there are so many invention scams!).

❖ Ads in trade publications

❖ Yellow Pages

✤ Referrals from clients
✤ Internet site

## Essential Equipment
✤ Home office: computer, software, printer, photocopier, fax machine, business phone, and answering system
✤ Internet service and site

## Recommended Training, Experience, or Needed Skills
✤ Legal training
✤ Experience with the patenting process
✤ A degree and/or knowledge in product development
✤ Ability to evaluate an idea for its market potential
✤ Read trade publications on future trends and marketing.

## Income Potential
$20,000 to $30,000

## Type of Business
$1/2$ meeting or talking with clients in your in-home office, $1/2$ doing outside research

## Best Customers
✤ People with innovative ideas
✤ Employees from different industries with ideas to improve a present product or introduce a new product to their industry

## Success Tips
✤ First and foremost, be honest!
✤ Have a list of experts and specialists with whom you work to gather information and to refer your client to for the next steps in the patenting process.

## Tips for Your Inventor-Clients
✤ The average patent acceptance process used to take about twenty months, but unfortunately, it may take several months

longer now because of the federal government's reorganization of its business practices.

❖ Avoid invention marketing companies that promote on radio and late-night TV. They are scams!

❖ Keep exact records of your idea.

❖ Build a model to prove your idea works.

❖ Join (legitimate) invention associations and network with other successful inventors.

❖ Have your invention evaluated by a professional in the industry you are targeting.

❖ Look in the *Thomas Register of Manufacturers* (check the reference section of your public library) to find companies that make items similar to yours to get the names and addresses of potential manufacturers (but do not spend money manufacturing the prototype until you have some orders).

❖ Do your own patent search at a patent depository library before you go to a patent attorney.

❖ Check with your business and/or patent lawyer before you sign any agreements concerning your invention.

❖ If you believe in your idea, *persist!*

### Additional Information
**Recommended Reading**

*Inventor's Desktop Companion* by Richard C. Levy (Detroit, MI: Gale Research, 1995)

*Inventor's Digest* by Affiliated Inventors Foundation, Inc., 2132 E. Bijou St., Colorado Springs, CO 80909-5950; $20/year for six issues

### Organizations

Inventor's Awareness Group, Inc.
1533 E. Mountain Rd., Suite B
Westfield, MA 01085-1458

An "all-volunteer consumer group formed in 1992 to serve and protect the dreams and aspirations of the independent inventor"; $25/year for membership. Send SASE for information. Its booklet *Invention. . .Truth or Consequences* ($5) is highly recommended for anyone with an invention idea.

U.S. Patent and Trade Office
Washington, DC 20231
Write or call the office's introductory switchboard at (703) 308-HELP (4357).

### On-line Sources

http://www.adlenterprises.com—Invention Management On-Line helps provide an inventor with information on prototype development and legal assistance. Sponsored by the consultancy Arthur D. Little Enterprises in Cambridge, Massachusetts.

http://www.ibm.com/patents—IBM's patent server that offers free on-line search access to IBM's database of more than two million patent filings dating back to 1971.

### Other Sources

✤ The Idea Machine, $59.95; an interactive CD-ROM designed to help the home-based, independent inventor protect ideas and develop and market new products. Based on the book *EUREKA! The Entrepreneurial Inventor's Guide to Developing, Protecting, and Profiting from Your Ideas* by Robert Gold (Upper Saddle River, NJ: Prentice Hall, 1994). Order from Cyber Knight International Corporation, P.O. Box 64, Spicewood, TX 78669.

✤ Inventor's Library—Business and Inventor Resource Center; sells many reports giving resources for inventors. Write for information to The Rite Co., 13520 Prairie Creek Rd., Platte City, MO 64079.

### *Additional Business Idea*

Speaker on inventions—making presentations to women's and mothers' groups to provide information; writing and selling your books and booklets on the topic

## ✎ 36 ✍
# LEATHER CRAFT

Leather is the oldest form of fabric. Different cultures—Native Americans, Chinese, Egyptians, and so on—have used different hand techniques to tan (vegetable, wood, or oil), to preserve, and to soften the hides. Today hides are prepared by machines and usually tanned through chemical processes. Leather is sold by the square foot and the ounce. As with any craft, you can make many of one piece or one-of-a-kind art pieces.

### Estimated Start-up Costs
$1,000 to $3,000

### Pricing Guidelines
* Material + time + what the market will bear
* Compare your products with others and their quality, and price yours accordingly.
* Selling one-of-a-kind products for collectors: one person sells leather figures from $400 to $3,000 apiece and higher, but this depends on your reputation as an artist.
* See also the craft pricing books listed at the beginning of this chapter.

### Marketing and Advertising Methods and Tips
* Exhibit at craft shows and fairs as well as leather trade shows.
* Perfect your skills to get accepted as a member of local and regional craft guilds for networking and prestigious shows.
* Decide what kind of leather items you will create, and market to the customers who want either beautiful but functional leather pieces or solely artwork.

### Essential Equipment
* Business cards and brochures
* Leather equipment and tools: shears, various punches, stamp, rawhide mallet, pins, needles, knives for cutting leather, lacing-gauge punch, slot-cutter, awl, stitch marker, and so forth
* Leather skins—most commonly used are calfskin, sheep-skin, and pigskin.
* Other tools: steel square, leather stencils, stamping tools, and accessories

### Recommended Training, Experience, or Needed Skills
Knowledge of basic leather-working skills—learn with courses at craft shops, adult evening schools, craft guilds, or an apprenticeship with a leather crafter.

### Income Potential
$10,000 to $20,000

### Type of Business
$1/2$ working at home, $1/2$ exhibiting at shows and fairs

### Best Customers
- ✤ Patrons at craft shows, folk art festivals, and trade shows
- ✤ Custom work and galleries
- ✤ Western saddle shops and leather accessories shops
- ✤ Horse shows and rodeos (have a table or booth)
- ✤ State fairs and sportsmen's shows
- ✤ Hunting, fishing, and hiking shops

### Success Tips
- ✤ Make a lot of "bread and butter," smaller items to sustain your business while at the same time developing more labor-intensive (and expensive) pieces that will be your "signature" pieces.
- ✤ Search for that unique product and make it the best!

### Additional Information
Write for the address of a guild nearest to you.

### Recommended Reading
*The Leather Crafters and Saddlers Journal,* 331 Annette Court, Rhinelander, WI 54501; $24/six issues (one year) or $48/fourteen issues (two years)

*The Leatherworking Handbook: A Practical Illustrated Sourcebook of Techniques and Projects* by Valerie Michael (New York: Cassell Academic, 1995)

**Organization**
The International Federation of Leather Guilds
P.O. Box 102
Arcadia, IN 46030

**Supplies**
Tandy Leather Company
P.O. Box 791
Forth Worth, TX 76101
Leathers, kits, tools, saddle trees, and hardware; also offers books and instructional videos. Write for a catalog ($3, refunded with order).

*Additional Business Idea*
Horse and riding-related products—read *Tools of the Cowboy Trade: Today's Crafters of Saddles, Bits, Spurs, and Trappings* by Casey Beard and Dale Degabriels (Boulder, CO: Gibbs Smith, 1997)

## ⊸ 37 ⊷
# LACE AND LACE CRAFTS

Lace is an ancient, decorative craft of openwork fabric dating as far back as ancient Egyptian times. Lace-making techniques were perfected as they came to Italy, France, and the rest of Europe over the ages, and many new patterns were created as sewing skills were taught to young girls. The Victorians of the last century especially loved lace and used it extensively. This is a labor-intensive needlework skill. If you create your own, you can sell it to specialty shops or make your own lace creations; or you can sew specialties using today's manufactured laces.

*Estimated Start-up Costs*
$2,000 for sewing machine and accessories plus lessons

# Tips for Matching Your Product with the Right Show

With over ten thousand arts and crafts shows and festivals from which to choose every year (according to *Sunshine Artist* magazine), you need to find the ones that will be the most profitable—in terms of money and potential customer leads generated—for your arts and/or handcraft business. Here are some tips to help you:

❖ Attend all the shows that you are considering entering. Talk to other exhibitors to find out what they do or do not like about that particular event.

❖ Match your crafts with the quality of a show's crafts—yours should not be higher or lower in quality.

❖ Have unique hang tags, brochures, and promotional literature with your products to tell your buyers why your arts and crafts are unique (your background, training, awards, method of creation, etc.). Tell "your story, your history."

❖ Make sure you have the necessary permits, tax certificates, and food licenses (if that is your product) for that state and region.

❖ Match your product with ethnic and theme shows.

## Pricing Guidelines

❖ This type of needlework is a fine art craft, so you should price your lace and lace crafts according to the time and skill involved.

❖ See the "Sewing Businesses" section on pages 204–205 for sewing business books that give pricing guidelines.

## Marketing and Advertising Methods and Tips

❖ Exhibit at trade and craft shows.

❖ Sell through craft, antique, and baby's wear stores and shops that take fine needlework like specialty gift shops.

✤ Sell through specialty catalogs.
✤ Display ads in fine needlework publications.

### Essential Equipment
Sewing machine, thread, bobbins, shuttles, sewing notions, assorted hand and machine needles, assorted scissors, thimble, and seam ripper

### Recommended Training, Experience, or Needed Skills
✤ Take private lessons (ask at your local sewing supply store for referrals).
✤ Practice with fine needlework until you perfect your skill.
✤ Courses and workshops
✤ Internet—look on the major Internet search engines for lace Web sites. Many are listed and offer lace-making instructors and courses.

### Income Potential
$5,000 to $15,000

### Type of Business
$3/4$ in home creating your lace; $1/4$ marketing, lecturing, and/ or teaching

### Best Customers
✤ Fine fabric stores, sewing and craft supply stores
✤ Mail-order sewing supply catalogs

### Success Tips
Perfect creating the styles of lace you enjoy the most and then create unique garments, potpourri pillows, sachets, and baby bonnets. Do the same if you purchase ready-made lace and create items for specialty shops (or your own catalog) like decorated hats, lace collars, wreaths, decorated hand towels, lace jewelry, lace ornaments, and so on.

## Additional Information
### Recommended Reading
*Anchor Manual of Needlework* (Loveland, CO: Interweave, 1990)

*Antique Lace Patterns* by Frances Bradbury (Owings Mills, MD: Stemmer House Publishers, 1985)

*Battenberg and Other Tape Laces: Techniques, Stitches, and Designs* by Butterick and Sara Hadley (Mineola, NY: Dover, 1988)

*Handwoven Laces* by Donna Muller (Loveland, CO: Interweave, 1992)

*Made with Lace: 40 Exquisite Lace Garments and Accessories* by Ginny Barnston (Radnor, PA: Chilton, 1997)

Dover Publications, 31 E. 2nd St., Mineola, NY 11501, has numerous books on lace making. Write for a current catalog.

Lark Books, 50 College St., Asheville, SC 28801; its catalog carries two books on bobbin lace making and a bobbin lace kit. Write for a current catalog.

### Organization
International Old Lacers (IOL)
Jo Ann Eurell, Membership Secretary
2103 Ikenberg Ct.
Urbana, IL 61801-8621
Send a LSASE for membership and other information.

### Supplies
Beggar's Lace
P.O. Box 481223
Denver, CO 80248
Offers a newsletter, books, and supplies; send for catalog.

Van Sciver Bobbin Lace
130 Cascadilla Park
Ithaca, NY 14850
Offers books, supplies, private lessons, workshops, and lectures.

Others listed in *Designer Source Listing* (see "Supplies" on page 168).

*Additional Business Idea*
Lace specialty items (nightgowns, pillows, etc.)—see *Crafting with Lace* by Joyce Elizabeth Cusick (Asheville, NC: Lark, 1995)

## ⊸ 38 ⊷
## METAL CRAFT

The term *metal craft* can cover a variety of art and craft techniques and types of metals such as bronze, gold, silver, tin, iron, steel, and a combination of these. Metal can be shaped solely for art pieces or combined to create functional pieces such as jewelry, hooks, frames, bowls, tableware, and many other items.

One couple takes old tin sheeting and recycles it into whimsical tin garden ornaments ranging from garden markers to scarecrows. They also make decorative metal household items.

### Estimated Start-up Costs
$1,000 to $10,000, depending on what equipment you need and whether you already have a home computer for inventory and small business management

### Pricing Guidelines
Follow the guidelines in the two craft pricing books listed on pages 164–165.

### Marketing and Advertising Methods and Tips
❖ Take samples of your work into craft shops or galleries and garden and gift shops.
❖ Network with members of craft and artist guilds and others in your industry.
❖ Be represented by a sales rep.
❖ Display color ads (can be expensive).
❖ Attend juried shows and fairs, and invite customers to sign a book that can build your mailing list. Then you can send postcards telling them of upcoming shows and exhibitions where you will be exhibiting.

✤ Apply to catalog houses to carry your best-selling items.
✤ Attend wholesale shows if you can mass-produce some of your products.

### Essential Equipment
✤ Business cards and brochures
✤ Studio or workshop
✤ Metal-working tools that are appropriate to your craft and metal type

### Recommended Training, Experience, or Needed Skills
✤ Art training, and training and experience in the techniques of the metal in which you are working
✤ Courses at art schools or craft centers
✤ Apprenticeship with a metal crafter

### Income Potential
$5,000 to $30,000, depending on the demand for your metalwork

### Type of Business
$\frac{1}{2}$ at home producing pieces, $\frac{1}{2}$ marketing and showing your product

### Best Customers
✤ Garden metal sculptures: gardeners, garden supply centers
✤ Interior decorators
✤ Customers at craft shows
✤ Readers of magazines advertising your products (i.e., mail-order customers)

### Success Tips
✤ Create a variety of products with varying price ranges to fit your customers' pocketbooks.
✤ Test-market your products at different places to see which is the best place to sell your items.

❖ Decide which metal(s) and markets you want as your spe-
    cialties.
❖ Keep current with the news and trends in your industry.
❖ Develop your style—your "signature" pieces and work.
❖ Listen to your customers, and do custom work or improve
    your line.


## *Additional Information*
### Recommended Reading

*The Complete Metalsmith: An Illustrated Handbook,* rev. ed., by Tim
    McCreight (Cape Elizabeth, ME: Brynmorgen Press, 1991)
*Metal: Design and Fabrication* by David and Susan Frisch (New
    York: Whitney Library of Design, 1998)
*Metals Technic: A Collection of Techniques for Metalsmiths* by Tim
    McCreight (Cape Elizabeth, ME: Brynmorgen Press, 1997)
*Metalwork for Craftsmen: A Step-by-Step Guide with 55 Projects* by
    Emil F. Kronquist (Mineola, NY: Dover, 1993)
*Metalworking: A Manual of Techniques* by Mike George (North
    Pomfret, VT: Crowood, 1991)
*Textile Techniques in Metal* by Arline M. Fisch (Asheville, NC: Lark,
    1996)
*Tinwork* by Marion Elliot, and *Wirework* by Mary Maguire; order
    both from Chester Book Company, 4 Maple St., Chester, CT
    06412.


## *Additional Business Ideas*

❖ Iron artistry (weather van⌐ s, hooks, wall sconces, etc.)—see
    *The Art of Blacksmithing* by Art W. Bealer (Edison, NJ: Books
    Sales, Inc., 1996)
❖ Jewelry making—see *101 Best Home-Based Businesses for
    Women* by Priscilla Y. Huff (Rocklin, CA: Prima, 1995) and *101
    Best Small Businesses for Women* by Priscilla Y. Huff (Rocklin,
    CA: Prima, 1996); also *Jewellery Making for Profit* by James E.
    Hickling (Wappeingers Falls, NY: Antique Collectors Club,
    1995).
❖ Wind chimes

## ᏚᎯ 39 ᏚᏚ
# SHOES (CUSTOM-MADE)

A number of women have started their own shoe design and production businesses. For example, two women friends who shared a love of horseback riding decided to design and make specialty riding boots for people who show horses because the boots they wore were so uncomfortable. They now have a multi-million-dollar business.

Another young woman who had suffered a foot malady due to childhood polio designs and makes custom shoes for people with disabilities. Still another woman owns a company that makes new shoes from the recycled parts of old ones. If you have a reason or idea for wanting to see something different in a shoe line, this may be a business for you.

### Estimated Start-up Costs
$15,000 to $45,000

### Pricing Guidelines
Follow industry guidelines, plus consider the profit margin you need to make.

### Marketing and Advertising Methods and Tips
✤ Internet site
✤ Trade shows
✤ Ads in trade publications of the industry—women's, hobby-ists, children's, athletics, outdoor enthusiasts, and others whom you are target-marketing
✤ Press releases of your start-up and the unique features of your shoes

### Essential Equipment
✤ Shoemaking equipment
✤ Promotional materials: samples, brochures, business cards, and business stationery
✤ Home office equipment and work space

## Recommended Training, Experience, or Needed Skills
❖ Fashion design training, background, and experience
❖ Shoemaking courses and apprenticeship
❖ Flair for design
❖ Sales training and business management
❖ Marketing skills

## Income Potential
You design and make the custom footwear: $20,000 to $45,000

## Type of Business
$1/2$ in home designing and producing, $1/2$ out of home marketing

## Best Customers
People for whom your footwear is especially designed and who can afford your custom work

## Success Tips
❖ Research the custom-made shoe industry so you can find the niche market that will create a demand for your shoes/ footwear.
❖ Draw on your background and interests to design a shoe that is unique to your market.
❖ Take shoemaking courses and/or apprentice with a shoe- maker to create a quality product.
❖ Talk with podiatrists and other experts in the field.

## Additional Information
### Recommended Reading
*Make Your Own Shoes: A Step-by-Step Guide for High Fashion, Low-Cost, and Perfect Fit* by Mary Wales Loomis; to order, send $19.95 + $3.50 (U.S. funds, made out to Mary Wales Loomis), 1487 Parrot Dr., San Mateo, CA 94402-3632

**Study**
Designer Shoe-Covering Course; Wonderful World of Hats, 897
Wade Rd., Siletz, OR 97380; $3 for catalog

*Additional Business Ideas*
* Bridal shoes
* Moccasins
* Doll shoes

## ꙮ 40 ꙮ
## T-SHIRTS

The T-shirt is a fashion staple today along with athletic shoes,
jeans, and baseball caps. Companies cashing in on this billion-
dollar industry include one-person screen-printing companies to
large-scale franchises, distributors, and sportswear licensers.
For a modest investment, you can start this business in a home-
based workroom and use your creative skills to design a profitable business in your community.

*Estimated Start-up Costs*
$5,000 to $9,000

*Pricing Guidelines*
$10 to $20 a T-shirt, depending on the size, logo, and profit margin you need to make

*Marketing and Advertising Methods and Tips*
* Your T-shirts are "walking billboards" so make them the best
  you can.
* Ads in local papers
* Direct mail to community sports groups and businesses
* Take samples to local retail clothing shops and Chamber of
  Commerce members.

❖ Know in advance upcoming commemorative events in your community and surrounding ones.

### Essential Equipment
❖ Screen-printing press (newer computerized printing presses can print multicolor designs several times more quickly than older presses, but these are very costly)
❖ Inks and spot dryer

### Recommended Training, Experience, or Needed Skills
❖ Work in a screen-printing shop.
❖ Take courses at local vo-tech or art schools.
❖ Study the industry.
❖ Attend trade shows.
❖ Hire a consultant if you intend to go for markets larger than your community (find consultants at trade shows, and expect to pay them $500 to $1,000 a day plus expenses).

### Income Potential
$35,000 +

### Type of Business
$3/4$ in home (design and production), $1/4$ marketing

### Best Customers
❖ Local businesses and community service groups
❖ Families holding large reunions
❖ Tourist shops
❖ Sports leagues
❖ Private and public schools

### Success Tips
❖ Work with smaller T-shirt mills that may be more receptive to small orders.

❖ Concentrate on quality shirts, artwork, and your logo or phrases (which should catch people's interest in 1.5 seconds!).

## Franchises, Distributorships, and Licenses
S. Morantz, Inc.
9984 Gantry Rd.
Philadelphia, PA 19115
(215) 969-0266
Sells the Moranz Screen-A-Print, which needs only eight square feet of floor space and prints on anything.

## Additional Information
### Recommended Reading
*Entrepreneur's Small Business Development Catalog,* "T-Shirt Screen-Printing"; $69.00 + $7.95 for shipping and handling. Call (800) 421-2300 for a catalog or credit card orders.

*Great T-Shirt Graphics 2* (Cincinnati, OH: North Light, 1995).

*Impressions,* Miller Freeman, Inc., P.O. Box 1265, Skokie, IL 60076; $36/year. Write for subscription information. Web site http://www.impressionsmag.com

*Print's Best T-Shirt Promotions 2* (Cincinnati, OH: North Light, 1995)

*Screen Printing Production Management* by Richard C. Webb (Cincinnati, OH: S.T. Publications, 1989)

*T-Shirt Retailers & Screen Printer,* WFC, Inc, 3000 Hadley Rd., South Plainfield, NJ 07080.

### Supplies
Dick Blick Art Materials Catalog
P.O. Box 1267
Galesburg, IL 61402-1267

## Additional Business Ideas
❖ Other products: aprons, jackets, tote bags, hats, and so forth
❖ Unique sweatshirts (not painted)—see *Sweatshirts with Style* by Mary Mulari (Radnor, PA: Chilton, 1993); and *More Sweatshirts with Style* by Mary Mulari (Radnor, PA: Chilton, 1996)

## ⊸ 41 ⊸

# WALL PIECES

Creating wall pieces is strictly a creative business. Your customers will either purchase your original pieces or commission you to make a wall piece for their home, business, or organization. The materials you use or will specialize in are your choice—wood, fiber, metal, paper, plaster, ceramics, or a combination of these. You will need a large work space to accommodate the sizes of your different works. It would be your choice (and the demand from your customers) if you want to do many smaller pieces or one-of-a-kind, larger works.

### Estimated Start-up Costs
$15,00 to $5,000

### Pricing Guidelines
$40 to $150 for smaller pieces; $500 + for larger ones, depending on the materials used, your time, and the customer demand for your pieces

### Marketing and Advertising Methods and Tips
✤ Photo ads in home magazines
✤ Networking with craft guilds, coops, and associations
✤ Craft shows and fairs
✤ Home furnishing trade shows
✤ Direct mail to real estate brokers and builders with an offer to decorate sample homes
✤ Direct mail to home furnishing stores
✤ Samples to interior decorators
✤ Teach courses at local adult evening schools and creative art learning centers.
✤ Write a how-to book on the topic (it establishes you as an expert).
✤ Exhibits at local libraries, museums, and bank and company
· lobbies

❖ Contract with a sales representative.
❖ Referrals from customers

### Essential Equipment
❖ Materials and related tools for your craft
❖ Promotional materials: professional photographs (slides, etc.) of your work for juried shows, brochures, and business cards
❖ Internet site (your own or on a professional craftspersons' site)
❖ Computer and software for inventory, billing, and desktop publishing of promotional materials

### Recommended Training, Experience, or Needed Skills
❖ Art and crafts training and background
❖ Knowledge of the arts and crafts and home furnishings industry
❖ Business management and art marketing knowledge

### Income Potential
$10,000 to $50,000, depending on the demand for your pieces

### Type of Business
$3/4$ in home designing, producing, and conducting business; $1/4$ marketing and attending show exhibits

### Best Customers
❖ Architectural firms
❖ Art enthusiasts and homeowners
❖ Contemporary and country home furnishing studios and stores
❖ Business and organizations (offices, lobbies)
❖ Interior decorators
❖ Museums, art galleries, and art centers
❖ Shopping malls

## Success Tips
✤ Perfect your art and craft.
✤ Constantly look for new avenues to market your work.
✤ Send press releases of your work (with a bio of your background, any awards, etc.) to consumer home decorating and interior decorating trade publications for possible features about your work.

## Additional Information
### Recommended Reading
*Decorating with Fabric and Wallcovering: 98 Projects and Ideas (Arts and Crafts, Home Decorating)* by staff of Cy DeCosse, Inc. (Minnetonka, MN: Cowles Creative Publishing, 1995)

## Additional Business Ideas
✤ Hand-painting custom floor cloths for country-style homes—see *The Complete Book of Floor Cloths: Designs and Techniques for Painting Great-Looking Canvas Rugs* by Kathy Cooper and Jan Hersey (Asheville, NC: Lark, 1997)
✤ Murals—see *Painting Murals* by Patricia Seligman (Cincinnati, OH: North Light, 1988)

∽ ● ∾

# MISCELLANEOUS CREATIVE BUSINESSES
✤ Crafts display supplier—making or finding rustic boxes, ladders, old fences, old (not antique) furniture, and so forth, and selling these to artists and craftspersons for displays at their shows or shops
✤ Crafts marketing consultant—serving crafts professionals and retailers
✤ Craft show production—see *How to Produce a Successful Crafts Show* by Kathryn Caputo (Harrisburg, PA: Stackpole, 1997)
✤ Sewing Businesses—recommended reading for sewing businesses:

*The Fashion Resource Directory* by Amy Holman Edelman (Fairchild Publications, 1992)

*How to Start a Home Sewing or Craft School* (#116) (1994; Success Publications, 3419 Dunham Rd., Box 263, Warsaw, NY 14569); write for ordering information and catalog.

*Marketing Today's Fashions* by Helena de Paola and Carol Stewart Mueller (Upper Saddle River, NJ: Prentice Hall)

*Sew to Success: How to Make Money in a Home-Based Sewing Business* by Kathleen Spike (Portland, OR: Palmer Pletsch, 1995)

*Sew Up a Storm: All the Way to the Bank* by Karen L. Maslowski (Cinncinnati: Sewstorm Publishing, 1995)

❖ For sewing supplies—see *Designer Source Listing, 1997-1998* by Maryanne Burgess (Carikean Publishing, P.O. Box 11771, Chicago, IL 60611-0771); (773) 728-6118; "best sourcebook of companies that sell sewing and needle arts supplies." Call or write for the cost of the current directory.

❖ Additional sewing business ideas include:

Making christening pillows

Embroidering christening cloths

Recycling vintage bits of linen into projects

Making ribbon flowers—see *The Artful Ribbon: Ribbon Flowers* by Candace Kling (Lafayette, CA: C & T, 1996)

Swag- and drapery-making—contact S. Morantz, Inc., 9984 Gantry Rd., Philadelphia, PA 19115; (215) 969-0266.

# Entertainment Businesses

*The economic dependence of women is perhaps the greatest injustice that has been done to us, and has worked the greatest injury to the race.*

—Nellie McClung

Entertainment is now big business in the United States. Just look at the millions being grossed by movies, pro sports, music, comedy, best-selling mystery and suspense books, and other amusements. You may or may not make millions in an entertainment business, but it can be lucrative for you if you find the right audience—and have fun at the same time. As you should for any of the businesses in this book, though, study the industry and persist to find your market niche in this creative industry.

## ᵔ 42 ᵔ
## COMEDY WRITING

If you have a "humorous slant" on everyday life and the world and an ability to put this into writing, you may want to try comedy writing. There is a demand for this talent with the growth of comedy clubs across the country. Many comedians write their own acts but need extra material, which you could provide.

If you find your humor "matches" that of a particular comedian, you can send him or her samples for consideration. This field is very competitive, but you can start with local comedians and comedy clubs and expand from there.

### Estimated Start-up Costs
$1,500 to $5,000

### Pricing Guidelines
❖ Gags only, $7 to $25 each
❖ Routines, $150 to $1,200 per minute
❖ New comics, five-minute routine for $180
❖ Top writers in this industry get as much as $2,550 for five-minute routines.

### Marketing and Advertising Methods and Tips
❖ Advertising in entertainment trade publications and writing trade publications
❖ Word of mouth
❖ Direct mail to comedians and comedy clubs
❖ Internet site and advertising

### Essential Equipment
❖ Computer with laser printer, access to Internet, and writing software
❖ Promotional materials: letters of introduction and video- and audiotapes of your work being performed

### Recommended Training, Experience, or Needed Skills
❖ Knowledge of the comedy industry and trends
❖ Some natural ability in humor and comedy writing
❖ Attend comedy-writing workshops.

❖ Experience writing for local comedians.
❖ Understand the audience(s) that the comedian will be entertaining.

## Income Potential
$12,000 to $35,000 +

## Type of Business
$1/2$ home business writing and marketing, $1/2$ marketing and observing comedians for whom you write (or for whom you want to write), as well as the studios and talent agencies you will want to visit

## Best Customers
❖ New stand-up comedians, comedy clubs, radio personalities
❖ Speech writers who need short, humorous fillers

## Success Tips
❖ Start by concentrating on marketing your comedy writing to local comedians and clubs.
❖ Send gags and routines via mail, e-mail, and fax to comedians for whom you believe your work is appropriate.
❖ Produce your own comedy scripts for local playhouses to get experience.

## Additional Information
### Recommended Reading
*The Comedy Market: A Writer's Guide to Making Money Being Funny* by Carmine Desena (New York: Berkley, 1996)
*Comedy Writing Secrets* by Mel Helitzer (Cincinnati, OH: Writer's Digest Books, 1997)
*The Comic Bible*, monthly publication for comics, sketch/improv artists, and writers. $55/six months; single copy $10. Order from Mary Ann Pierro, Publisher, Pierro Movie Syndicate, The Comic Bible, P.O. Box 995, Kings Park, NY 11754-0995. E-mail ComicBible@aol.com.

**Organization**
 Comedy Writers Association
 c/o Robert Makinson
 P.O. Box 304
 Brooklyn, NY 11202-3304
 Newsletter published semiannually; annual convention held in New York City. Publication for sale (and others): *How to Sell Comedy Material*. Send a LSASE for membership and publications' ordering information.

### *Additional Business Ideas*

* Humor writing—many publications use humor writing, slanted to their readers. If you are knowledgeable in a craft or hobby, have some business expertise, and can write with humor, you will have many places to sell your pieces.
* Comedy play- and scriptwriting for local theater groups
* Humorous writing for greeting card companies and manufacturers of bumper stickers, badges, and buttons (or produce your own)—for more information on how you can begin writing captions for cards and other products, please send a LSASE to Sandra Louden, Box 9701, Pittsburgh, PA 15229-0701; and Oatmeal Studios Greeting Cards, Box 138, Rochester, VT 05767. Review *How to Write and Sell Greeting Cards, Bumper Stickers, T-Shirts and Other Fun Stuff* by Molly Wigand (Cincinnati: F & W Publications, 1992).
* Write and illustrate a humorous book (if you are so talented or can find an illustrator to work with you) for a particular trade, business, or organization.
* Write and illustrate cartoons—see *Getting Started Drawing and Selling Cartoons* by Randy Glasbergen (Cincinnati, OH: North Light Books, 1993)

## ↜ 43 ↝
# STORYTELLING

Do you love to tell stories and have a dramatic flair? Storytelling is the ancient form of handing down information and tales from ages past. It was used for communication and entertainment before the written word. Today, storytellers are sought to entertain children and even adults (stage shows, etc.). You may find even more markets than are mentioned here.

### Estimated Start-up Costs
$500 to $3,000 (if you do not have a computer)

### Pricing Guidelines
$25 to $300 per event

### Marketing and Advertising Methods and Tips
❖ Direct-mail promotional pieces and audio- and/or videotapes of your performances to your targeted audiences
❖ Word-of-mouth referrals
❖ Ads in parents' publications and local newspapers
❖ Performances at public events (e.g., folk festivals, fairs, Octoberfests)
❖ Ad on your community's business Web site

### Essential Equipment
❖ Audiovisual equipment: sound system with recording capabilities, lights, and props
❖ Books and materials from which you gain your stories
❖ Promotional literature, tapes, and business cards
❖ Home office: computer, word processing and desktop publishing software, printer, and modem

### Recommended Training, Experience, or Needed Skills
❖ Background, training, education, and/or experience in drama and acting
❖ Ability to relate stories that evoke descriptive images in your listeners' imaginations
❖ A love of storytelling and people
❖ A good memory and understanding to relay the stories to your listeners

## Income Potential
Good part-time business ranging from $5,000 to $30,000 a year, depending on your schedule and the groups hiring you

## Type of Business
$\frac{1}{2}$ in home practicing your presentations, researching folk tales, and so forth; $\frac{1}{2}$ storytelling

## Best Customers
❖ Schools, institutions, and group homes for mentally and physically challenged individuals
❖ Day and overnight camps
❖ Senior citizens centers, nursing homes, and hospitals with recreational therapy departments
❖ Public library programs for children
❖ Bookstore chains like Barnes & Noble and Borders Books that host children's events, folk and ethnic fairs, and other events
❖ Parents who hire you for their children's parties

## Success Tips
❖ Develop your own interpretation and presentation of stories.
❖ Constantly evaluate your presentations to improve your performances.
❖ Practice regularly.

## Additional Information
### Recommended Reading
*The Musician's Guide to Making and Selling Your Own CDs and Cassettes* by Jana Stenciled (Cincinnati, OH: Writer's Digest Books, 1997); use the same principles to record your stories.

*The Story Bag: A National Storytelling Newsletter.* Send a LSASE to The Story Bag, 5361 Javier St., San Diego, CA 92117-3215 for subscription information.

*The Storyteller's Guide: Storytellers Share Advice for the Classroom, Boardroom, Showroom, Podium and Central Stage* by William Mooney, David Holt, and Bill Mooney (Little Rock, AR: August House, 1996)

*The Storyteller's Start-up Book: Funding, Learning, Performing, and Using Folktales: Including Twelve Tellable Tales* by Margaret Reed MacDonald (Little Rock, AR: August House, 1993)

### Organization
Storytellers Association
P.O. Box 309
Jonesborough, TN 37659
Send a LSASE for membership information. Publishes *The Inside Story,* a bimonthly newsletter.

### Additional Business Idea
Writing folk tales—new or from old legends and cultures, for children's publishers and publications; find many markets in *Children's Writer's and Illustrator's Market* (Cincinnati, OH: Writer's Digest Books, annual).

## ⤙ 44 ⤚
# FAN CLUB MANAGEMENT
If you personally know a celebrity or have taken note of an entertainer in the movie, music, television, theater, writing, sports, or another public industry, you might propose managing a fan club related to that person's fame and notoriety. However, most fan clubs are started on their own by enthusiastic supporters of a celebrity who join together to hear about the latest news and happenings in relation to their favorite famous person without his or her official endorsement. It is a fun hobby for those fans and may be a lucrative business for you.

### Estimated Start-up Costs
$3,500 to $6,000, unless the celebrity pays for the costs

### Pricing Guidelines
Your money would be made from membership fees, ranging from $12 to $25 each, and from the commission or percentage you

would receive in selling your celebrity's related merchandise. In some cases, you will need to purchase a license to market your products.

## Marketing and Advertising Methods and Tips
* Classified ads in the fan, entertainment, and industry publications related to the field of your celebrity
* Direct mail to people who send fan letters
* Radio and cable television ads

## Essential Equipment
Home office: computer, laser printer, desktop publishing software, fax, telephone with answering system, and mailing software

## Recommended Training, Experience, or Needed Skills
* Public relations experience, training, and/or education
* Good communication and writing skills
* Creativity for brainstorming ideas for promotions, events, and so forth
* Having worked in fan club management before is extremely helpful.

## Income Potential
$7,000 to $25,000, depending on the popularity status of your celebrity, what products you sell and distribute, and so on. This is often a part-time income, and it is "a fun business," says Linda Kay of the National Association of Fan Clubs.

## Type of Business
$3/4$ in home conducting business, $1/4$ out of home sponsoring the events and conducting other publicity

## Best Customers
* Fans and supporters of the celebrity
* Hometown neighbors of the celebrity

## Success Tips

✤ Network with other fan club managers to pick up success tips.
✤ Stay on top of the latest promotional products, contests, and packages you can offer the fans.

## Recommended Reading

*Fan Club Directory: Over 2400 Fan Clubs and Fax-Mail-Internet and E-mail Addresses in the U. S. and Abroad*, 4th ed., by Patrick R. Dewey (Jefferson, NC: McFarland, 1997)

## Organization

National Association of Fan Clubs
Linda Kay, President
P.O. Box 7487
Burbank, CA 951510-7487

Publishes *Fan Club Monitor* newsletter (send a LSASE for membership information), *Fan Club Booklet*, and *Directory of Fan Clubs*. E-mail lknafc@aol. com for information.

## Additional Business Idea

Mailing list management services for fan clubs—see *How to Start and Profit from a Mailing List Service* by Allegato (1991); seventy-five-minute audio program; $19.95; order from The New Careers Center, Inc., 1515 23rd St., P.O. Box 339-DT, Boulder, CO 80306.

<hr>

## ⊰ 45 ⊱
# LOCAL RADIO OR TV SHOW

If you have experience and knowledge on certain topics, you might want to consider hosting a radio and/or television show from your own home studio or at an already established studio. Consider just a few of the radio and television shows from one community: a women who owns a health and organic food store hosts a weekly call-in radio show on natural foods; a college professor hosts a radio show from his college's communications building featuring guest speakers; a young couple presents area artists and their works on a local cable television show; a woman who heads a nonprofit group for people with disabilities hosts an information cable television show from her home in her wheelchair; a local horticulturist hosts a radio and cable television show and gives gardening and plant care tips.

If you are outgoing and a good communicator, hosting a show may be the future for you.

### Estimated Start-up Costs
$12,000 to $20,000

### Pricing Guidelines
Your money is made from your advertisers, made up primarily of local businesses that can spend an average of $100 to $200 a month to $1,000 + .

### Marketing and Advertising Methods and Tips
❖ Direct mail to businesses
❖ Networking with Chambers of Commerce and other local business groups
❖ Word-of-mouth referrals
❖ Contests
❖ Broadcasting live from local events

### Essential Equipment
❖ For your own studio: basic audio equipment, including cartridge tape recorders, audio mixer, reel-to-reel tape machine, commercial-grade VCRs, editing controller, camcorders, tripods, microphones, and video modulator
❖ FCC licensing (takes at least six months)
❖ Antenna, transmitter, satellite dish, and so forth
❖ For your own cable television show: wardrobe and props

### Recommended Training, Experience, or Needed Skills
❖ Attend broadcasting, communications, and filmmaking courses at your local high schools or colleges.

❖ Work and/or volunteer at either a radio or television station or both at your local high school or college with facilities for students to learn broadcasting.
❖ The education, training, and technical background in audio-visual and broadcasting to run your own studio
❖ Background and experience in hosting a show
❖ Knowledge of your topic so you are credible to your listeners or viewers
❖ Interesting and informative material to give people a reason for wanting to tune in

### Income Potential
$5,000 to $60,000, depending on your advertisers

### Type of Business
❖ In-home studio: $3/4$ programming and running the show, $1/4$ out getting new advertisers
❖ Radio show or television show: $1/2$ in home planning and writing your material; $1/2$ out of home, doing the show, gathering information, or filming

### Best Customers
❖ Local businesses, newspapers, health services, private schools and colleges

### Additional Information
### Recommended Reading
*Cable Television Technology and Operations: Hdtr and Ntsc Systems* by Eugene R. Bartlett (New York: McGraw-Hill, 1990)
*Producer's Masterguide: The International Production Manual for Motion-Picture, Broadcast-Television Commercials, Cable and Videotape Industry* by Shmuel Bension (New York: Producers Masterguide, 1997)
*Radio Production: A Manual for Broadcasters* by Robert McLeish (Newton, MA: Butterworth-Heinemann, 1994)
*Radio Production: Art and Science* by Michael C. Keith, Ph.D. (Boston: Focal Press, 1990)

*Radio Station Operations: Management & Employee Perspectives,*
   Wadsworth Series on Mass Communications, by Lewis B.
   O'Donnell (Belmont, CA: Wadsworth, 1989)
*Television Operations Handbook* by Robert Oringel (Stoneham, MA:
   Focal, 1984)

**Other Source**
*How to Talk to Anyone, Anytime, Anywhere! The Secrets of Good
   Communication,* audiotape, by Larry King and Bill Gilbert (New
   York: Random House, 1994)

*Additional Business Idea*
Short documentary filmmaker for television

## ⊸ 46 ⊱
## PONY RIDES AND PETTING ZOO
If you love animals and children (and bringing the two together),
you may want to look into offering pony rides and a traveling
petting zoo as a business; or instead of traveling with your
animals, you could have people come to your farm and participate in added attractions like hay rides, crawling through hay
mazes, building scarecrows, walking through a pumpkin patch,
milking a goat or cow, and other fun activities.

### Estimated Start-up Costs
❖ $2,000 to $5,000 if you already have the animals
❖ Additional costs involve advertising, licenses, permits, animal
   care, and insurance fees for liability coverage.

### Pricing Guidelines
❖ For pony rides, $1 to $3 a ride
❖ Admission to petting zoo, $1 to $2 per child; $5 to $7 per
   family
❖ For traveling to an event, $100 to $500 for the day, depend-
   ing on how large the event, what sort of animals you have

(farm or exotic), and mileage; this charge may or may not include a percentage of the admissions and rides.
❖ $1 for a quick photo of child with the animal

### Marketing and Advertising Methods and Tips
❖ In farm: ads in pet and parent publications; flyers at pet, grocery, and department stores; direct mail to preschools, day care centers, and homes for special-needs children
❖ Traveling: direct mail to boroughs, towns, and organizations that have annual fairs
❖ Promotional materials: business cards, brochures, flyers, and photos
❖ Internet site

### Essential Equipment
❖ Small animals that are child- and people-friendly (also healthy and with proper inoculations)
❖ Temporary yet sturdy fences
❖ Trailers and crates if you travel
❖ Animal harnesses, bridles, and saddles
❖ Food for children to feed your animals

### Recommended Training, Experience, or Needed Skills
❖ Knowledge of the nature of each animal you have
❖ Ability to choose animals with good natures
❖ Love and understanding of children
❖ Physical stamina to care for and transport the animals and the necessary equipment
❖ Business management skills

### Income Potential
❖ This is primarily a seasonal business if you live where there are cold winters, so it may be a part-time business.
❖ $5,000 to $30,000, depending on how large the fairs and events are that you attend

## Type of Business
$^1/_2$ in home if you offer a traveling petting zoo; full-time at home if your customers come to your farm

## Best Customers
❖ Parents and grandparents of young children
❖ People with special needs who respond well to animals
❖ Promoters of city and state fairs, festivals, and community events
❖ Company picnics
❖ "Grand openings" of malls
❖ Business's special promotions

## Success Tips
❖ If possible, work or volunteer in a petting zoo to see how it is operated both on site and at an event.
❖ Make sure your animals are clean, safe, and people-friendly.
❖ Have adequate liability insurance.
❖ Have a variety of pets: kittens, puppies, ponies, pygmy goats, miniature horses, miniature donkeys, iguanas, hedgehogs, pot-bellied pigs, and so forth.

## Additional Information
### Recommended Reading
Animal care books: Write to Storey's How-To Books for Country Living, Schoolhouse Road, Pownal, VT 05261, for the latest catalog.

Career Success with Pets: How to Get Started, Get Going, Get Ahead by Kim Barber (New York: Howell, 1996)

### Organizations
International Association of Fairs and Expositions
P.O. Box 98
304 E. Cairo
Springfield, MO 65801

Outdoor Amusement Business Association, Inc.
4600 W. 77th St.
Minneapolis, MN 55435

### Additional Business Idea
Show business—see *How to Get Your Pet into Show Business* by
Arthur J. Haggerty (New York: Howell, 1994)

## ❧ 47 ☙
# SCIENCE SHOWS

Many schools cannot afford to take class trips to science centers
or museums. If you have an expertise in an area of science—
animals, reptiles, space, electricity, the science of bubbles, and
other areas—and can make the topic both informative and exciting, you may want to think about planning science shows to present to schools and institutions. You could also give science
parties for birthdays and scouting banquets or hold after-school,
weekend, or summer classes—all geared for fun activities while
learning science.

If you are a retired science teacher or have stopped teaching to have children, you could be a tutor or a consultant to
schools to help them set up science fairs.

### Estimated Start-up Costs
$1,000 to $5,000 (if you already have a computer)

### Pricing Guidelines
❖ Charge fees per child if you hold in-home classes; $10 per
  child (for five to ten children for one hour).
❖ School programs run from $400 for two one-hour programs
  to $1,200 for a full day of programs and individual class
  visitations.
❖ $7 to $19.95 for the cost of your own how-to book on fun
  and exciting science experiments

❖ $1,000 to $2,000 for a workshop to instruct teachers and schools in an area of science or how to hold science fairs

## Marketing and Advertising Methods and Tips
❖ Direct mail to school boards, school principals, and parent-teacher groups
❖ Promotional materials: business cards, videos of your performances, and brochures
❖ Internet site with photos of your shows

## Essential Equipment
Van or truck to carry your equipment, sound system, props, and materials

## Recommended Training, Experience, or Needed Skills
❖ A degree or certificate in the area of science that your shows cover
❖ A flair for entertaining and amazing children (they love humor, too)

## Income Potential
❖ In home, $40 to $50 an hour
❖ For schools and other groups, $30,000 to $60,000 a year, depending on how often you perform

## Type of Business
$1/4$ in home (more if you have classes in your home or workshop), $3/4$ out of home to do the shows

## Best Customers
❖ Schools: private, public, and charter; and homeschool groups
❖ Learning and/or creative learning centers
❖ Children's organizations: YMCAs, scouting groups, recreation centers, and camps
❖ Cable television stations

## Success Tips

✤ Observe a number of school programs and evaluate what you liked (or did not like) about their performances.

✤ Know your subject and how to present it in an exciting and entertaining manner to children to get them enthused about science.

✤ Demonstrate through your workshops how schools can have science programs and fairs economically and with the facilities and equipment they already have.

✤ Get feedback from the students and the adults as to the effectiveness of your programs—did they learn?

## Additional Information
### Recommended Reading

*101 Science Surprises: Exciting Experiments with Everyday Materials* by Roy Richards (New York: Sterling, 1994)

*175 Amazing Nature Experiments* by Rosie Harlow and Gareth Morgan (New York: Random House, 1992)

*175 More Science Experiments to Amuse and Amaze Your Friends* by Terry Cash (New York: Random House, 1991)

*365 Simple Science Experiments with Everyday Materials* by E. Richard Churchill (New York: Black Dog and Leventhal, 1997)

## Additional Business Ideas

Educational consultant for science fairs—giving workshops on how schools (private, public, charter) and homeschooling groups can put on productive science shows

꞊ ● ꞊

# MISCELLANEOUS ENTERTAINMENT BUSINESSES

✤ Puppet shows—performing for nursery schools, day care centers, church school programs, primary school grades, community summer park programs, day camps, and so forth.

You can purchase or make your puppets. If you are trained in a field of psychology, puppets can also be used for therapy.
❖ Recommended reading for puppet shows:

*Amazingly Easy Puppet Plays: 42 New Scripts for One-Person Puppetry* by Dee Anderson (Chicago: American Library Association, 1996)

*Fantastic Theater: Puppet, and Plays for Young Performers and Young Audiences* by Judy Sierra (Bronx, NY: Wilson, 1991)

*Hand Puppets*, rev. ed. (Mineola, NY: Dover, 1990)

*Hand Puppets: How to Make and Use Them* by Laura Ross (Mineola, NY: Dover, 1990)

*The Little Pigs Puppet Book*, vol. 1, by Cameron N. Watson (Boston: Little, Brown, 1990)

❖ Organization—Puppeteers of America, 5 Cricklewood Path, Pasadena, CA 91107. Send a LSASE for membership information.

# Environmental and Green Businesses*

*Gardening stimulates all your senses and helps you stay active and creative.*

—Anonymous

Gardening will continue to be a growing interest in the next century as many people have it as an ongoing hobby to beautify their properties and communities. Recycling and recycled products will also continue to be in demand as the world searches to feed, house, warm (or cool), and power itself while at the same time attempting to save its resources. There is a movement, for example, in Philadelphia, Chicago, and other cities, to employ persons to grow fresh fruits and vegetables in abandoned lots. Mushroom and fish culture are also being considered as alternative industries.

As a result of this "green thumb" madness and the quest for clean food, air, and water, many businesses are starting to serve

*Make sure you have the necessary licenses and permits to sell your produce, plants, and run a business. Check with your county extension agent for any regulations concerning raising and selling of certain plants and so forth.

these markets. If you are knowledgeable in gardening, have an idea for a recycled product, or want to start a service business that is related to the environment, you may well start on a profitable venture that is almost guaranteed to prosper into the next century.

## Additional Information
### Recommended Reading

*Gale Environmental Almanac* by Gale Research (Detroit, MI: Gale Research); environmental topics and sources. Check your library's reference section for availability.

*Pay Dirt: How to Raise and Sell Herbs and Produce for Serious Cash* by Mimi Luebbermann (Rocklin, CA: Prima, 1997)

*Profitable Plants—Your Guide to the Best Backyard Cash Crops,* booklet; send $1 for shipping to Homestead Design, P.O. Box 2010, Port Townsend, WA 98368-0080; resources and tips for growing and marketing more than twenty high-value crops.

*Small Farm Today,* Missouri Farm Publishing, Inc., c/o Ridge Top Ranch, 3903 W. Ridge Trail Rd., Clark, MO 65243-9525; $21/yr. 6 issues; sample copy $4.

### Publishers of Gardening Books
Write for current listings or catalogs.

Interweave Press, 201 E. Fourth St., Loveland, CO 80537-5655; gardening, herbs

Rodale Press, 33 E. Minor St., Emmaus, PA 18049

Sterling Publishing Company Inc., 387 Park Ave. South, New York, NY 10016-8810

Storey's How-To Books for a Country Living, Schoolhouse Road, Pownal, VT 05261; http://www.StoreyBooks.com; gardening, raising crops, herbs, and more

### Organizations
American Horticultural Society
7931 E. Boulevard Dr.
Alexandria, VA 22308-1300

Membership of $25/year includes *American Gardener* magazine, admission to flower shows and arboretums, and a free spring and fall seed exchange; (800) 777-7931.

American Landscape Horticulture Association
2509 E. 1000 Oaks Blvd., Suite 109
Westlake Village, CA 91362
Send a LSASE for membership.

National Landscape Association
1250 I St., NW, Suite 500
Washington, DC 20005
Send a LSASE for membership information.

The Co-Op America Business Network
1612 K St., NW, Suite 600
Washington, DC 20003
$60 membership fee; lists members in its *Co-op America National Green Pages*, featuring more than 100,000 consumers and businesses that demonstrate caring and respect for the environment. Send a LSASE for information.

### Local Government Assistance
U.S. Department of Agriculture, Cooperative Extension Service—
The USDA has an extension office in every county in the United States. Originally formed to assist farmers, these offices operate in conjunction with state universities and are good sources for information on plants and insects. In recent years, they have also assisted in forming craft cooperatives and providing information on small business start-ups. Look in your telephone directory's government pages or call directory assistance for the number of the office nearest you.

### Home Study
Lifetime Career Schools
"Flower Arranging and Floristry," "Landscaping"
101 Harrison St.
Archbald, PA 18403-1997

**Other Source**
Herb Growing and Marketing Network
P.O. Box 245
Silver Spring, PA 17575
http://www.herbnet.com

## ৵ঞ 48 ঞ৵
# COMPOST AND SOIL PRODUCTION

Many municipalities and landfills are not accepting garden wastes and lawn and hedge clippings. You can show new gardeners how to turn their garden refuse, pet droppings (not from meat-eating animals), and table scraps (not meats, cheeses, etc.) into valuable compost for their yard and garden. If you have grain- or grass-eating animals (horses, goats, rabbits, cows) and organic (nonchemical) garden and yard waste, you could also mix your own compost/fertilizer mix and sell to special gardening centers or organic gardeners.

You could also buy wholesale quantities of perlite, bone meal, lime, and sterilized and organic soil (or use your own) and create special soils for different plants, such as cacti, African violets, and so forth, for indoor gardeners.

### Estimated Start-up Costs
$3,000 to $10,000

### Pricing Guidelines
$5 to $10 a bag; or by the yard, ton, or whatever amount you choose; you can charge what the market will bear and for the value and the uniqueness of your soil and compost

### Marketing and Advertising Methods and Tips
❖ Direct mail to gardening centers
❖ Samples to garden shops, florists, and greenhouses
❖ Sales representatives

❖ Exhibits at garden consumer and trade shows (have plants grown with ordinary soil and your soil)
❖ Ads in gardeners' publications
❖ Talks to gardening groups
❖ Hold courses and workshops at your home or at local gardening centers on composting and mixing potting soils.
❖ Internet Web site

### Essential Equipment
❖ Space needed for mixing and preparing compost and soils
❖ Bags for compost and soil
❖ Gardening tools, wheelbarrows, shredders, and barrels
❖ Bins for shifting piles of decomposing compost
❖ Shovels and a small front-end loader to load and shift soil, compost, and equipment
❖ Garden shed with work table
❖ Van or truck for deliveries
❖ Tests for soil components
❖ Sources of phosphate, potash, organic plant materials, and animal wastes

### Recommended Training, Experience, or Needed Skills
❖ Knowledge and experience of the different soil requirements of indoor and outdoor plants.
❖ Knowledge of the chemistry and "formulas" of soil and compost
❖ Gardening and horticultural education, training, and experience
❖ Take gardening courses at local horticultural and vo-tech schools.
❖ Contact and work with your cooperative extension agents for information on soils, compost, and testing.

### Income Potential
$10,000 to $35,000 +, depending on the size of your operation

### Type of Business
$3/4$ in home preparing compost and soils, $1/4$ marketing

## Best Customers
* Hobbyist gardeners
* Small greenhouse growers
* Florists, plant shops, and gardening centers

## Success Tips
* Promote the effectiveness and benefits of using your soils and composts.
* Experiment and do trials to find the best composts and soils for popular plants.

## Franchises, Distributorships, and Licenses
Agronics, Inc.
6808 Academy Parkway, E., NE, Suite A3
Albuquerque, NM 87109
Biological farming products; total soil management. Write for information.

## Additional Information
See the resources cited beginning on page 225.

## Recommended Reading
*Don't Call It Dirt!: Improving Your Garden Soil* by Gordon Lloyd (Rochester, NY: Bookworm, 1976)

*Easy Composting (Environmentally Friendly Gardening)* by James Ball, Robert Kourik, and Roberta Spieckerman (San Ramon, CA: Ortho, 1992)

*Let It Rot! The Gardener's Guide to Composting* by Stu Campbell (Pownal, VT: Garden Way, 1992)

*The Rodale Book of Composting*, rev. ed., by Deborah L. Martin and Grace Gershuny (Emmaus, PA: Rodale, 1992)

*Rodale's Successful Organic Gardening: Improving the Soil* by Erin Hynes (Emmaus, PA: Rodale, 1994); potting formula mixes

*Start with the Soil* by Grace Gershundy (Emmaus, PA: Rodale, 1993); soil mix formulas; resources for soil care supplies, test kits, worms, plant information sources, and composting supplies

**Supplies**
See the "Resources" chapter of *Start with Soil* by Grace Gershundy (Emmaus, PA: Rodale, 1993).

*Additional Business Idea*
Weeds away and mulch service—specializing in a gardening service that organically gets rid weeds (with your special gardening tools) and covers customer's flower beds and small gardens with mulch to prevent regrowth; maintaining the beds as needed or decided by your contract

## ~~ 49 ~~
## EDIBLE LANDSCAPING

People love to eat what they have grown. They also wish to have fruit and vegetables that are free of sprays and chemicals. With your landscaping design know-how, you will be able to plan landscaping designs that combine both beauty and practicality with lots of good eating!

*Estimated Start-up Costs*
$2,500 to $3,000

*Pricing Guidelines*
* $25 to $30 an hour, $50 to $100 an hour if you have a degree in horticultural or landscape design
* Additional fees if you are contracted to install the trees, shrubs, and plants

*Marketing and Advertising Methods and Tips*
* Classified ads in local newspapers' business sections
* Direct mail to wholesale growers of fruit and berry trees and plants
* Press release of this different type of landscaping
* Booths at local and regional gardening shows

❖ Courses and workshops at hardware stores, farm and gardening centers
❖ Word-of-mouth referrals
❖ Business cards and brochures with color photos of some of your gardens
❖ Talks to gardening clubs

### Essential Equipment
❖ Gardening and horticultural reference books
❖ Assorted gardening tools and hoses
❖ Van or truck
❖ Gardening-related and desktop publishing software

### Recommended Training, Experience, or Needed Skills
❖ Degree or certificate in landscape design or horticulture
❖ Work for a landscaping service
❖ Creativity in design and planting

### Income Potential
$25,000 to $50,000 full-time

### Type of Business
$1/2$ in home designing, planning, and conducting business; $1/2$ on-the-job work

### Best Customers
❖ Individual homeowners
❖ Group homes for individuals with mental or physical disabilities (they can participate in the harvesting, etc.)

### Success Tips
❖ Charge a design fee, but credit it toward the entire bill if the customer decides to have you install the plantings.
❖ Offer a yearly maintenance service (for pruning, getting rid of pests [organic methods], etc.).

❖ Describe in your promotional materials the benefits of combining edible fruit-producing trees and plants.
❖ Keep up with the latest horticultural methods in the industry.


### Additional Information
**Recommended Reading**
*The Complete Book of Edible Landscaping* by Rosalind Creasy (New York: Random House, 1982)
*Designing and Maintaining Your Edible Landscaping Naturally* by Robert Kourik (Portland, OR: Metamorphous, 1986)


### Additional Business Ideas
❖ Birdscaping—designing gardens to attract different species of birds for amateur ornithologists. See *The Bird Garden* (National Audubon Society) by William J. Weber (New York: Dorling-Kindersley, 1996).
❖ Backyard wildlife habitats—contact the National Wildlife Federation, 8925 Leesburg Pike, Vienna, VA 22184, to order the low-cost packet on how to establish a backyard wildlife habitat. You can invite your customers to participate in this worthwhile program and have their backyards "certified" by the National Wildlife Federation as being suitable for wildlife. Also see *Attracting Birds and Butterflies: How to Plan and Plant a Backyard Habitat* by Barbara Ellis (Boston: Houghton-Mifflin, 1997).


## ❧ 50 ❧
## (HOME) FRUIT AND VEGETABLE STAND

On my road alone, there are three home fruit and vegetable stands. One is a run by a retired farmer, one by a husband and wife, and one by a grandmother (whose young grandchild also helps with the business). They open the growing season with spring (forced) bulbs in pots and close after Christmas and the selling of live and cut trees and greens. They grow most of the produce themselves, but sometimes they also sell the special herbs, plants, and assorted goods of other local growers.

Another man and wife who have two greenhouses sell a wide variety of perennials by the roadside, not far from their house. Their perennials are in pots that are set in long boxes under a protective canopy away from the sun, and they supply red wagons for their customers to carry their pots as they stroll up and down the rows. The quality of their foods and plants and their friendly and old-fashioned (it seems, these days) customer service, bring many loyal customers to return year after year.

### Estimated Start-up Costs
$5,000 to $10,000

### Pricing Guidelines
Survey the prices of fruits and vegetables in local grocery stores and make yours competitive. Remember, you can charge more as "specialty," "gourmet," and "heirloom" vegetables become popular with chefs and cooking enthusiasts.

### Marketing and Advertising Methods and Tips
❖ Offer to sponsor a "farm market day" weekly in nearby towns, inviting other local growers to have booths to sell their produce in a parking lot or area in the center of town.
❖ Get together with your county extension office to publish a small directory listing all the area's farm stands. Have these directories available to hand out at local stores, news agencies, community centers, libraries, and so forth.
❖ Make eye-catching roadside signs.
❖ Offer attractive additions for sale like outdoor lawn and garden ornaments, wind chimes, and birdhouses.
❖ Offer free recipes for the fruits and vegetables you sell.

### Essential Equipment
❖ Access to farm land (own or rent); depending on your crops, one to two acres or more
❖ Gardening equipment
❖ Wagon/stand that can be towed into your fields and back out to a roadside area

❖ Display signs, bags, baskets, scales, and hoses
❖ Cash register
❖ Small tractor
❖ Van or truck

### Recommended Training, Experience, or Needed Skills
Gardening skills and farm and greenhouse experience

### Income Potential
$20,000 to $50,000 + , depending on your traffic and whether you have "gourmet" crops

### Type of Business
$3/4$ at home growing and selling your produce, $1/4$ marketing to other outlets

### Best Customers
Community consumers and restaurant chefs

### Success Tips
❖ Diversify, unless you have a specific crop that is in demand in your area. For example, grow Indian corn (to eat and for the corn stalks) and pumpkins for Halloween and Thanksgiving as many people decorate in a big way for these holidays.
❖ Specialize in "gourmet" crops and find outlets for them (e.g., restaurants and chefs who will pay very well to offer these to their customers).
❖ Make sure you have a safe parking area for your customers and that you are allowed to sell produce from your location.

### Additional Information
#### Recommended Reading
*Backyard Market Gardening: The Entrepreneur's Guide to Selling What You Grow* by Andrew Lee (Burlington, VT: Good Earth, 1995)

*Market Gardening: Growing and Selling Produce* by Ric Staines (Burlington, VT: Good Earth, 1992)

*The New Organic Gardener: A Master's Manual of Tools and Techniques for the House and Market Gardener* by Eliot Coleman (Broomall, PA: Chelsea Green, 1995)

*Small Farm Today*, 3903 W. Ridge Trail Rd., Clark, MO 65243-9525; $21/year, six issues; sample copy $4

### Additional Business Ideas

❖ Growing heirloom crops—there is a great demand by chefs and restaurants for special varieties of lettuce, tomatoes, peppers, and other vegetables, many which are old kinds grown years ago in early America or in Europe. Culinary herbs are also in demand. For information on organically grown seeds and heirloom and traditional varieties, see "Seeds of Change," P. O. Box 15700, Santa Fe, NM 87506-5700. Write for a catalog, or visit http://www.seedsofchange.com.

❖ Hydroponic gardening (the practice of growing plants without soil; plants are grown directly in a water-nutrient solution that contains the minerals necessary for plant nutrition and growth)—selling to restaurants, cooking schools, chefs, and others. See *Beginning Hydroponics: Soilless Gardening: A Beginner's Guide to Growing Vegetables, House Plants, Flowers, and Herbs without Soil* by Richard E. Nichols (Philadelphia: Running Press, 1990); and *Hydroponics for the Home Gardener* by Stewart Kenyon (Toronto: Key Porter, 1992).

❖ "Pick Your Own Fruits/Vegetables"—if you have the land, then plant strawberry beds, berry bushes (blackberry, raspberry, blueberry, etc.), plum bushes, grapes, and so forth, as well as assorted vegetables, and place small display ads in your free, classified papers. People provide their own containers (or you can sell some) and pick their own fruits and vegetables, which you weigh on your scale and charge per pound.

❖ "Share the Farm"—many people who live in towns or on small properties would love to have space for larger gardens. If your have the land, you could rent them different-sized plots to raise their vegetables and/or flowers.

## ∼ 51 ∼
# HEDGE TRIMMING AND LANDSCAPE LIGHTING

Many people do not mind cutting their lawns, but they do not have the equipment or the time to trim, prune, or maintain their hedges. If you have experience and the knowledge of how to trim different kinds of hedges and shrubs, you may want to start this green service business.

You can also offer to install landscape lighting—not the kind that requires the digging of deep trenches and an electrician but the kind that comes already boxed.

### Estimated Start-up Costs
$2,000 to $5,000

### Pricing Guidelines
$20 to $35 an hour for hedge trimming and for the installation of landscape lighting that the home- or business owner chooses

### Marketing and Advertising Methods and Tips
❖ Classified ads in local papers
❖ Lawn sign visible from the road near the property on which you are working
❖ Word-of-mouth referrals from satisfied customers and gardening centers
❖ Yellow Pages

### Essential Equipment
❖ Hedge trimmers (both battery operated and electric), pruners, and rakes
❖ Electrical extension cords
❖ Wheelbarrow, shovels, and trowels
❖ Van or truck
❖ Heavy gloves, protective eyewear, and face masks

❖ Area to place clippings or save money for a chipping machine to do the chipping on site

### Recommended Training, Experience, or Needed Skills
❖ Knowledge of different varieties of shrubs and hedges and how to cut and shape them
❖ Experience and skill in cutting the plants
❖ Strength and stamina
❖ For landscape lighting—knowledge of the lights you carry and how to install them. Follow the manufacturer's recommendations.

### Income Potential
$15,000 to $20,000 a season

### Type of Business
$1/4$ in home for conducting business, $3/4$ out of home

### Best Customers
Homeowners, businesses, and organizations

### Success Tips
❖ Know the care of each type of hedge or shrub that you are asked to trim.
❖ Be fast and efficient, and clean up thoroughly after you are finished.
❖ Make sure the manufacturer of the lighting systems that you use offers guarantees if the lighting malfunctions.

### Additional Information
#### Recommended Reading
*Garden Craftsmanship in Yew and Box* by Nathaniel Lloyd (Wappingers Falls, NY: Antique Collectors Club, 1995)
*The Landscape Lighting Book* by Janet Lennox Moyer (New York: Wiley, 1992)

*Living Fences: A Gardener's Guide to Hedges, Vines, and Espaliers* by Ogden Tanner (Shelburne, VT: Chapters, 1996)

### Additional Business Ideas
❖ Evergreen and holly tree grower—selling wholesale to florists to sell to their customers for seasonal decorations
❖ Hedge and flowering shrub designer—planning and designing the landscape for the home- or business owner who wants hedges and flowering vines but is not sure about which ones would be best for her property and needs.
❖ You can also cut hedges into topiaries for special events.
❖ Plant mazes for future fun and attractions in large gardens.

## ◁ 52 ▷
## INTERIOR LANDSCAPING

Some scientific studies report that houseplants not only provide an esthetic presence in a home's or building's decorating scheme but actually help filter out impurities in the air. Houseplants, however, have very different water, light, soil, and temperature requirements than outdoor plants do. You can guide customers with suggestions for the best houseplants that will grow, thrive, and beautify their home and/or office.

### Estimated Start-up Costs
$5,000 to $10,000

### Pricing Guidelines
$40 to $75 an hour, or charge a fee for a project—including designing and purchasing the plants (which could run $1,000 + )

### Marketing and Advertising Methods and Tips
❖ Yellow Pages
❖ Ads in local papers and magazines
❖ Referrals from architectural firms and real estate brokers

❖ Direct mail followed up with visits to greenhouse owners, plant and florist shops, and garden centers
❖ Word-of-mouth referrals
❖ Direct mail to new office centers and businesses, organizations' buildings, and other places with lobbies and public areas

## Essential Equipment
❖ Library of houseplant care books
❖ Home office: computer with design capabilities, printer, photocopier, business phone with answering system, and related software
❖ Promotional materials: portfolio with photos of your work and prices and fees, business cards, and brochures
❖ Van
❖ Watering cans, mister, soil, and houseplant tools (pruners, pots)

## Recommended Training, Experience, or Needed Skills
❖ Degree, experience, or knowledge in horticulture and plant design
❖ Volunteer to design family members' and friends' homes and businesses to get experience.
❖ An aesthetic sense of arrangement that pleases your customer and yet fits within the budget

## Income Potential
$15,000 part-time, $35,000 to $55,000 full-time

## Type of Business
$1/2$ in home designing and planning, $1/2$ doing on-site work and marketing

## Best Customers
❖ Affluent homeowners
❖ Businesses, organizations, and institutions with lobbies and offices

## Success Tips

✤ Find your customer niche—those places and people with whom you communicate the best.

✤ Network with other interior plant designers.

✤ Make sure you have any licenses or permits you may need.

✤ Offer a plant maintenance plan with your service, or have good referrals you can make.

## Additional Information

### Recommended Reading

*The Complete Book of Houseplants: A Practical Guide to Selecting and Caring for Houseplants* by John Evans (New York: Penguin Studio, 1994)

*Decorating with Silk and Dried Flowers: 80 Arrangements Using Floral Materials of All Kinds (Arts & Crafts for Home Decorating)* by staff of CyDeCosse (Minnetonka, MN: Cowles Creative Publications, 1994)

*Environmental Interiorscapes: A Designer's Guide to Interior Plantscaping & Automated Irrigation Systems* by Stuart D. Snyder (technical) (New York: Whitney Library of Design, 1995)

*Interior Plantscapes: Installation, Maintenance and Management* by George H. Manaker (Upper Saddle River, NJ: Prentice Hall, 1996)

*Silk Flowers: Complete Color and Style Guide for the Creative Crafter* by Judith Blacklock (Radnor, PA: Chilton, 1995)

## Franchises, Distributorships, and Licenses

Totally Tropical Interiors, Ltd.
4310 12th St. NE
Calgary, Alberta T2E 6K9, Canada

Silk plants, trees, and decorating accessories. Write for information.

## Additional Business Ideas

✤ Baby- and pet-safe plant consultant—advising parents, day cares, preschools, and pet owners on nontoxic plants. See *Baby-Safe Houseplants and Cut Flowers: A Guide to Keeping Chil-*

*dren and Plants Safely under the Same Roof* by John and Delores Alber (Pownal, VT: Garden Way, 1993)

❖ Add these services to your business (or specialize in them): live plant cleaning and repotting, silk plant cleaning

❖ Natural pest control—review *Dead Snails Leave No Trails: Natural Pest Control for Home and Garden* by Loren Nancarrow and Janet Hogan Taylor (Berkeley, CA: Ten Speed Press, 1996)

## ⋙ 53 ⋘
# TOPIARY BUSINESS

This is a fun green business that you can start for little money and with little experience. This venture involves training plants to grow around templates and mock topiaries, ceramic animal forms, chicken wire frames, three-dimensional stencils, and other forms. People and businesses use them for accents in their gardens or to attract attention. Practice at this craft will only improve your skill, and your imagination will always keep you creating a new "green piece."

Other options with this business are to put your customers' plants in the ground and train them to grow around a permanent form or to cut and trim them ornamentally.

### Estimated Start-up Costs
$500 to $1,000

### Pricing Guidelines
❖ Small topiaries run from $10 to $110
❖ Charge $20 to $100 an hour to build one in a customer's yard + $20 an hour for any assistants + the cost of materials.

### Marketing and Advertising Methods and Tips
❖ Flyers at gardening centers
❖ Referrals from landscape designers and satisfied customers
❖ Photo ads in your local newspapers

✤ Teach courses at local garden centers, vo-tech schools, and community colleges.
✤ Business cards and color brochures
✤ Direct mail to businesses saying that you can replicate a topiary of their logo or initials
✤ Exhibits at garden and flower shows
✤ Free pieces at charity auctions

### Essential Equipment
✤ Plants and medium pots for holding soil and water (there is a shortage of sphagnum moss, so check for substitutes recommended by the plant industry)
✤ Hedge and plant shears
✤ Chicken wire, floral foam, twine and fishing line, cutouts around which plants can grow
✤ Tools for building the frames

### Recommended Training, Experience, or Needed Skills
✤ Horticultural degree, certificate, training, or hands-on experience
✤ Knowledge and skill of the plants best suited for topiary plant culture
✤ Building skills for making the frames
✤ Creativity in originating the topiary ideas, which can range from small, tabletop pieces to large, permanent, and life-size ones

### Income Potential
$15,000 to $35,000 full-time

### Type of Business
$1/2$ in home workshop, $1/2$ at customers' homes and marketing

### Best Customers
Flower shops and garden centers, schools, zoos, individuals' gardens, gift shops, craft and garden shows

### Success Tips
❖ Find the topiaries that you make best.
❖ Let your imagination run wild making animal shapes and training vines to grow into shapes against the walls.
❖ Start with small, indoor topiaries.
❖ Practice until you perfect your skill.

### Additional Information
#### Recommended Reading
*The Book of Topiary* by Charles H. Curtis and W. Gibson (Boston: Tuttle, 1986)

*The Complete Book of Dried Flower Topiaries: A Step-by-Step Guide to Creating 25 Stunning Arrangements* by Richard Felber and Carol Endler Sterbenz (Philadelphia: Courage Books, 1990)

*Herb Topiaries* by Sally Gallo (Loveland, CO: Interweave, 1992)

*Quick and Easy Topiary and Green Sculpture* by Jenny Henry (New York: HarperCollins, 1996)

#### Organizations
Send a LSASE to the associations listed in the beginning of this chapter to see whether they have any publications for sale on topiaries.

### Additional Business Ideas
❖ Foundation forms for topiaries—creating these for people who want to create their own topiaries but who do not want to do the building of the forms or the templates
❖ Flower growing and drying—selling these to craft and floral shops or individuals who come to your home shop

## ∼ 54 ∼
## WATER GARDENING DESIGN

One of the most soothing sounds in a garden is the sound of water trickling or lightly splashing; however, not everyone's garden is located near a stream, pond, or lake. The National Pond

Society says that more than two million households in the
United States are pond keepers and purchase many products
(plants, pond forms, fish, fountains, pumps, etc.) to maintain
them and that the trend is rapidly growing. Many people are also
putting these ponds inside their home sunrooms to enjoy pond
keeping year round.

With your business, though, you can create water gardens
that will add beauty and charm to your customers' backyard
gardens. Water never fails to attract birds, butterflies, dragon-
flies, and even a frog or two. It completes a mini-ecosystem in
a garden setting.

You can design the gardens and install them yourself and/or
subcontract any excavation and/or electrical work that may be
needed for installation.

### Estimated Start-up Costs
$5,000 to $15,000

### Pricing Guidelines
❖ $50 to $75 an hour if you have a degree in horticulture
❖ $1,500 + for directing the installation of a home pond
❖ Add a service for pond maintenance, including spring and
   fall preparation.

### Marketing and Advertising Methods and Tips
❖ Flyers at gardening centers
❖ Classified ads in local newspapers
❖ Yellow Pages
❖ Word-of-mouth referrals
❖ Press releases
❖ Exhibits at local garden shows
❖ Join local gardening and business clubs.
❖ Talks to garden clubs
❖ Internet site that features local businesses; offer some photos
   of your ponds that you have designed or installed.

## Essential Equipment
❖ Home office: computer with design software
❖ Books on water gardening and plants

## Recommended Training, Experience, or Needed Skills
❖ Knowledge of pond installation, water plants, fish, and so forth
❖ Work for or observe landscape services that install ponds.
❖ Take courses at local schools.

## Income Potential
$25,000 to $80,000

## Type of Business
$1/3$ in home designing, $2/3$ working on site

## Best Customers
❖ Individual gardeners
❖ Institutions—hospitals, mature adult homes, rehabilitation centers
❖ Businesses with outdoor gardens
❖ Architects and interior designers (for their customers)
❖ Professionals' offices
❖ Businesses and hotel lobbies

## Success Tips
❖ This was primarily a seasonal business in the cooler climates, but now that more people are installing indoor ponds, you can advertise and work year-round.
❖ Teach courses on pond gardening at local adult evening schools during the off-season months.
❖ Have good materials and subcontractors on whom you can depend and trust.
❖ Be able to suggest all sizes of ponds to fit your customers' budgets.

## Additional Information
### Recommended Reading
*The American Horticultural Society Complete Guide to Water Gardening* by Peter Robinson (New York: Dorling-Kindersley, 1997)

*Catfish Ponds and Lily Pads: Creating and Enjoying a Family Pond* by Louise Riotte (Pownal, VT: Storey, 1997)

### Organization
National Pond Society
286 Village Parkway
Marietta, GA 30067

Publishes *Pondscapes Magazine,* a full-color magazine that features a December (Christmas) issue that is a wealth of resources for pond keepers; $24/eight issues. Write or call for information: (770) 859-9282.

### Supplies
Lilypons Water Gardens, 6800 Lilypons Rd., Box 10, Buckeystown, MD 21717; catalog, $5

Paradise Water Gardens, 78 May St., Whitman, MA 02382; catalog, $4

Van Ness Water Gardens, 2460 N. Euclin Ave., Upland, CA 91786; catalog, $2

## Additional Business Ideas
❖ Growing water plants
❖ Raising ornamental pond fish

༝ ● ༝

# MISCELLANEOUS ENVIRONMENTAL BUSINESSES

❖ Recycled products creator—send a LSASE for information to the National Recycling Coalition, 30th St., SW, Suite 305, Washington, DC 20007. Also see *Choose to Reuse: An Ency-*

clopedia of Services, Businesses, Tools and Progress That Facilitate Reuse by Nikki and David Goldbeck (Woodstock, NY: Ceres Press, 1995)

* Xeriscaping consultant (a type of landscaping with plants and shrubs, etc., that conserves and uses little water)—see *Xeriscape Plant Guide* by Rob Proctor (Golden, CO: Fulcrum, 1996); and *Xeriscape Color Guide* by Denver Water, American Water Works Association, and Fulcrum Publishing (Golden, CO: Fulcrum, 1998). Also contact the Center for the Development of Hardy Landscape Plants, Dr. Harold Pellet, P.O. Box 39, Chenhassen, MN 55317; and Planetary Design Corp., 2601 E. Airport Dr., Tucson, AZ 85706; supplies information on salt-tolerant landscape plants.

* Building stone walls (dry)—small, decorative for gardens, low walls, using local stones from customers' property or ones discarded from local farm fields or from landscape supply centers. See *Step-by-Step Outdoor Stonework* edited by Mike Lawrence (Pownal, VT, Storey, 1995); and *Stonework: Techniques and Projects* by Charles McRaven (Pownal, VT: Storey, 1997)

# Food-Related Businesses

*Tell me what you eat, and I will tell you what you are.*
—A. Brillat-Savarin

Americans have a love-hate relationship with food. We love to eat, but we hate what it does to our bodies. Despite the fitness craze, we Americans will always enjoy the little indulgences of our favorite foods. Specialty foods, sauces, beverages, healthy snacks, and convenience services are all predicted to have record growth in the next century.

## Additional Information
### Recommended Reading
*Fancy Food,* 20 N. Wacker Dr., Suite 1865, Chicago, IL 60606; 800-229-1967; $34/year

*From Kitchen to Market: Selling Your Gourmet Food Specialty,* 2nd ed. by Stephen F. Hall (Dover, NH: Upstart, 1996)

*Gourmet News,* P.O. Box 3047, Langhorne, PA 19047; 215-788-7112; $55/year

*Income Opportunities;* features an annual issue devoted to food entrepreneurs and businesses every August; P.O. Box 55207, Boulder, CO 80323-5207; $11.97/twelve issues

National Business Library, *Small Business Catalog*, "Make Money with Your Family Recipe," $49.95 + $6.50 for shipping and handling; (800) 947-7724

### Organizations
National Association for the Specialty Food Trade, Inc.
120 Wall St., 27th Floor
New York, NY 10005-4001
Must have had your food products on store shelves for at least a year before you can join. Sponsors a specialty food trade show.

Also check with your state department handling food licensing and other matters to see whether they have any assistance programs for your food specialty.

### Home Study
International Correspondence Schools
"Catering/Gourmet Cooking"
925 Oak St.
Scranton, PA 18515

Lifetime Career Schools
"Cooking"
101 Harrison St.
Archbald, PA 18403

## ❧ 55 ❧
## BARBECUE SET-UPS
In this business, you are a type of caterer and/or consultant with barbecue cooking and grilling. Your food service business can include advising your customers as to the best equipment to purchase, holding grilling lessons, or setting up and cooking barbecues for picnics. You could add another service in the spring or fall of cleaning the grills.

*Estimated Start-up Costs*
$500 to $3,000, depending on whether you have to use a commercial kitchen for any of your precooking and preparation

*Pricing Guidelines*
- ❖ $20-$30 an hour for a grilling lesson or consultation
- ❖ $500 to $1,500 for conducting a barbecue for a picnic
- ❖ $30 to $50 + to clean up a barbecue grill and equipment

*Marketing and Advertising Methods and Tips*
- ❖ Business cards
- ❖ Classified ads in local newspapers

## Tips and Places to Sell Your Specialty Food

You can read about many success stories of people who have made "big bucks" with their specialty salsa, sauce, condiment, cakes, cookies, and other foods, but few make it without having many doors slammed in their faces and making their share of mistakes. To make your food sell well, here are few tips and markets:

- ❖ Tip 1: Start with local distributors and shops, and market aggressively until you have established a good customer base. Then and only then should you move onto wider regions.
- ❖ Tip 2: Fit your product to the store and neighborhood. Supermarket chains only deal in volume, plus the fees to get on their shelves can be prohibitive. Try to build up a relationship with the stores that will carry your product. Offer to give demonstrations, free samples, and testing.
- ❖ Tip 3: After your product has been on store shelves for at least a year, exhibit it at trade shows.

* Press releases about your unusual service
* Booth at a local fair to sample your cooking
* Word-of-mouth referrals
* Screen-printed barbecue hats and aprons with your business name and logo on them

### Essential Equipment
* Barbecue equipment and related cooking utensils: portable charcoal or gas grills, briquettes, liquid or electric starter, glazes, marinades, skewers, spatulas, tongs, instant-read thermometer, carving board, insulated containers for food, grill brush, and clothes and towels for clean-up

---

* Tip 4: Your packaging can make or break the sales of your food, so get some feedback about it from customer test marketing.
* Tip 5: Persuade restaurants and chefs to taste your food, and evaluate their responses.
* Tip 6: Sell your foods in a small specialty catalog or through direct-mail orders.
* Tip 7: Start selling at farmer's markets and stands where you can build a loyal customer base and possibly meet food buyers.
* Tip 8: Develop a press packet and advertising copy to use in your press releases and ads in trade food journals.
* Tip 9: Try other ways of marketing your product: home shopping channels, giveaways at charity auctions, Internet Web site, a self-authored cookbook based on your product, and talks, courses, or seminars about selling an original food.
* Tip 10: Be your own best salesperson and representative. Give a history and story about the background of your food and yourself.

❖ Woods for smoking (hickory, apple, cherry, oak, mesquite, grapevine, alder)
❖ Van or small truck

### Recommended Training, Experience, or Needed Skills
❖ Take courses at local vo-tech or culinary schools.
❖ Work for a catering business that does barbecues and picnics.
❖ Experiment and try recipes on your own grill until they are perfected, and have them taste-tested by family and guests.
❖ Knowledge and training of proper food handling and preparation to prevent food spoilage and poisoning

### Income Potential
$15,000 to $25,000 (you may have to do other type of commercial cooking in the off season)

### Type of Business
$\frac{1}{2}$ in home preparing and holding lessons, if you teach in your home kitchen; $\frac{1}{2}$ on site barbecuing

### Best Customers
❖ Homeowners: graduations or family picnics, reunions, outdoor celebrations
❖ Businesses: company picnics
❖ School fairs and community festivals

### Success Tips
❖ Make sure you get any licenses and permits necessary to handle and cook food. Some states permit you to cook from your kitchen; others require that you use a commercial kitchen or build a separate one with a separate entrance.
❖ Make your barbecue event memorable with special food presentations.
❖ Perfect your recipes.

## Questions to Ask Yourself About Your Specialty Food Product

1. What is the best retail price for my product?
2. What is the best location for my product? Should it be by itself or with other products?
3. How fast is my product moving? Is it selling better at some locations than others? If so, why?
4. Can my packaging and presentations be improved? If so, how? What do the customers say?
5. How committed (timewise, financially, emotionally) can I be to my product?

♣ Be well organized and hire good assistants for the day if you should need help.

### Additional Information
#### Recommended Reading
*The Barbecue Book: Everything You Need to Know about Barbecues* by Gail Duff (Happy Camp, CA: Prism, 1994)

*The Classic Barbecue and Grill Book* by Marlena Spieler (New York: Dorling-Kindersley, 1996)

*The Complete Book of Outdoor Cookery* by Helen Evans Brown and James A. Beard (New York: Marlowe, 1997)

*The Grilling Encyclopedia: An A-Z Compendium on How to Grill Almost Anything* by A. Cort Sinnes (New York: Atlantic Monthly Press, 1994)

*Great American Grilling* by Sunset Publishing Corporation (Menlo Park, CA: Sunset, 1996)

*The Great Barbecue Companion: Mops, Sops, and Sauce and Ribs* by Bruce Byorkman (Freedom, CA: Crossing, 1996)

*How to Run a Catering Business from Home* by Christopher Egerton-Thomas (New York: Wiley, 1996)

*How to Start a Home-Based Catering Business,* 2nd ed., by Denise
   Vivaldo (Old Saybrook, CT: Globe Pequot, 1996)

### Additional Business Ideas
* Create your own barbecue sauce or meat marinades.
* Design and sew barbecue aprons and hats.

## ❧ 56 ❧
# CAKE DECORATING

Once cakes were either homemade or bought at the local bakery.
Now, however, ready-made cakes can be bought and decorated
on the spot at many large grocery stores. Therefore, to succeed
at this business, you will have to offer something unique that
your customers can buy nowhere else. If you do children's birthday cakes, you will have to know the latest popular characters,
hobbies, sports, and games and add decorative touches that
are exclusive.

   If you create wedding cakes, you will have to offer different
kinds of cakes, decorations, and so forth. First, get the basic
skills and perfect them. Next, study your competition. Then
decide what is not being offered. Depending on your area and
your niche, your creativity will know no bounds!

### Estimated Start-up Costs
$200 to $1,000

### Pricing Guidelines
$15 to $1,200 + a cake

### Marketing and Advertising Methods and Tips
* Children's cakes—parents' publications; flyers at toy and
   children's clothing stores; referrals from party planners, children's party entertainers, and parents; newspapers ads
* Wedding cakes—booths at bridal shows, referrals from bridal
   consultants and families of brides, newspaper ads

❖ All-occasion—ad in businesses newsletters, flyers in senior citizen centers for wedding anniversaries; flyers in party goods stores
❖ Referrals from event planners and caterers
❖ Portfolio of photos of your cakes from which your customers can choose

### Essential Equipment
❖ Access to commercial oven (if required in your state)
❖ Baking pans, cake tins: tube, sandwich, muffin, Swiss (jelly) roll, loaf, springform
❖ Utensils and ingredients
❖ Cake decorations, boxes, platforms, and other accessories
❖ Vehicle for delivery
❖ Promotional materials
❖ Answering system with your telephone

### Recommended Training, Experience, or Needed Skills
❖ Work in a cake decorating department of a grocery store or bakery.
❖ Take courses at local schools.
❖ Take the time to perfect your skills.
❖ Volunteer to decorate for relatives' and friends' special occasions.
❖ Be creative and artistic.

### Income Potential
$4,000 to $5,000 part-time, $20,000 + full-time

### Type of Business
$3/4$ in home making the cakes and conducting business, $1/4$ traveling to clients' homes to show cake photos and delivering cakes

### Best Customers
Parents, brides, anniversary couples, businesses, restaurants, caterers, retirement and nursing homes, school faculties

### Success Tips

❖ Develop your style and specialty.

❖ Novelty cakes sell better in an upscale and urban neighborhood.

❖ Remember that your cakes must taste extraordinarily delicious as well as look beautiful!

### Additional Information
#### Recommended Reading

*American Cake Decorating Magazine*, P.O. Box 1385, Sterling, VA 20164-8440; $19/year

*Cake Decorating (Work Station)* by Jenny Harris and Sara Carter (Los Angeles: Price Stern Sloan, 1997)

*First Steps in Cake Decorating: Over 100 Step-by-Step Cake Decorating Techniques and Recipes* by Janice Murfitt (New York: Sterling, 1996)

*National Business Library, Small Business Catalog,* "Cake Decorating," $49.95 + $6.50 for shipping and handling. Call (800) 947-7724 for a catalog or credit card orders.

*The Wedding Cake Book* by Dede Wilson (New York: Macmillan, 1997)

### Additional Business Ideas

❖ Create special wedding cake toppings (sugar flowers, figures, etc.)

❖ Make specialty cheesecakes.

❖ Teach cake decorating.

## ⚶ 57 ⚶
## COOKING SCHOOL

Six years ago, Winnie McClennen (a gourmet cook) and Peggi Clauhs—mother and daughter—had a building on their old farm property remodeled into a kitchen, and they decided to offer cooking lessons to the community. The response to their cooking school was so overwhelming that they now have full classes at least three to four times a week as well as sponsor bus trips to gourmet shops, restaurants in Philadelphia and New York, farmers' markets, and overseas culinary tours to France, Italy, and other European destinations.

Their classes consist of teaching their students to cook a full-course, gourmet meal in keeping with the season, which everyone then eats together. For those who want instruction and technique but not a full meal, they offer morning demo classes that run about two hours followed by a continental breakfast. Peggi and Winnie also sell kitchen tools, gadgets, and cookware and have become authorized dealers of the manufacturer of the kitchen appliances in their "Cooking Cottage."

Peggi Clauhs says, "One tip that really helped us to get going was to have a local newspaper food writer do a feature story on our business. To have an endorsement in a newspaper (article) is as good as gold!"

### Estimated Start-up Costs
$15,000 to $23,000

### Pricing Guidelines
$25 to $55 for a class, $70 for one-day field trips

### Marketing and Advertising Methods and Tips
* Press release of the opening of your cooking school
* Brochures—Peggi and Winnie send out seasonal brochures of the schedules of their meals and trips to students and those who request them. Full payment is made upon registration.
* Word-of-mouth referrals
* Networking with others in business associations

### Essential Equipment
* Fully equipped kitchen (check with your state's licensing and permits)
* Utensils and ingredients
* Space large enough to accommodate students

### Recommended Training, Experience, or Needed Skills

* Professional education or training in the area(s) of cooking that you are instructing (Peggi and Winnie are members of the International Association of Culinary Professionals.)
* Patience and teaching skills
* Ability to communicate well to your students

### Income Potential

$15,000 to $50,000 (with full classes)

### Type of Business

Full-time instructing, planning, and managing the business

### Best Customers

* Cooks for other restaurants
* Men and women who love cooking as a hobby

### Success Tips

* Have the right mixture of cooking knowledge and expertise, business and communication skills.
* Encourage repeat business with new menu offerings, appearances of guest specialty cooks (pastry cooks and specialty chefs), and special outings.
* Peggi and Winnie will schedule classes for groups that request it. They have also had birthday cooking parties for children.
* Like Peggi and Winnie, you can offer related cooking utensils and cookware for sale, as well as gift certificates for birthdays, showers, and seasonal gifts.
* Love people and love to cook!

### Additional Information

#### Recommended Reading

*Alphabet Cooking: From Angel-in-a-Cloud to Zebra Cooking Cups: Fun Recipes for Children A-Z* (Lincolnwood, IL: NTC/Contemporary Books, 1998)

*The Guide to Cooking Schools,* 9th ed., Shaw Guides (Coral Gables, FL: Shaw Associates Educational Publishers, 1997)

**Cooking Seminars/Schools**
   Karen Lee's Cooking Seminars
   142 West End Ave.
   New York, NY 10023
Weeklong and weekend cooking instruction workshops in fusion cooking, Italian cuisine, and more, taught in the Manhattan kitchen of Karen Lee, nationally recognized teacher, caterer, and cookbook author. Write or call for details: (212) 787-2227.

   Ritz-Carlton Hotel
   Ritz-Carlton Cooking School
   475 Amelia Island Parkway
   Amelia Island, FL 32034
Two-day classes held at the resort taught by chefs of the hotel's award-winning restaurant. Package includes hotel stay, dinner, and continental breakfast. Write for a schedule of the monthly workshops offering a variety of cooking.

   See also Shaw Guides for listing of other cooking schools

*Additional Business Idea*
Specialty chef—specializing in pastry, salads, desserts, or ethnic foods, and giving cooking lessons in people's homes or yours

## 58
# FLAVORED HONEYS
Honey is a natural sweetener produced by honeybees and can range in color from white to almost black, depending on the bees' origins. Honey has been used for cooking and sweetening foods, and as remedies for colds, sore throats, and other common ailments.
   With the interest in organic and natural foods, the popularity of honey has increased. Flavored honeys can be used for tea,

toppings, and spreads. You can raise your own honey—even in urban areas—or buy it from local beekeepers. Flavor your honeys with herbs and spices, make honey jellies, and sell these as specialty foods.

### Estimated Start-up Costs
$500 to $5,000, depending on whether you raise the bees yourself

### Pricing Guidelines
Flavored honeys: $4 to $5 a pound or the competitive rates (check with the industry rates or organic food store prices of organic honey)

### Marketing and Advertising Methods and Tips
✤ A stand at farmer's markets
✤ Your own roadside stand
✤ Ads in classified paper
✤ Samples to targeted customers (shops, gift basket businesses, etc.)
✤ Advertising in food catalogs
✤ Internet Web site (your own or with a community business group)

### Essential Equipment
✤ Beekeeping equipment and hives
✤ Decorative jars and labels
✤ Access to commercial kitchen; check with your state agency dealing with food licensing to see whether you need a license or permit to sell your honeys.
✤ Promotional materials: business cards and brochures
✤ Home office: computer with desktop publishing software to produce your flyers, brochures, and labels

### Recommended Training, Experience, or Needed Skills
✤ Take beekeeping courses at an agricultural college, or work with a beekeeper until you can start your own hive.

❖ Knowledge of basic food preparation and cooking with honey and herbs
❖ Knowledge of the different herbs and their propagation
❖ Business management expertise and sales experience

### Income Potential
$5,000 to $25,000, depending on the markets you reach

### Type of Business
3/4 in home preparing your honeys and doing marketing via telephone and fax, 1/2 out of home marketing your product

### Best Customers
❖ Small specialty food shops, gift basket business owners, food catalogs
❖ Tea shops, restaurants, bakeries

### Success Tips
❖ Experiment and taste-test your honeys to find the best products.
❖ If you raise the bees, make sure you work with another beekeeper for care tips.

### Additional Information
#### Recommended Reading
*The Basic Beekeeping and Honey Book* by Louise G. Hanson and Lily A. Davis (New York: McKay, 1977); lemon-, parsley-, and strawberry-flavored honeys

*Joy with Honey: More Than 200 Delicious Recipes That Make the Most of Nature's Own Sweetener* by Doris Mech (New York: St. Martin's, 1995)

*The New Complete Guide to Beekeeping* by Roger A. Morse (Woodstock, VT: Countryman, 1994); beekeeping basics as well as information on bottling, nutritional labeling, and recipes

**Organization**

American Bee Breeders Association
P.O. Box 905
Moultrie, GA 31776
Send a LSASE for membership details.

### Additional Business Ideas

❖ Sell bee-related products—see *Bee Hive Product Bible* by Royden Brown (Bassendean, WA: Avery, 1993); and *Bee Products: Properties, Applications, and Apitherapy* by A. Mizrahi and Yaacov Lensky (New York: Plenum, 1997)

❖ Sell flavored vinegars or oils—see *The Best 50 Flavored Oils and Vinegars* by David DiResta (San Leandro, CA: Bristol, 1997); *Flavored Vinegars* by Michael Chirello with Penelope Wisner (San Francisco: Chronicle Books, 1996); *Flavored Oils* (San Francisco: Chronicle Books, 1995), which includes recipes for making flavored vinegars, too; and *Herbal Vinegar* by Maggie Oster (Pownal, VT: Storey, 1994)

## ❧ 59 ❧
# JAMS AND JELLIES

Once our great-grandmothers and grandmothers did much of their own canning and preserving of homegrown and/or wild berries, grapes, and other fruits and vegetables. Of course, today we can purchase these in any grocery store, and few of us have time to make our fruit concoctions. However, special jams, jellies, preserves, and butters are always a real treat and welcome gift, and thus there a number of markets for these sweet fruit products.

If you enjoy this home art and have access to low-cost fruits (or grow your own or pick wild fruits), you may want to think about doing this on a commercial basis. As with all the food businesses, check to see what licenses, kitchen specifications, and ingredient labels you are required to have to sell this type of food product. This is a good business for a person who enjoys both growing her own fruits and turning them into delectable products.

### Estimated Start-up Costs
$600 to $1,200, depending on whether you need access to a commercial kitchen

### Pricing Guidelines
❖ Research the going rate for jams and jellies at different stores.
❖ Calculate your costs and profit margin.
❖ Jams and jellies can sell from $4.50 to $7 a jar, depending on the ingredients, labeling, and so forth.

### Marketing and Advertising Methods and Tips
❖ Samples at food shows and fairs
❖ Samples at farm stands, indoor farmers' markets, gift and country shops, gift basket businesses, and special bakeries
❖ Direct mail to food catalogs and cable television shopping networks

### Essential Equipment
❖ Food equipment: jars, strainers, canner, lids, pectin, assorted fruits (picked at their recommended ripeness), decorative labels, and jar coverings
❖ Office equipment: computer with desktop publishing software for your special label designs, software for inventory and mail order (if you take your business in that direction)
❖ Promotional materials: brochures and hang tags that detail your business's "story"
❖ Van or truck for deliveries
❖ Your own fruit- and berry-producing trees and plants or access to wholesale growers'

### Recommended Training, Experience, or Needed Skills
❖ Knowledge of how to preserve fruits
❖ Knowledge of growing requirements of the berry and fruit plants you use
❖ Take related food-preparation courses.
❖ Make and taste-test your recipes, and get feedback from others.

*Income Potential*
$25,000 to $40,000 (more if you expand your production operation)

*Type of Business*
³/₄ in home (or in a kitchen that meets the required food standards), ¹/₄ out marketing your product

*Best Customers*
❖ Attendees of food shows and fairs
❖ Farm stands and farmers' markets
❖ Gift and country shops
❖ Gift basket businesses
❖ Special bakeries and food catalogs
❖ Cable television shopping networks

*Success Tips*
❖ Research the jellies, jams, and so forth, that are being sold, and see what "niche" your product can fill (i.e., different fruits and combinations thereof):
  Jellies: apple, crabapple, blackberry, boysenberry, dewberry, currant, elderberry, grape, mayhaw, mint, peach, plum, black or red raspberry, loganberry, rhubarb, strawberry, and any other fruits common to your region (ground cherry, cacti, etc.)
  Jams: apricot, blackberry, boysenberry, dewberry, loganberry, red raspberry, youngberry, blueberry, cherry, currant, fig, gooseberry, grape, orange marmalade, peach, pear, plum, rhubarb, strawberry, spiced tomato, and more
  Other jellies: cactus, pepper, violet
  Butters and spreads: apple, pear, and other suitable fruits
❖ Search constantly for new markets for your jams and jellies.

*Additional Information*
**Recommended Reading**
*Art of Preserving* by Jan Berry (Berkeley, CA: Ten Speed Press, 1997)

*The Big Book of Preserving the Harvest* by Carol Costenbader
(Pownal, VT: Storey, 1997)

*Canning and Preserving without Sugar*, 4th ed., by Norma M.
MacRae (Old Saybrook, CT: Globe Pequot, 1996)

*Jams, Jellies, or Preserves: Make Beautiful Gifts to Give (or Keep)* by
Linda Ferrari (Rocklin, CA: Prima, 1996)

*A Passion for Preserves: Jams, Jellies, Marmalades, Conserves,
Butters* by Frederica Langeland (New York: Friedman/Fairfax,
1997)

*Rodale's Successful Organic Gardening: Fruits and Berries* by Susan
McClure and Lee Reich (Emmaus, PA: Rodale, 1996)

**Other Source**
Check with your local USDA county extension office (look in
your telephone directory's white or government pages, or call
information) for pamphlets on growing berries and fruits as well
as publications on making jams, jellies, and preserves.

**Additional Business Ideas**
✤ Make fruit "leathers" and dried fruit mixtures as healthy
snack and energy foods; read *Making and Using Dried Foods* by
Phyllis Hobson (Pownal, VT: Gardenway, 1994)
✤ Give classes on making jams and jellies, canning, and so
forth—potential to make $500 a week if you charge $40 per
student for a three-hour class (not including supplies).

⟫ **60** ⟪

# PERSONAL CHEF AND SUPPERS-TO-GO

With today's hectic work schedules plus kids' school and extracurricular activities, many families scramble to eat something
other than fast food. After an exhausting day, cooking is the
last thing many a man or woman wants to do. That is where a
personal chef is now becoming an answer to many families'
mealtime dilemma. If you really love to cook and have the
knowledge, training, and experience, being a personal chef—
cooking meals at your clients' homes—may be just the right
answer for everyone.

As an add-on (or alternative business) to your personal chef business, you can have a selection of frozen suppers-to-go that customers can call and have delivered ahead of time or on the spur of the moment, chosen from a list of meals that you send them ahead of time.

### Estimated Start-up Costs
$10,000 to $15,000

### Pricing Guidelines
$50 to $75 one-time registration fee (to purchase the containers, foil, wrap, tape, etc., in which to freeze and store the food) + $280 to $300 a month for fifteen meals for a family of four or twenty meals for a single person

### Marketing and Advertising Methods and Tips
* Advertising in local newspapers
* Co-op coupon advertising with other businesses
* Word-of-mouth referrals
* Flyers at grocery, organic foods, and fish and meat markets
* Press releases to local media
* Donate a gift certificate at a charity auction.
* Teach a culinary course at an adult evening school.

### Essential Equipment
* Cooking equipment needed to prepare the different cuisines you offer in your business
* Cookbooks, recipes, computer and recipe software
* Vehicle for carrying food and cooking equipment
* Promotional materials: business cards, brochures, menu and ordering lists

### Recommended Training, Experience, or Needed Skills
* A love of cooking
* Some professional cooking education, training, certifications,

and experience (e.g., working as a chef in a restaurant, for a caterer, etc.)
❖ Well organized
❖ Knowledge of basic nutrition
❖ Good people skills

### Income Potential
$30,000 to $100,000 + , depending on the number of clients and your background and reputation

### Type of Business
$1/4$ in home organizing and managing your business, $3/4$ cooking in your customers' homes and food shopping (the good news is that you can cook during the day and prepare most of the client's meals at one time)

### Best Customers
Two-income families, single professionals, seniors with independent-living housing

### Success Tips
❖ Ideally, if you are a certified chef, you can charge accordingly.
❖ Plan meals that are interesting and appealing to your customers, and offer a choice of cuisines as well as special diets (low-fat, diabetic, etc.).
❖ Check with your local and state officials as to the licenses and permits you need.
❖ If you raise your herbs, fruits, and vegetables, you can save money as well as have better-tasting meals.

### Franchises, Distributorships, and Licenses
Entrees On-Trays Inc.
3 Lombardy Terrace
Fort Worth, TX 76132
(817) 735-8558

One of the oldest home-operated dinner delivery services in America. Write or call for information.

Also see the U.S. Personal Chef Association below.


### Additional Information
**Recommended Reading**

*Chef Magazine*, 20 N. Wacker Dr., Suite 1865, Chicago, IL 60606; (800) 229-1967; $36/year

*The Chef's Companion: A Concise Dictionary of Culinary Terms*, 2nd ed., by Elizabeth Riely (New York: Van Nostrand Reinhold, 1996)

*Get in There and Cook: A Master Class for the Starter Chef* by Richard Sox and David Ricketts (New York: Clarkson Potter, 1997)


**Organizations**

U.S. Personal Chef Association
3615 Highway 528, Suite 107
Albuquerque, NM 87114
(800) 995-2138
$199/year for membership; call or send a LSASE for information; http://www.uspca.com.

American Culinary Foundation
10 San Bartola Rd.
P.O. Box 3466
St. Augustine, FL 32085-3466
Send a LSASE for membership information.

International Association of Culinary Professionals (IACP)
304 W. Liberty St., #201
Louisville, KY 40202
(502) 581-9786
Call or send a LSASE for membership information.


### Additional Business Idea
Guest chef—featuring your own television show on your local cable television channel; teaching cooking classes in adult

evening courses; serving as a guest chef at restaurants and cooking schools; demonstrating cooking equipment and food preparation at home trade shows

## ✎ 61 ✑
# VEGETARIAN CONSULTANT

In her 1996 book *Clicking* (HarperCollins), Faith Popcorn says some fourteen million Americans are vegetarian. With health consciousness growing and the environmental concerns many people have over the cost in financial and environmental terms to raise meat animals, many more people are predicted to become or want to become vegetarian. Many people, however, wonder what vegetarian foods they should eat to get the correct balance of nutrients their bodies need, and what foods and recipes they can prepare that are both vegetarian and tasty. If you have the knowledge of vegetarian eating and nutrition, you can be a consultant and help individuals get started on this healthy-style diet.

### Estimated Start-up Costs
$4,000 to $12,000, plus the cost of any certifications you may want to earn

### Pricing Guidelines
$35 to $75+ an hour

### Marketing and Advertising Methods and Tips
❖ Advertising in local newspapers
❖ Word-of-mouth referrals
❖ Flyers at groceries and organic foods markets
❖ Press releases to local media
❖ Donate a gift certificate at a charity auction.
❖ Teach a culinary course at an adult evening school.

## Essential Equipment
* Basic cooking equipment
* Reference books on vegetarian cooking and nutrition

## Recommended Training, Experience, or Needed Skills
* Degree or certificate in nutrition
* Familiar with and knowledgeable about cooking vegetarian meals
* Knowledge about the different types of vegetarian diets (lacto-ovo, etc.)

## Income Potential
$8,000 to $20,000 +, depending on whether you add on other food services (like being a professional chef or cooking vegetarian "suppers-to-go")

## Type of Business
$\frac{1}{2}$ in home planning and possibly cooking vegetarian meals, $\frac{1}{2}$ consulting with or teaching customers how to cook vegetarian

## Best Customers
* People interested in becoming vegetarian
* Group homes or mature adult homes, restaurants (you will need a degree, license, and/or certificate to plan vegetarian meals for institutions, etc.)

## Success Tips
* Be able to fit the vegetarian meals into the lifestyle of your customers as far as ease of cooking and affordability.
* Be on call for questions and support.
* Offer a wide variety of choices and recipes from which your customers can choose.
* Make sure the meals you plan are tasty.

## Additional Information
### Recommend Reading
*Become a Vegetarian in Five Easy Steps!* by Christine H. Beard (Ithica, NY: McBooks, 1996)

*Becoming Vegetarian: The Complete Guide to Adapting a Health Vegetarian Diet* by Vesanto Melina (Seattle, WA: Book Publishing, 1995)

*The Complete Book of Vegetarian Cooking* by Veronica Sperling and Christine McFadden (New York: Smithmark, 1996)

*Vegetarian Times,* P.O. Box 420235, Palm Coast, FL 32142; $29.95/year

### Organizations

American Association of Vegetarian Dietitians and Nutrition Educators
3835 State Rte. 414
Burdett, NY 14818
Publishes the book *Course Book in Vegetarian Nutrition;* runs a speaker's bureau; offers a correspondence course, "VegeDine," for general public. Send a LSASE for membership information.

American Vegan Society (AVS)
56 Dinshah Lane, P.O. Box H
Malaga, NJ 08328-0908
Send a LSASE for membership information.

North American Vegetarian Society (NAVS)
P.O. Box 72
Dolgeville, NY 13329
Send a LSASE for membership information.

### Additional Business Ideas

Vegetarian cooking instructor—charge $20 to $45 per person a class in your kitchen or your customer's.

# MISCELLANEOUS FOOD BUSINESSES

❖ Cooking demonstrator—working at a cookware or health food store; $150 for two hours

❖ Food-of-the-month—if you prepare assorted cakes, popcorn, breads, sauces, and mustards, start a food-of-the-month mail-order business.

✤ Food writer—$500 + an article for a major magazine
✤ Food gift baskets—see *The Perfect Basket: Make Your Own Special Occasion Baskets* by Diane Phillips (New York: Hearst, 1994)
✤ Menu planner—planning a family's meals for a month, tailored to their preferences. Supply recipes for each day.

# Health-Related Businesses

*Good health is taken for granted . . . until you have to pay for it.*
—Anonymous

According to the American Federation of Home Health Agencies, over 15 percent of the country's gross national product is spent on health care. With an aging population and rapid medical technological advances, people want affordable, readily available care and health services. If you have a health-related education, training, and/or experience, here are a few ventures that may prove lucrative.

### Additional Information
**Recommended Reading**

*How to Start and Manage a Nursing Service Business, How to Start and Manage a Nursing Home Care Business,* and *How to Start and Manage a Home Health Care Business,* by Jerre G. Lewis and Leslie D. Renn; order from Lewis and Renn Associates, 10315 Harmony Dr., Interlochen, MI 49643; $14.95 each + $3 for shipping and handling.

*Making Money in a Health Services Business on Your Home-Based PC,* 2nd ed., book and CD, by Rick Benzel (New York: McGraw-Hill, 1997)

*The Nurse's Guide to Starting a Small Business* by Betty Hafner (Greenport, NY: Pilot Books, 1992); order from Pilot Books, (800) 79-PILOT.

*The WomanSource Catalog and Review: Tools for Connecting the Community of Women,* by Illen Rosoff (ed.) (Berkeley, CA: Celestial Arts, 1997); almost two thousand books, periodicals, organizations, and more—a holistic, centralized information source of life from health care to the environment and politics for women.

### Organizations

National Association for Home Care
228 Seventh St. SE
Washington, DC 20003
http://www.nahc.org
Send a LSASE for your inquires.

National Nurses in Business Association (NNBA)
1000 Burnett Ave., Suite 450
Concord, CA 94520
"Promotes the growth of health-related businesses owned and operated by nurses." Publishes *How I Became a Nurse Entrepreneur* ($24.95, including shipping and handling) and a directory of nurse entrepreneur businesses (a good networking source). Write for membership costs and information.

### Sources for Persons with Disabilities

Abilities Expos—nationwide trade shows featuring products, employers of people with disabilities, support services, daily living aids, books and publications, computers and software, and so forth. E-mail: abilities@expocon.com or http://www.expocon.com.

Disabled Businesspersons Association (DBA), 9625 Black Mt. Rd., Suite 207, San Diego, CA 92126-4564; largest nonprofit organization for entrepreneurs and professionals with disabilities. Write for more information.

Disability Product Postcards, P.O. Box 220, Horsham, PA 19044-0220; an advertising packet of companies serving the needs of people with disabilities. Write to be put on the mailing list.

### Supplies
*Home Health Care* catalog by Sears Home Healthcare, 9804 Chartwell, Dallas, TX 75238; write for a catalog of health maintenance and rehabilitation products.

### ⊸ 62 ⊱
# FIRST AID AND CPR INSTRUCTOR

When a young mother, an intensive care nurse, used her emergency training to dislodge a piece of food from her young daughter's throat, she started thinking that all parents and persons who work with children should know how to utilize cardiopulmonary resuscitation (CPR). After talking to several other nurses and individuals, this woman and some colleagues decided to start their own business of offering on-site CPR, first aid, and other requested special health programs and instructions.

These nurses-turned-entrepreneurs discovered that many people do not have the time or the inclination to go into a hospital to take these courses. So they go to into people's homes, businesses, and organizations to offer instruction in an easy-to-follow and less intimidating manner so that people can learn and (hopefully) apply these measures in an emergency situation. Classes are offered at times convenient for their customers, and they take turns working the different shifts. Many businesses are also looking into scheduling these programs as a way to get insurance cost reductions.

### Estimated Start-up Costs
$500 to $3,000

### Pricing Guidelines
❖ $25 to $35 per participant
❖ Group rates

## Marketing and Advertising Methods and Tips
* Press releases to local newspapers and media for possible coverage and articles
* Direct mail (brochures) to health clubs, food establishments, nursing homes, churches, department stores, colleges with nursing programs, businesses and utility companies, and camps
* Flyers on community bulletin boards
* Word-of-mouth referrals

## Essential Equipment
* Practice dummies
* Manuals, visual aids, and other related materials
* Audiovisual equipment and videotapes
* Wipeboard for writing instructions

## Recommended Training, Experience, or Needed Skills
* Certification by the American Red Cross or American Heart Association
* Additional nursing, first aid, and emergency procedures education, training, and experience
* Good teaching and communication skills

## Potential Income
$5,000 to $10,000 part-time, $20,000 to $30,000 + full-time and with employees

## Type of Business
$1/4$ in home, planning lessons and marketing; $3/4$ on site teaching

## Best Customers
* Family, parenting, and church groups
* Babysitters
* Day and overnight camps, scouting and youth groups
* Businesses, department stores, restaurants
* Doctors' offices, nursing programs

❖ Nursing and group homes
❖ Public and private schools

## Success Tips
❖ Be certified and have experience teaching.
❖ Offer your programs in a nonthreatening method (more hands-on and practical tests—many people have fears of written tests).
❖ Be flexible with your scheduling and where you teach to fit your customers' preferences.
❖ Offer a variety of additional health-related programs—get feedback from your students and customers as to what they want and need.

## Franchises, Distributorships, and Licenses
Santigo Data Systems Inc./Medical History
1801 Dove St.
Newport Beach, CA 92660
Emergency medical history information; write for information.

## Additional Information
### Recommended Reading
The American Red Cross First Aid and Safety Handbook by Kathleen Handal (Boston: Little Brown, 1992)
Baby and Child Emergency First Aid Handbook: Simple Step-by-Step Instruction for the Most Common Childhood Emergencies by Mitchell J. Einzig (Deephaven, MN: Meadowbrook, 1996)
First Aid and CPR, 3rd ed. (Boston: Jones and Bartlett, 1997)

### Organizations
American Heart Association
7272 Greenville Ave.
Dallas, TX 75231-4596

American Red Cross
431 18th St., NW
Washington, DC 20006

Sponsors many first aid, CPR, and water safety classes. Look in the white pages of your telephone directory for an office nearest you, or contact your local health care agency or hospital for courses on emergency first aid care.

### Additional Business Idea
Health service referral business—see *How to Start and Manage a Referral Services Business* by Jerre G. Lewis and Leslie D. Renn; order from Lewis and Renn Associates, 10315 Harmony Dr., Interlochen, MI 49643; $14.95 + $3 for shipping and handling.

## ☙ 63 ❧
# HEALTH INSURANCE CONSULTANT
With the dilemma of all the health insurance policies and programs that exist, many self-employed people and people who are losing their health insurance coverage because of the death of a spouse, job loss, or other situation need a professional to help them evaluate and choose the best affordable health insurance plan for them. You will need training and licensing to offer such advice, but your services should be in demand with our country's ongoing health care crisis.

### Estimated Start-up Costs
$5,000 to $10,000 (does not include the cost of your education and training)

### Pricing Guidelines
$30 to $100 an hour

### Marketing and Advertising Methods and Tips
❖ Referrals from medical professionals
❖ Talks to small and home-based business owners groups
❖ Talks at senior citizens' centers
❖ Column on health insurance (you pay) in local papers

❖ Referrals from satisfied customers
❖ Ads in local papers

### Essential Equipment
❖ Home office equipment: computer, software, printer, business telephone, and answering system
❖ Internet access
❖ Manuals and literature of health programs and plans

### Recommended Training, Experience, or Needed Skills
❖ Insurance training, education (in the health insurance field), and licensing
❖ Ability to communicate and educate your customers and make "sense" out of the myriad of health plans available
❖ Patience and understanding
❖ Ability to be impartial and give the facts and information your customer needs

### Income Potential
$35,000 to $50,000 full-time

### Type of Business
$\frac{1}{2}$ in home conducting business and doing research, $\frac{1}{2}$ meeting with clients

### Best Customers
❖ Small and home-based business owners
❖ Relatives of mature adults (the "sandwich" generation)

### Success Tips
❖ Be discreet in dealing with your customers.
❖ Be ethical and honest in striving to offer your clients the best health insurance for them.
❖ Keep up-to-date with the latest trends in the health insurance industry by subscribing to industry journals, attending trade shows and seminars, taking courses, and so forth.

*Additional Information*
**Recommended Reading**
*The Complete Book of Insurance: The Consumer's Guide to Insuring Your Life, Health, Property, and Income* by Ben G. Baldwin (Chicago: Probus, 1996)
*Health Insurance: How to Get It, Keep It, or Improve What You've Got* by Robert Enteen (New York: Demos Vermande, 1996)
*1997 Mercer Guide to Social Security and Medicare*, 25th ed. by Dale R. Detlefs, Robert J. Myers, and J. Robert Treanor (Louisville, KY: Mercer, 1997)
*Understanding Medical Insurance: A Step-by-Step Guide*, 3rd ed. book and CD, by Jo Ann C. Rowell (Albany, NY: Delmar, 1995)

**Organization**
American Association of Insurance Management
c/o Paige Proctor
P.O. Box 3517
Bloomington, IL 61701
Publications, conferences. Send a LSASE for membership information.

*Additional Business Idea*
Publish a health insurance newsletter for consumers.

## ◈ 64 ◈
# HOMEOPATHIC COUNSELOR

Homeopathy is a natural and safe complement to traditional medicine. Its philosophy is to trigger the body's own self-healing abilities through the use of homeopathic remedies that will treat common afflictions. Homeopathic medicines are used to treat allergies, colds, headaches, children's illnesses, menstrual problems, and other conditions. As a homeopathic counselor, you will help your clients find sources of homeopathic remedies to help alleviate symptoms of persistent problems. Your counseling will not eliminate conventional medicines prescribed by a medical physician but rather be natural and safe additions to work with conventional medical treatments.

### Estimated Start-up Costs
$5,000 to $10,000

### Pricing Guidelines
$25 to $30 for an hour-long consultation, depending on the evaluation, and what education and training you have

### Marketing and Advertising Methods and Tips
✤ Classified ads
✤ Referrals from clients
✤ Flyers in health/organic food stores
✤ Referrals from health care professionals
✤ Talks to groups

### Essential Equipment
✤ Home office: computer, printer, desktop publishing software; desk, office chairs, office to receive clients (unless you meet with them in their home); telephone with answering system
✤ Promotional materials: business cards, brochures, and manuals

### Recommended Training, Experience, or Needed Skills
✤ Medical training and background
✤ Training or courses in homeopathic medicine
✤ Work and/or apprentice with a homeopathic professional.

### Income Potential
$25,000 to $35,000

### Type of Business
Full-time in home (if you receive clients in your home office), $3/4$ out of home if you visit them

## Best Customers

❖ People who have an interest in natural and safe products that will improve their general well-being
❖ People with multiple allergies
❖ People in chronic pain

## Success Tips

❖ Check to find out what licenses, restrictions, and so forth you are required to obtain and/or follow before you begin to see clients.
❖ Work with medical professionals (consult, assist) who believe in homeopathic medicine.
❖ Keep up-to-date with the latest findings.

## Additional Information

### Recommended Reading

*Everybody's Guide to Homeopathic Medicines: Safe and Effective Remedies for You and Your Family* by Stephen Cummings and Dana Ullman (Boston: Houghton-Mifflin, 1997)

*Healing Homeopathic Remedies* by Nancy Bruning (New York: Dell, 1996)

*Spontaneous Healing: How to Discover and Enhance Your Body's Natural Ability to Maintain and Heal Itself* by Andrew Weil (New York: Ballantine, 1996)

### Organization

International Foundation for Homeopathy
2366 Eastlake Ave., #301
Seattle, WA 98102
Send a LSASE with any inquiries for information.

Homeopathic Educational Services
2124 Kittredge St.
Berkeley, CA 94704
http://www.homeopathic.com/
Resource of homeopathic books, tapes, medicines, software, correspondence courses, and general information on homeopathy.

### Additional Business Ideas

❖ Aromatherapy consultant—see *Aromatherapy Blends and Remedies: Over 800 Recipes for Everyday Use* by Franzesca Watson (New York: HarperCollins, 1996)

❖ Herbalist—see *The A-Z Guide to Healing Herbal Remedies* by Jason Elias and Shelagh Ryan Masline (New York: Dell, 1997); *Herbs for Your Health* by Steven Foster (Loveland, CO: Interweave, 1997); *Herbs for Health* magazine, published by Interweave Press; $24/year; (800) 456-6018

❖ Franchise/business opportunity/direct sales—Herbalife offers weight management, nutritional, and personal care products. For information on becoming a distributor for Herbalife, contact Sam and Kay LaRocca, 4003 Forest Dr., Aliquippa, PA 15001; http://www.1second.com/herbal.htm.

## ❧ 65 ☙
# MEDICAL HEALTH AND RECORDS MANAGEMENT

Many hospitals are cutting back on staff, while other health services are increasing. They may not have the funds to hire a medical records expert, so they often ask understaffed and stressed staff who do not have the time (or the expertise) to do an adequate job. They still need to organize, code, and maintain their present medical records, and your background and service business will allow them to operate more efficiently.

### Estimated Start-up Costs

$5,000 to $7,000 (does not include training and courses)

### Pricing Guidelines

$40 to $60 an hour; also go by present rate recommended by the profession

### Marketing and Advertising Methods and Tips

❖ Résumé and promotional materials sent to target customers, followed up by telephone calls for a personal interview

❖ Referrals from clients
❖ Answering newspaper advertisements for medical records technicians and offering to subcontract your services

## Essential Equipment
❖ Home office: computer and medical records software, laser printer, and reference books
❖ Promotional materials: brochures, business cards, and résumé

## Recommended Training, Experience, or Needed Skills
❖ Degree, certificate, training, and experience in the medical records field
❖ Work experience in one or more medical offices

## Income Potential
$30,000 to $40,000 full-time, depending on number of clients

## Type of Business
$^1/_5$ in home conducting business, $^4/_5$ in the clients' offices and visiting potential clients

## Best Customers
Small hospitals, clinics and health centers, and health professionals' offices

## Success Tips
Master the needed training, and then work in one or more offices (or visit them) to see the systems and particular methods they use.

## Additional Information
### Recommended Reading
*The Clinical Documentation Sourcebook: A Comprehensive Collection of Mental Health Practice Forms, Handouts, and Records* (New York: Wiley, 1997)

*Health Care and Information Ethics: Protecting Human Rights* by
Audrey R. Chapman, ed. (Kansas City, MO: Sheed & Ward,
1997)
*Legal Aspect of Health Information Management* by Dana C. McWay
(Albany, NY: Delmar, 1996)

### Organization
American Health Information Management Association
919 N. Michigan Ave., Suite 1400
Chicago, IL 60611
Courses (including home study) in medical record technology
and coding. Write for information.

### *Additional Business Ideas*
Medical librarian consultant—offering your professional librarian or librarian technician services to small hospitals, medical
associates' offices, health clinics, and women's health centers
    Contact the Medical Library Association, Suite 300, 6 N.
Michigan Ave., Chicago, IL 60602-4805. For a catalog of
home-study courses, including library technology, write Graduate School, U.S. Dept. of Agriculture (USDA), Stop 9911, Room
1112 South, 1400 Independence Ave., SW, Washington, DC
20250-9911.

## ৯৯ 66 ৯৯
# POSTSURGERY AND
# RECUPERATIVE CARE-GIVING AGENT
Because changes arise continuously in what and how much
health insurers will pay for hospital care, many people who need
postoperative care, speech or physical therapy, and others in
various states of recovery are being moved to their homes
instead of having longer hospital stays. Your business can offer
home health care for persons who need assistance until they can
take care of themselves or enter a more total health care facility
if needed.

## Estimated Start-up Costs
$7,000 to $40,000

## Pricing Guidelines
$40 to $50 an hour

## Marketing and Advertising Methods and Tips
- Yellow Pages
- Newspaper ads
- Referrals from former clients and health care workers
- Flyers and brochures at senior adult activity centers

## Essential Equipment
- Home office: computer, business-related software, business telephone and answering system; cellular phone and pager (optional)
- Promotional materials: business cards and brochures

## Recommended Training, Experience, or Needed Skills
- Recommended to have a nursing degree and home health care experience related to the needs of persons to whom care is given
- Work and management experience in the home health care field
- Make sure you have the licenses and permits required to run such a business.

## Income Potential
$20,000 to $50,000 +, depending on how often you work and whether you are in partnership or have staff

## Type of Business
- For a sole proprietorship (you are the caregiver): $1/4$ in home, $3/4$ in patients' homes

❖ For a sole proprietorship or partnership (you schedule the caregivers and do the care): $1/2$ in home, $1/2$ out of home interviewing and caring for your patients

## Best Customers
❖ People with surgical operations who need daily or periodic checks and monitoring of their medications
❖ People needing assistance in daily living skills as they recuperate

## Success Tips
❖ This business requires much time and organization. As a nurse or licensed therapist, you may want to start by working for a visiting nurses or larger home care agency to learn how such a business is conducted and what is expected of the caregivers.
❖ You will want to start small and find out whether you just want to specialize in one kind of home health care or many.
❖ It is recommended to start as a private service, because of the complexity of dealing with Medicare and other government agencies.
❖ Your niche may be home services (cooking, shopping, running errands) with a minimum of actual medical care needed.

## Additional Information
### Recommended Reading
Professional medical and nursing manuals and texts
*Perioperative Medicine: The Medical Care of the Surgical Patient* by David R. Goldman and Frank H. Brown (New York: McGraw-Hill, 1993)

### Organization
National Association for Home Care
228 Seventh St., SE
Washington, DC 20003
http://www.nahc.org

## Additional Business Ideas

✤ Total referral service for home health care—arranging and scheduling lawyers who make house calls, food delivery services, mobile dog grooming services, and other services that can come to the home for the individual's needs

✤ See also "Home Health Care" in *101 Best Home-Based Businesses for Women* by Priscilla Huff (Rocklin, CA: Prima, 1995)

### ∽ 67 ∾
# MASSAGE THERAPIST

With the growth of alternative therapies and natural medicine, massage therapy has gained acceptance and respect with its recognized effectiveness at relieving stress and muscle aches, as well as promoting healing. Massage therapists work out of home offices, in conjunction with other services, or make calls to businesses and individuals at their jobs.

## Estimated Start-up Costs
$1,200 to $6,000

## Pricing Guidelines
$40 to $65 per session

## Marketing and Advertising Methods and Tips

✤ Business cards and flyers on community bulletin boards
✤ Recommendations and referrals from athletic trainers and other therapists
✤ Develop a clientele by working in conjunction with beauty salons, spas, health clubs, and related businesses.
✤ Offer a gift certificate at charity auctions.
✤ Network with small and home-based business associations.

## Essential Equipment

✤ Massage tables, chairs, and related products and equipment

❖ Home office if you see clients in your home or in an attached building

## Recommended Training, Experience, or Needed Skills
❖ Courses and programs that lead to being a certified professional
❖ Fulfilling requirements for a license, which is required in most states

## Income Potential
$15,000 to $35,000

## Type of Business
❖ Full-time in home if you see clients exclusively in your home office
❖ Other times in a salon or clients' homes and/or offices, or part-time in a clinical setting

## Best Customers
❖ Athletes and people working in physical occupations (to relax and help with muscle strain)
❖ Children with special needs who respond well to massage therapy to ease their contracted muscles
❖ Business employees who need to relieve muscle tension caused by stress

## Success Tips
❖ Work to develop a routine of regular customers.
❖ Keep up with the latest trends and findings in the profession.

## Additional Information
### Organization
American Massage Therapy Association
820 Davis St., Suite 100
Evanston, IL 60201-4444

Publishes *Massage Therapy Journal;* write for membership information and benefits.

### Recommended Reading
*Massage Magazine,* 1315 W. Mallon, Spokane, WA 99201

*Mosby's Fundamentals of Therapeutic Massage* by Sandra Fritz (St. Louis: Mosby, 1995)

*Mosby's Visual Guide to Massage Essentials* by Sandra Fritz (St. Louis: Mosby, 1997)

*Therapeutic Massage and Bodywork: 750 Questions and Answers* by Jane S. Garofano (Stamford, CT: Appleton & Lange, 1997)

### Additional Business Ideas
❖ Sports massage—contact the American Massage Therapy Association.

❖ See "Reflexologist" in *101 Best Home-Based Businesses for Women* by Priscilla Huff (Rocklin, CA: Prima, 1995).

## ❧ 68 ☙
## ROLFER

Rolfing is a technique of connective tissue manipulation that involves body manipulation and movement education. Developed by Ida P. Rolf, Ph.D., Rolfers strive to bring the various portions of the body (head, neck, torso, pelvis, legs, and feet) into a balance and support of one another. Rolfing sessions can result in clients' greater ease in movement and breathing, improved balance and stability, and an increased sense of well-being.

Rolfing is performed in a ten-session process, with many clients choosing to return six months to two years later for evaluation and for concentration on more specific problems.

### Estimated Start-up Costs
$2,000 to $9,000

## Pricing Guidelines
Follow the training guidelines for consultation fees.


## Marketing and Advertising Methods and Tips
❖ Press releases and promotional articles to explain and define
   Rolfing
❖ Talks and demonstrations at health clubs and health centers
❖ Business cards and flyers
❖ Network and have referrals from other professionals who
   are alternative therapists (massage therapists, reflexologists,
   acupuncturists, etc.).
❖ Exhibit at health shows and malls featuring health profes-
   sionals, agencies, and so forth.


## Essential Equipment
❖ Cushioned table and/or bench, towels
❖ Health questionnaires
❖ Business telephone with answering system
❖ Scheduling book
❖ Books on Rolfing


## Related Training, Experience, or Needed Skills
❖ Training at the Rolf Institute (see page 292) or by a certified
   Rolfer
❖ Continuing education courses
❖ Work with or observe a Rolf practitioner for experience and
   practical knowledge.


## Income Potential
$20,000 to $30,000


## Type of Business
In home full-time if you see clients in your professional office

## Best Customers
Those with chronic muscle tension, postural problems, stress-related tension, uneven gait, and poor self-esteem

## Success Tips
❖ Study and work with others in this field.
❖ Keep up with the latest trends and findings in the profession.
❖ You may have to introduce the benefits of Rolfing to your community through demonstrations and talks.

## Additional Information
### Recommended Reading
*Balancing Your Body: A Self-Help Approach to Rolfing Movement* by Mary Bond (Rochester, VT: Inner Traditions, 1996)

### Organization
Rolf Institute
P.O. Box 1868
Boulder, CO 80306
(303) 449-5903
Write or call for more information about Rolfing and a *Directory of Certified Rolfers and Rolfing Movement Teachers.*

## Additional Business Idea
Reiki practitioner—see *A Complete Book of Reiki Healing: Heal Yourself, Others, and the World around You* by Bridgitte Muller and Horst H. Gunther (Mendocino, CA: Liferhythm, 1995); and *Reiki: Beyond the Usui System* by Karyn Mitchell (Oregon, IL: Mind Rivers, 1997)

## ❧ 69 ❧
# SPEECH PATHOLOGIST
According to the American Academy of Private Practice in Speech Pathology and Audiology (AAPPSPA), over twenty-eight million Americans have some degree of hearing loss, and over

fourteen million Americans have a speech or language problem. Many of these people do not realize that several of these problems can be eliminated or minimized. Speech-language pathologists and audiologists are the professionals who can help identify and treat these conditions.

If you have the education and experience in this field, you may want to open a practice to help those with communication problems.

### Estimated Start-up Costs
$3,000 to $5,000 (after college expenses)

### Pricing Guidelines
$45 to $75 an hour (follow recommendations for your profession)

### Marketing and Advertising Methods and Tips
* Schools—private, public, organizations, and county units providing services for children and adults with physical and mental disabilities
* Referrals from educators, physicians, psychologists, and other professionals
* Yellow Pages
* Networking with other speech pathologists and audiologists

### Essential Equipment
* Business cards and stationery
* Home office equipment and furniture if you receive clients in your home
* Telephone with answering service, fax machine
* Computer with billing and medical claims software
* Materials related to helping your clients

### Recommended Training, Experience, or Needed Skills
* College degree and training

❖ Current state license to practice in the field of audiology or speech-language pathology
❖ Certificate of Clinical Competence (CCC) from the American Speech-Language-Hearing Association (ASHA) in audiology or speech-language pathology
❖ Experience with all ages of clients with speech and/or hearing problems

### Income Potential
$35,000 to $65,000

### Type of Business
❖ In-home office: $3/4$ in home, $1/4$ out of home meeting with clients
❖ At agencies or clients' homes: $1/4$ in home planning, $3/4$ out of home

### Best Customers
❖ Children and adults with mental and/or physical disabilities
❖ Recovering stroke victims
❖ People with stuttering problems

### Success Tips
❖ Keep up with your professional organization on the latest information (see AAPPSPA on page 295).
❖ Keep current with the latest findings and trends in your profession by attending conferences, seminars, and continuing education courses and by networking with other speech pathologists.
❖ Have considerable experience with the problems with which you deal.
❖ Solicit feedback from past clients.
❖ Track the effectiveness of your treatments.

## Additional Information
### Recommended Reading
*Business Approach for Establishing Private Practice in Speech Language and Audiology* by Sharon Berlye Wexler (Springfield, IL: Thomas, 1986)

*Marketing Speech—Language Pathology and Audiology Services: A How-To Guide* by Cindy B. Matthews (San Diego: Singular, 1992)

### Organization
American Academy of Private Practice in Speech Pathology and Audiology (AAPPSPA)
c/o Membership Chairperson
507 New London Turnpike
Norwich, CT 06360-6552
Send a LSASE for membership information.

## Additional Business Idea
Sign language instructor—read *Essential ASL: The Fun, Fast, and Simple Way to Learn American Sign Language* by Martin L. A. Sternberg (New York: HarperCollins, 1996)

∞ ● ∞

# MISCELLANEOUS HEALTH BUSINESSES
❖ Strategic health care planner—see *Strategic Healthcare Management: Applying the Lessons of Today's Management Experts to the Business of Managed Care* by Ira Studin (Linn, MO: Irwin, 1995); and *Strategic Healthcare Management: Mastering Essential Leadership Skills* by George H. Stevens (San Francisco: Jossey-Bass, 1991)

❖ On-line medical researcher—using your medical background and computer search skills to research treatments for illnesses

# Home Services

*Old houses mended, cost little less than new before they're ended.*
                                                          —Colly Cibber

We once had time to do the extra chores around our homes and yards. Now, it seems we barely have time to make our beds and eat because of our hectic work, family, and extracurricular activities! Our lifestyles are forcing us to contract and hire more and more home services to do the chores that we once had time to do. Here are just a few of the many entrepreneurial opportunities that are opening up.

## ～ 70 ～
## WINDOW CLEANING

In the early part of American history, one indication of a man's wealth was the number of windows that were in his house. If that were true today, we would all be wealthy, for few buildings or homes do not have windows—and all need cleaning (inside and out)! If you do not mind manual work, this is a much needed service. Depending on your community, there may be quite a few competitors, so before you embark on this venture, research the type of customers they serve and look to see whether a "niche" market exists that you can reach.

### Estimated Start-up Costs
$1,000 to $6,000 (liability and disability health insurance may be high in cost)

### Pricing Guidelines
* Charge by the window, pane, or job, depending on what the market will bear
* Residential: $12 to $25 an hour; commercial, $25 to $35 an hour
* Check with the industry and manual guidelines

### Marketing and Advertising Methods and Tips
* Yellow Pages
* Business section of your local papers
* Coupon advertising with other businesses
* Word-of-mouth referrals
* Flyers to new housing development residents, senior citizens' housing, and businesses; visit new businesses, giving your business cards and brochures to their receptionists.
* Direct mail to builders and real estate brokers
* Referrals from interior decorators, landscape contractors, and house painters

### Essential Equipment
* Ladders, platforms, scaffolding (you can rent or only do windows that can be reached by a ladder)
* Cleaning solutions, buckets, rags
* Truck or van

### Recommended Training, Experience, or Needed Skills
* Read industry manuals.
* Work in a window-cleaning business.

❖ Pay attention to detail and efficient methods.
❖ No fear of heights
❖ Physical stamina

## Income Potential
$25,000 to $50,000

## Type of Business
$1/4$ in home for managing your business, $3/4$ out of home at your clients' locations

## Best Customers
Homeowners, small professional and business offices

## Success Tips
❖ Efficient and courteous service will encourage repeat business.
❖ Look for those customers not being served, or add an additional service like screen cleaning, cleaning the windows from the inside, or installing screens or storm windows for the seasons in older homes.
❖ You can start out by working as a subcontractor for construction clean-up crews, apartment preparation firms, and/or already established window-washing companies.
❖ Take time to learn the proper methods that will not scratch or damage your customers' windows.
❖ Have adequate insurance coverage.

## Additional Information
### Recommended Reading
*American Window Cleaner*, 27 Oak Creek Rd., El Sobrante, CA 94803; (510) 222-7080; $35/year; http://www.awcmag.com. "Voice of the professional window cleaner" and "a trade publication written for window cleaners by window cleaners." Includes a number of articles and information for professional window cleaners—many of them women who own window-

cleaning business or are in partnership with their spouses or other women. Back issue ($6), "Women in the Industry," July-August 1993.

*Beginner's Guide to Window Cleaning* by Michael Omalia (Las Vegas, NV: Ready Books, 1992)

*Cleaning Business Magazine,* Cleaning Consultant Services, Box 1273, Seattle, WA 98111; $20/year, four issues; covers how to start a cleaning and window-washing home business.

*How to Start and Manage a Window Washing Service* by Jerre G. Lewis and Leslie D. Renn; order from Lewis and Renn Associates, 10315 Harmony Dr., Interlochen, MI 49643; $14.95 + $3 shipping and handling.

*How to Start a Window Cleaning Business: A Guide to Sales, Procedures, and Operations* by Judy Suval; $25; order from Cleaning Consultant Services, Box 1273, Seattle, WA 98111. Write for catalog; this company has many other cleaning business-related materials: books, magazines, software, videotapes, seminars, licensing information, and more. Visit http://www.cleaningconsultants.com.

### Organization
International Window Cleaning Association
Box 48426
Niles, IL 60648
(301) 340-9560
http://www.iwca.org

### *Additional Business Idea*
Window blind cleaning—for equipment, consider Li'l Baby Blind Cleaning Machine; contact S. Morantz, Inc., 9984 Gantry Rd., Philadelphia, PA 19115; (215) 969-0266. Call or write for information.

## ⊷ 71 ⊷
# CLOSET/STORAGE/PANTRY ORGANIZATION
Take a look into any home and you will see many closets as crowded as a teenager's school locker (or worse!). Many of us

do not have the time or know-how to straighten and organize our closets (or other storage areas, like pantries). If you enjoy creating order out of chaos and have a good system that you think will work for others, too, you may want to think about starting this much needed home service.

## Estimated Start-up Costs
$3,000 to $20,000

## Pricing Guidelines
$40 to $100 an hour, or a fee per project

## Marketing and Advertising Methods and Tips
❖ Yellow Pages
❖ Direct mail to real estate brokers, builders, and remodeling contractors
❖ Demonstrations at stores that carry closet and storage organizers/units
❖ Business cards
❖ Exhibit at local home shows and fairs.
❖ Prepare a portfolio of "before and after" photos of closets and storage spaces you have organized.
❖ Show slides or videos of organizing tips to community and business groups.

## Essential Equipment
❖ Assorted tools for installing the units and remodeling
❖ Storage and closet units; you may need to find storage space to store units that you purchase or make yourself.
❖ Individual shelves, boxes, wire baskets, shoe racks/holders, extra drawers, and storage compartments
❖ Home office: telephone with answering system, fax machine, computer (to keep records), and design software

## Recommended Training, Experience, or Needed Skills
❖ Volunteer to do relatives', friends', and organizations' storage spaces to get experience.

❖ Contact the manufacturers of home organizing units to see if they offer training and/or workshops.

❖ Look for home repair courses and adult evening courses held at local vo-tech schools and colleges.

## Income Potential
$8,000 to $50,000 + , depending on whether you are a one-person business or hire subcontractors and employees

## Type of Business
$1/4$ in home for designing units and marketing your business, $3/4$ in your clients' homes or offices

## Best Customers
❖ Homeowners of all income levels who need more space and organized closets and storage areas

❖ Real estate agents—many times if their clients' closets and other spaces are organized, it looks good to prospective home buyers.

❖ Builders who want to have closet and storage systems installed in their new homes

❖ Remodeling contractors may want to subcontract you in connection with their projects.

❖ Businesses—office and warehouse organization can increase profits and efficiency.

## Success Tips
❖ Research the competition and see what niche you can fill.

❖ Get the necessary skills by taking home repair courses, installing closet and storage systems for people you know, or working for such a business or franchise.

## Franchises, Distributorships, and Licenses
Closet Classics
3311 Windquest Dr.
Holland, MI 49424
Write for information.

## Additional Information
### Recommended Reading
*Entrepreneur's Small Business Development Catalog*, "Professional Organizer," $69 + $7.95 for shipping and handling. Call (800) 421-2300 for a catalog or credit card orders.

*Organize Your Closet: And Other Storage Ideas* by Debra Melchior (Lincolnwood, IL: Publications International, 1993)

### Video
*Storage and Closet Organization* by Vvmec 2404 ($60); (Charlotte, NC: Baker & Taylor); ISBN 6302057760

### Organization
National Association of Professional Organizers
1033 La Posada Dr., #220
Austin, TX 78752-3880
(512) 206-0151

## Additional Business Idea
"Do-it-yourself" closet and storage kits—designing the closet and making the pieces (or subcontracting someone to do it); writing up the instructions and diagrams

### ❧ 72 ❧
# HANDY WOMEN

In this business, you (or your "handy" women) do simple household repairs and services like painting, wallpapering, installing shelves and household fixtures, repairing screens, replacing window panes, and just about any small, household chore that the homeowner wishes. Note: You need a license and/or permit to do major plumbing and electrical work.

Dee, a single fifty-year-old, started her interior repair business when she volunteered to help some older relatives do minor repairs and maintenance on their homes. As a youngster, she often assisted her father, a builder, at his work sites. When friends saw her work, they began to request that she do repairs in their homes. Dee is now so busy, she is looking for other women to work with her. She says, "My customers are mostly mature and older adults who cannot fix things as they once could."

### Estimated Start-up Costs
$1,000 to $3,000

### Pricing Guidelines
❖ Have a set fee for certain jobs.
❖ Offer free estimates to senior citizens.

### Marketing and Advertising Methods and Tips
❖ Flyers and business cards to senior citizen centers and independent living homes
❖ Classified ads in local, free classified newspapers
❖ Word-of-mouth referrals from satisfied customers
❖ Exhibits at home shows
❖ Referrals from real estate brokers and remodeling contractors
❖ Magnetic vehicle signs with your business advertisement and information

### Essential Equipment
❖ Full line of basic tools used for home repairs
❖ Ladder and truck or van
❖ Telephone with answering system
❖ Computer with billing software

### Recommended Training, Experience, or Needed Skills
❖ Basic knowledge of household maintenance repairs—take courses at vo-tech schools, adult evening schools, and community colleges
❖ Good communication and people skills
❖ Knowledge of other household concerns: programming VCRs, assembling furniture and gifts (toys for grandchildren),

painting and wallpapering, cleaning windows, replacing lightbulbs and hinges, hanging Christmas lights, and so forth
❖ If possible, work with a repair or building service contractor for experience.

## Income Potential
$20,000 to $50,000 + , full-time

## Type of Business
Full-time in customers' homes (you can work your hours around your family if you have child care coverage)

## Best Customers
❖ Mature adults living in independent living homes, apartments, or their own homes
❖ Working couples who do not have the time or inclination to do minor household chores or repairs
❖ Real estate brokers and apartment owners who need repairs made before a new owner or tenant moves in

## Success Tips
❖ Be customer oriented: you will need to work well with older people and give them good service.
❖ Be prompt, professional, and efficient. Up to 80 percent of your business could be repeat customers.
❖ Check with your insurance agent as what type of coverage you should have.
❖ If you are "handy," this type of service will be in great demand because many contractors really do not want to handle such small jobs.

## Additional Information
### Recommended Reading
*The Family Handyman Helpful Tips: Quick and Easy Solutions Time-saving Tips, Tricks of the Trade* by Reader's Digest (Pleasantville, NY: Reader's Digest Books, 1995)

*500 Terrific Ideas for Home Maintenance and Repair* by Jack Maguire (New York: Budget Books, 1997)

*The Woman's Hands-On Repair Guide* by Lyn Herrick (1997); order from Storey's How-To Books for Country Living, Schoolhouse Road, Pownal, VT 05261; www.StoreyBooks.com

### Additional Business Ideas

❖ Wallpapering and painting business—see *101 Best Home-Based Businesses for Women* by Priscilla Huff (Rocklin, CA: Prima, 1995)

❖ Handy repair referral service—customers will call you for a referral of a specific contractor, and you will get a commission for every job they receive through you.

## ⤙ 73 ⤙
# LAPTOP INVENTORY SERVICE FOR HOME OWNERS

For insurance and assessment purposes, home owners need an inventory of their belongings to make sure they will be covered in the event of a disaster or theft. With this service, you can bring your laptop computer to your customer's home and inventory each item they want listed. When you are finished, you can give them an itemized printout as well as a 3.5-inch disk or a CD-ROM that contains the list.

### Estimated Start-up Costs
$5,000 to $8,000

### Pricing Guidelines
$30 to $50 an hour; $60 to $100 per visit, includes itemized list, disk, and written report

### Marketing and Advertising Methods and Tips
❖ Referrals from insurance agents, friends, family, and business associates

❖ Information brochures that explain your service and the need for it
❖ Exhibit at local home shows.
❖ Speak to business association groups.
❖ Direct mail to insurance agents, real estate agents, appraisers, estate planners, and estate lawyers; follow up with visits.
❖ Yellow Pages
❖ Classified advertising
❖ Internet Web site to explain your business service

### Essential Equipment
❖ Laptop computer, disks, desktop computer, and business suite software
❖ Optional: video camera in the event you would also like to offer a video recording of clients' inventories
❖ Business telephone and answering system

### Success Tips
❖ Know how insurance agents and law enforcement officials prefer to have items inventoried in the event of loss and/or theft.
❖ Good communication and people skills
❖ Volunteer to take inventories of your friends' and family's possessions to gain experience.
❖ Must be discreet about your customers' possessions

### Income Potential
$25,000 to $50,000, depending on the number of inventories you do a year

### Type of Business
$1/4$ in home marketing and conducting business, $3/4$ out of home marketing and working in customers' homes

### Best Customers
New home owners, home owners with valuable collectibles

## Success Tips

❖ Offer free consultations and estimates to home owners so they get to meet with you and ask questions about your service.

❖ Much of your business will come from referrals as people will be wary to have an unknown person come into their house; build your networking circle so you will be well known and trusted.

❖ Keep customers' inventories confidential.

❖ Check with your own insurance agent about being bonded. You should be bonded in the event you damage or lose customer property. Attach that bonding as a rider to your standard business insurance policy.

## Franchises, Distributorships, and Licenses

Easy Method Property Documentation
P.O. Box 3715
Evergreen, CO 80437-3715

Photographic property documentation services (video). Send a LSASE for information.

## Additional Information

### Recommended Reading

*The Household Inventory Guide: Ideas and Lists for Stocking, Restocking, and Taking Stock of Your Home* by Carol Phillips (Lexington, KY: Ipp Press, 1993)

*Protecting the Family Jewels: How to Inventory Your Home without Losing Your Mind* by Kathleen Gura (Redlands, CA: Enterpress, 1988)

## Additional Business Idea

Find appraisers (and buyers if home owners request them) for people's collectibles—take a commission for each appraisal.

## ‹ॐ 74 ॐ›
## RECORDS AND INFORMATION SEARCHER

If you like to find information, almost like a quest, then you might like to search public records for businesses and individuals who do hot have the time or know-how to obtain the information they need. Discretion and professionalism are imperative in this business, and you should follow proper procedures and regulations in this information business.

### Estimated Start-up Costs
$5,000 to $9,000

### Pricing guidelines
* $25 to $50 + an hour, depending on the project involved and how much data you are asked to retrieve
* Give estimates or have a rate sheet for certain kinds of document searches.

### Marketing and Advertising Methods and Tips
* Direct mail to lawyers, real estate agents, private investigators, and political workers
* Brochures to individuals who are seeking deed information, genealogy records, and so forth, on a wide range of topics requiring Internet research (e.g., stocks, jobs, travel destinations, history, etc.)

### Essential Equipment
* A computer with a hard drive, fax/modem (high speed), printer, and access to the Internet and selected databases
* Telephone with answering system, fax machine, and cellular phone
* Notebooks and folders
* Business cards and business stationery

## Recommended Training, Experience, or Needed Skills
* Computer courses at colleges and schools on information retrieval procedures
* Seminars on information brokering
* Work in your county's courthouse.

## Income Potential
$5,000 to $15,000 part-time, $20,000 to $35,000 full-time

## Type of Business
$\frac{1}{2}$ in home doing research with your phone, fax, and Internet computer searches; $\frac{1}{2}$ out of home searching public records and libraries

## Best Customers
* Lawyers, real estate agents, private investigators, and political workers
* Individuals who are seeking information on a wide range of topics (Internet research) (e.g., stocks, jobs, travel destinations, history, etc.)
* Students searching for colleges
* Small businesses
* Organizations interested in historical data

## Success Tips
* Be thorough and fast.
* You may want to specialize in searching for certain records and information and in the clients that your business serves.

## Franchises, Distributorships, and Licenses
The National Locator
1119 S. Mission Rd., #105
Fallbrook, CA 92028-3225
Write for information.

## Additional Information
### Recommended Reading

*Find Public Records Fast: The Complete State, County and Courthouse Locator* by Michael Sankey and Carl R. Ernst (Lanham, MD: National Book Network, 1997)

*Information Broker's Handbook* by Sue Rugge with Alfred Glossbrenner (New York: McGraw-Hill, 1995); excellent book on information retrieval, workshops, and seminars; includes a disk of business-related forms and additional resources.

*Researching Public Records: How to Get Anything on Anybody* by Vincent Parco (Secaucus, NJ: Citadel, 1994)

*The Sourcebook of Public Records: The Definitive Guide to Searching for Public Records Information at the State Level* by Michael L. Sankey and Carl R. Ernst (Tempe, AZ: Business Resources Bureau, 1997)

*Your Personal Netspy: How You Can Access the Facts and Cover Your Tracks Using the Internet and Online Services* (New York: Wolf New Media, 1996)

## Additional Business Idea

Expert locator—finding experts on all kinds of topics for researchers, students, writers, and individuals seeking interviews and advice

## ༣ 75 ༣
# RELOCATION CONSULTANT

Over the past few years, many companies have "downsized" and laid off workers at all skill and management levels. Many companies are moving to locations out of state or out of country, and employees who are moving with their companies need information about their new surroundings. On the other hand, employees who have been let go need a number of services: job placement assistance, neighborhood and home selection, finding and evaluating schools and religious organizations, and selecting a moving company. To get started, you can volunteer to work with a local company that is relocating, and then build a client base from this experience.

## Estimated Start-up Costs
$15,000 to $30,000

## Pricing Guidelines
* Work on a retainer, per-individual, or commission basis.
* Real estate agents in the proposed communities could pay you a commission for setting up a home purchase (20 to 25 percent).

## Marketing and Advertising Methods and Tips
* Direct mail to companies that are reported to be moving or opening other facilities in other locations
* Advertising in business trade publications
* Networking with business owners in local associations
* Internet Web site

## Essential Equipment
* Home office equipment: computer, fax/modem, telephone with conferencing capabilities and an answering system, fax, photocopier, and laser printer
* Promotional materials: business cards and brochure explaining your background, expertise, and the specific services your business offers
* Career counseling and assessment forms and articles
* Access to the Internet to retrieve information about housing

## Recommended Training, Experience, or Needed Skills
Degree, license, and/or work experience in real estate, human resources, job counseling, and helping individuals and families relocate and regroup into new communities and homes

## Income Potential
$5,000 to $10,000 part-time, $20,000 to $40,000 full-time

## Type of Business
Full-time in home if you have an office that receives clients

## Best Customers

✤ Workers who have been or are going to be replaced or relocated

✤ People returning to the workplace after raising children or recovering from illness or injuries

✤ Companies that are moving or opening new operations either locally or farther away

## Success Tips

✤ Start with small businesses and their employees who are in transition, or deal with displaced individuals who have been laid off because of downsizing.

✤ Develop a network of resources and contacts in your community and around the country so you can offer complete evaluations of a new community before you look for paying customers.

✤ It will take persistence and patience to help your clients.

## Additional Information

**Organization**

Employee Relocation Council
1720 N St. NW
Washington, DC 20036
Write for more information.

## Additional Business Idea

Publish a newsletter for people and families who have to relocate, profiling thriving areas in the United States.

## ◆ 76 ◆

# "SMART" HOMES DESIGNER

This is a business that uses your creative skills and/or knowledge of efficient home designs. If you are a licensed architect, you can actually draw up the blueprints for builders of your clients' homes. If you are not an architect and have drafting experience and knowledge of computer design software, you can help clients with ideas in home planning (floor plans) or remodeling projects. A third alternative is to start a home decorating service that makes use of the items that your clients already have; rearrange them in a more ergonomic fashion and add a few accessories for an affordable new look.

## Estimated Start-up Costs
* Architect: $20,000 to $45,000
* Home planning consultant: $5,000 to $7,000
* Home decorating service: $1,000 to $3,000

## Pricing Guidelines
* Architect: could run from $4,500 to $20,000 for special home plans
* Home planning consultant: $30 to $40 an hour or a flat fee
* Home decorating service: $30 to $40 an hour or a flat fee per room or for the entire home

## Marketing and Advertising Methods and Tips
* Yellow Pages
* Classified ads in local newspapers
* Exhibits at home shows
* Referrals from satisfied customers
* Portfolio of homes you have planned, designed, or decorated
* Referrals from paint, wallpaper, and fabric stores

## Essential Equipment
* Architect: drafting table, computer with computer-aided design (CAD) software, printers, blueprint-sized photocopier, and cellular phone
* Home planning consultant: drafting table, computer with software design capabilities, laser printer, photocopier, telephone with answering system; names of decorators, builders, remodeling contractors, furniture stores, and other home accessory stores

❖ Home decorating service: computer for business management, telephone with answering system, business cards, portfolio of "before and after" photos of homes you have redesigned, paints, brushes, stencils, ladder, tape measures, rags, sponges, and decorating idea books for reference

### Recommended Training, Experience, or Needed Skills
❖ Architect: license after schooling and apprenticeship
❖ Home planner consultant/designer: drafting, design courses, work experience with a builder or remodeling contractor. Check for licensing requirements.
❖ Home decorator: considerable experience with sewing, painting, stenciling, textiles, fabric, and home design; experience working in a home decorating firm

### Income Potential
❖ Architect (for individuals and couples): $40,000 to $100,000 +
❖ Home planning consultant: $10,000 to $30,000
❖ Home decorator: $10,000 to $50,000

### Type of Business
❖ Architect: $1/2$ in home working on the plans and designs, $1/2$ on the job site
❖ Home planning consultant: full-time in home working on the floor plans and meeting with clients
❖ Home decorator: $1/2$ working in home preparing and sewing the materials, $1/2$ working on site in the client's homes

### Best Customers
Home owners who want energy-efficient, well-planned spaces decorated to their tastes at affordable prices

## Success Tips

❖ Architect: house plans should be affordable yet efficient and environmentally friendly, with technology (if your client can afford it) that will go into the next century.

❖ Home planning consultant/designer: plans should fit the lifestyles of the homeowner and family but also offer creative use of space and be efficient and environmentally friendly.

❖ Home decorator: your service should use the furnishings the homeowner already has but offer new features like window treatments, painting and stenciling, home accessories like dried and silk flower arrangements, and so forth. Your niche will be that you can offer a new "look" but at much more affordable prices than completely remodeling or refurnishing.

## Franchises, Distributorships, and Licenses

The Homemaker's Idea Company
1420 Thorndale Ave.
Elk Grove Village, IL 60007-6751
Decorating, not interior design; baskets and other home decorating products. Write for information.

## Additional Information

### Recommended Reading

*Be Your Own Home Decorator* by Pauline B. Guntlow; order from Storey's How-To Books for Country Living, Schoolhouse Road, Pownal, VT 05261; http://www.StoreyBooks.com

*Energy Efficient Homes (Best Home Plans)* by Elizabeth L. Hogan (Menlo Park, CA: Sunset, 1993)

*Environmental Design: Architecture and Technology* by Margaret Cottom-Winslow (Glen Cove, NY: PBC International, 1996)

*The Healing House: How Living in the Right House Can Heal You Spiritually, Emotionally, and Physically* by Barbara Bannon Harwood (Carson, CA: Hay House, 1997)

**Organization**
American Society of Interior Designers (ASID)
608 Massachusetts Ave., NE
Washington, DC 20002
http://www.asid.org
Send a LSASE for membership qualifications and information.

**Home Study**
International Correspondence Schools
"Drafting," "AutoCAD (Computer-Aided Design)"
925 Oak St.
Scranton, PA 18515

*Additional Business Idea*
Designing living spaces for retirees—see *Elderdesign: Designing and Furnishing a Home for Your Later Years* by Rosemary Bakker and Thomas Kenny (New York: Penguin, 1997)

꾕 ● ꕤ

# MISCELLANEOUS HOME SERVICES

✤ Collections compiler—helping people display, organize, and catalog their personal collections
✤ Household management service—helping supervise household chores such as moving details. Concentrate on and offer the services that you prefer to handle and are needed.

# Baby Boomer and
# Senior Services

*How old would you be if you didn't know how old you was?*

—Satchel Paige

It is a fact: the huge baby-boom generation is rapidly approaching the retirement age. The U.S. Bureau of the Census also reports that by the year 2020, approximately fifty-three million elderly persons will be living in our country. As the number of seniors continues to grow, the person looking for an entrepreneurial opportunity would do well to target a business idea toward the mature and senior adult population.

**Additional Information**
**Recommended Reading**
Check your public library's reference section for these books.

*Older Americans* by Ronald Manheimer (Detroit, MI: Gale
     Research, 1993)
*Statistical Record of Older Americans* by Arsen J. Darnay, ed.
     (Detroit, MI: Gale Research, annual)

**Organizations**
National Aging Information Center
330 Independence Ave. SW, Room 4656
Washington, DC 20201

National Association of Senior Living Industries
184 Duke of Gloucester St.
Annapolis, MD 21401-2523

## ✑ 77 ✑
# FINANCIAL SERVICES

Good news and bad news for baby boomers: the good news is that medical experts predict boomers will live longer than their parents; the bad news is that only half of them have planned how they will support themselves financially. If you have a financial planning background and education, this is a business service sure to grow in demand—even with the competition that exists. Despite what is commonly thought, and because of the changing economics in our country, financial planning and services are not for just the wealthy.

You will be evaluating a client's entire financial life and sources of income and making recommendations based on his or her financial commitments and goals. Long-term relationships are often established with clients involving planning for college education, retirement, estate planning, and periodic revisions because of a change of employment, illness, divorce, or death.

### Estimated Start-up Costs
$5,000 to $12,000

### Pricing Guidelines
Depending on the consulting and investments made, fees can run from $250 to $300 for a simple financial plan and $50 to $250 an hour for a retainer fee. Some charge a percentage of income, and still others take a commission on the sale of stocks, bonds, insurance, and so forth. Much depends on who your

clients are, the complexity of their finances, and your qualifications and reputation.

### Marketing and Advertising Methods and Tips
* ❖ Free seminars at senior citizen centers
* ❖ Column on financial planning in your local and regional publications (you pay)
* ❖ Radio appearances (or host a show) on this topic
* ❖ Referrals from family, friends, and business acquaintances, as well as professionals you know—bankers, accountants, attorneys, and others
* ❖ Yellow Pages
* ❖ Send out a newsletter to all who inquire or use your services.
* ❖ Network within business associations.

### Essential Equipment
* ❖ Computer with Internet access, printer, telephone with conferencing capabilities and answering system, fax, photocopier, and business suite software
* ❖ Home office suitable for interviewing clients

### Recommended Training, Experience, or Needed Skills
* ❖ Degree in accounting (and/or certified public accountant [CPA] designation), economics, or a financially related field; or courses leading to a certificate to be a certified financial planner (CFP)
* ❖ If you also sell stock, insurance, or real estate, you will need a license.
* ❖ Ability to review your clients' assets and create a plan or make a recommendation that they can comprehend and follow as well as help increase their finances.

### Income Potential
$15,000 to $50,000 +, depending on the number of clients you have

## Type of Business
Full-time in home meeting with clients and drawing up plans

## Best Customers
* Baby boomers, especially people in their fifties
* Recently widowed or divorced people who need to have their income stabilized and need financial advice
* Young professionals, parents, and business owners who want to set up long-range financial plans
* Businesses and government agencies that need information on budgeting, cost cutting, accounting, investing, and financial management

## Success Tips
* Start small and look for groups and individuals (your niche market) who are not being served by other financial services and planners in your community.
* Develop quality expertise in the financial fields in which you are dealing.
* Be honest, ethical, and professional, and act confident in your ability to help your client.
* Get the qualifications you need to best serve your clients, and stay informed of the latest information in this industry.

## Franchises, Distributorships, and Licenses
Financial Education Services, Inc.
8200 Humboldt Ave. S, #215
Minneapolis, MN 55431
Money management seminars. Write for information.

## Additional Information
### Recommended Reading
*The Beardstown Ladies' Stitch-in-Time Guide to Growing Your Nest Egg: Step-by-Step Planning for a Comfortable Financial Future* by the Beardstown Ladies' Investment Club (New York: Hyperion, 1997)

*Last Chance Financial Planning Guide: It's Not Too Late to Plan for Your Retirement If You Start Now* by Anthony Spare and Paul Ciotti (Rocklin, CA: Prima, 1997)

### Organizations
Institute of Certified Financial Planners
3801 E. Florida Ave., Suite 708
Denver, CO 80210

The National Association of Personal Financial Advisors
355 W. Dundee Rd., Suite 200
Buffalo Grove, IL 60089

### Additional Business Ideas
❖ Financial services—college planning, business loans, and so forth
❖ Financial seminars—see *The Financial Planner's Seminar Kit: Everything You Need to Turn Prospects into Clients* by James H. Wilson (White Plains, NY: Longman Financial Service, 1985); may be out of print so check also in your public library.

## ◆ 78 ◆
# GERONTOLOGY CONSULTANT

Gerontology is the study of aging and the special problems of the elderly. With seniors being the fastest-growing segment of America's population, they will influence many aspects of our society. As an expert in this field, you can act an independent adviser and expert to help community organizations, businesses, and families with older relatives deal with issues of aging.

Your work will involve assisting your clients to adjust to the changes and challenges of this population while helping provide better services to seniors.

### Estimated Start-up Costs
$500 to $10,000, depending on the materials you will need for your services (e.g., multimedia, videos, manuals, books)

### Pricing Guidelines
$25 to $45 an hour

### Marketing and Advertising Methods and Tips
* Promotional materials: brochures, business cards, and so forth, sent to medical institutions, nursing schools, businesses, colleges, psychologists, and local and county government officials
* Yellow Pages
* Articles and columns on aging issues in local and regional publications
* Advertise on local cable television programs.
* Speak at community and business groups.
* Publish a newsletter on aging issues.

### Essential Equipment
* Home office equipment: telephone with answering system and fax; computer with Internet access for research and networking, desktop publishing software, inkjet or laser color printer, and photocopier
* Promotional materials (including videotapes on this topic that you have purchased or made for your presentations)
* Listing of resources at all levels—local, county, state, national—for senior citizens

### Recommended Training, Experience, or Needed Skills
* Degree, education, and experience in gerontology, sociology, and/or psychology
* Before you market your services as a consultant, it is good to work in agencies or homes that handle affairs of the aged.

### Income Potential
$25,000 to $45,000

### Type of Business
$1/2$ in home marketing, conducting business, and planning your presentations; $1/2$ out of home meeting with clients and making presentations

## Best Customers
✤ Hospitals and nursing homes
✤ Government agencies
✤ Mental health foundations and institutions
✤ Nursing schools
✤ Businesses and marketing research groups
✤ Community colleges
✤ Professional conferences
✤ Families needing counseling services and guidance as to the problems experienced by elderly relatives
✤ Radio and cable television shows

## Success Tips
✤ Become an expert and write a book on aging issues and your experiences in this field.
✤ Stay current about the political and social issues surrounding aging through continuing education, journals, and other resources.
✤ Constantly market your consulting services through follow-up calls, press releases of upcoming talks you will be doing, and so forth.
✤ Have the understanding and compassion needed for the counseling you do.

## Franchises, Distributorships, and Licenses
Heartland Retirement Services
902 Watston Ave.
Madison, WI 53713-3255

## Additional Information
### Recommended Reading
*The Encyclopedia of Aging and Elderly* by F. Hampton Roy and Charles Russell (New York: Facts on File, 1992)
*The Human Elder in Nature, Culture, and Society (Lives in Context)* by David L. Gutman (Boulder, CO: Westview, 1997)

### Additional Business Idea

Seminars on aging—giving seminars and workshops on the aspects of our aging population and how it affects business markets, health care, family issues, lifestyles, and more. See *Entrepreneur Magazine: Organizing and Promoting Seminars* by *Entrepreneur Magazine* (New York: Wiley, 1997)

## ᗷ 79 ᗒ
# NOSTALGIA-RELATED PRODUCTS

Baby boomers (and their parents) love nostalgia products: old radio and television shows, old movies and cartoon characters, famous sports stars, old toys (bikes, yo-yos, etc.), and so on. The baby boomers in their fifties comprise a $900 million market— one third of all dollars spent by American consumers (American Association of Advertising Agencies). If you can obtain the license to sell nostalgia-related products or originate products related to the memories of today's mature adults, you could have a thriving venture selling products via mail order or at shows and fairs.

*Note:* When a toy or product has an important anniversary date, it is a good time to bring forth your product. You will have to do the research *before* that date on many of the once popular products so you will be ready to market your wares on the anniversary or milestone. Look in your public library at collectibles' price guides (collectible items) and reference books like *Chronicle of America* (Mount Kisco, NY: Chronicle Books, 1989) for anniversary dates of certain products.

### Estimated Start-up Costs
$3,000 to $10,000

### Pricing Guidelines
Depends on what the market will bear, price within the range of similar reproductions, and other considerations.

### Marketing and Advertising Methods and Tips
* Send samples to mail-order catalogs that carry nostalgia-related products.
* Press releases (with good photos) to publications geared to the mature adult readership
* Exhibit at specific collectible trade shows and gift trade shows.
* As your budget permits, advertise on local cable television shopping shows; from that response, apply to the larger national shopping television networks to see whether your product will be accepted on their shows.
* Internet Web site

### Essential Equipment
* Home office: computer with design software capabilities, peripherals, telephone with answering system, and fax
* Promotional materials: photo cards and brochures with professional photos

### Recommended Training, Experience, or Needed Skills
* Creativity to develop new ideas for nostalgic items
* Experience in marketing research and marketing new products
* Take courses in marketing and mail-order business basics if you will also be selling through the mail.

### Income Potential
$20,000 to $30,000 + , depending on the success of the product

### Type of Business
$1/2$ in home doing marketing and fulfilling orders

### Best Customers
* Those that remember the years when your product v popular

❖ People who collect memorabilia items
❖ Hobbyists

## Success Tips

❖ Thoroughly research the existing products related to your idea(s) to see whether the market is too saturated.
❖ Test-market your product idea(s) before you invest large sums of money to have it manufactured or purchase a quantity of materials to make your product(s). Then if these findings are positive, go onto further development and possibly find sales representatives to sell your products.
❖ Advertising is crucial, and you may want to consult with a home-based advertising specialist for advice.

## Additional Information
### Recommended Reading

*American Nostalgia* by Charlene Beeler (Waco, TX: Prufrock Press, 1992)

*40's and 50's Designs and Memorabilia: Identification and Price Guide (Confident Collector)* by Anne Gilbert (New York: Avon, 1994)

*The Lyle Price Guide to Collectibles and Memorabilia* by Tony Curtis (Perigee, NY: 1994)

*60's and 70's Designs and Memorabilia: Identification and Price Guide (Confident Collector)* by Anne Gilbert (New York: Avon, 1994)

## Additional Business Idea

Collectibles broker—see the following business start-up guide: Entrepreneur's Small Business Development Catalog, "Collectibles Broker," $69 + $7.95 for shipping and handling. Call (800) 421-2300 for a catalog or credit card orders.

### ⋙ 80 ⋘
# RETIREMENT LIFE PLANNER

'ith the baby boomer generation noted for its lack of planning retirement and many social programs in jeopardy (or facing a dire forecast), retirement planning may be in for overnight growth. As baby boomers realize that they must seriously plan for their retirement years, they will begin searching for financial planners and specialists to help them.

As a retirement life planner, you can offer referrals to financial experts (as mentioned earlier), home health care providers, types of senior housing and living, career counseling for those wanting to start a business or go back to school, insurance specialists, investment counselors, and help with any other concerns your clients have in planning their retirement years.

### Estimated Start-up Costs
$2,500 to $4,000

### Pricing Guidelines
Fees of $100 to $1,500, depending on the involvement asked for by your client

### Marketing and Advertising Methods and Tips
* Ads in local publications
* Column on retirement planning in your local and regional publications (you pay)
* Radio appearances (or show) on this topic
* Referrals from family, friends, business acquaintances, and social workers
* Yellow Pages
* Send out a newsletter to all who inquire or use your services.
* Network within business associations.

### Essential Equipment
* Home office set up for receiving clients (or you can opt to visit them in their homes), telephone and answering system, computer with word processing and desktop publishing software for writing up reports
* Promotional materials: business cards and brochures with testimonials from satisfied clients, portfolio of brochures and

information on the services and experts to help them with other aspects of retirement living

### Recommended Training, Experience, or Needed Skills
* Financial planning certification, accounting, and/or banking experience
* Education and/or experience in working in social service programs serving the needs of the elderly
* Good communication and people skills

### Income Potential
$15,000 to $45,000

### Type of Business
$1/_2$ in home compiling reports and recommendations for your clients; $1/_2$ meeting with clients in their homes (if they cannot meet in your home office) and giving seminars, doing interviews, and gathering resources for your clients

### Best Customers
* Baby boomers, especially people in their fifties
* Young professionals, parents, and individuals who want to set up long-range retirement plans
* Businesses that want to add your services as benefits to employees who are taking early retirements

### Success Tips
* This is a challenging business in that you will have to first educate people in your community as to why they need your service, and then give them the best information and referrals that will offer them the soundest information and advice.
* The personal attention that you can give your clients will be more desireable than dealing with a larger retirement planning firm.

### Additional Information
**Recommended Reading**

*The Best of Retirement Planning* by Marion E. Haynes (Menlo Park, CA: Crisp, 1995)

*Retirement Places Rated/The Single Best Sourcebook for Planning Your Second Home: Your Guide to Planning Your Retirement,* 4th ed. by David Savageau (New York: Macmillan General Reference, 1995)

*10 Minute Guide to Long-Term Retirement Planning (10 Minute Facts)* by Mark Battersby (New York: Macmillan General Reference, 1996)

*Your Personal Guide to Pre-Retirement Planning;* order for $5 from Pilot Books, 127 Sterling Ave., P.O. Box 2102, Greenport, NY 11944-2102; (800) 79-PILOT.


### Additional Business Idea
Small business consultant—see *100 Best Retirement Businesses* by Lisa Angowski Rogak Shaw (Dover, NH: Upstart, 1994); and *The Senior Citizen's Guide to Starting a Part-Time Home-Based Business;* over forty ideas for $5.95; order from Pilot Books at (800) 79-PILOT.


### ◆ 81 ◆
# SPECIFIC PRODUCT DEVELOPMENT: ASSISTANCE PRODUCTS

As we grow older, we face the possibility of experiencing physical limitations caused by medical problems and age itself. If you have developed an idea or living assistance product to make life easier for seniors, you may make money while having the satisfaction of helping others.


### Estimated Start-up Costs
$3,000 to $8,000 +

## Pricing Guidelines
* Depends on the cost of marketing and the profit margin you wish to make
* Make your price competitive with others in similar lines unless your product is totally new.

## Marketing and Advertising Methods and Tips
* Send samples to mail-order catalogs that carry products for senior adults.
* Press releases (with good photos) to publications geared to the mature adult readership
* Exhibit at product trade shows
* Ads in magazines, such as *Modern Maturity*, that reach the mature audience
* As your budget permits, advertise on local cable television shopping shows; from that response, apply to the larger national shopping television networks to see whether your product will be accepted on their shows.
* Internet Web site
* Brochures with photos or illustrations and ordering information

## Essential Equipment
* Equipment, tools, and work area needed to produce your product
* Computer with billing, desktop publishing, mailing, and inventory software; peripherals
* Telephone with answering system

## Recommended Training, Experience, or Needed Skills
* Training and experience in working with seniors (nursing, assisting in therapy, life skills, etc.) and knowledge of their special needs
* Creativity and mechanical inclinations to come up with new ideas or improvements on present products

## Income Potential
$15,000 +, depending on whether you produce your product, like a special wheelchair shopping bag or unique cane, or whether you have it patented and manufactured

## Type of Business
$3/_4$ in home producing your product, conducting business, and brainstorming new ideas; $1/_4$ out of home marketing and selling your product

## Best Customers
❖ Mature adults
❖ Individuals of all ages with physical disabilities
❖ Retirement homes
❖ Day care centers for seniors
❖ Private and public agencies serving senior adults

## Success Tips
❖ Thoroughly test-market your idea.
❖ Consult with marketing experts and patent attorneys to determine whether it is worth it to invest the time and money to get a patent.
❖ Marketing experts say consumers at this age do not buy many new items but will purchase familiar products that have been improved.

## Additional Information
### Recommended Reading
*The Complete Idiot's Guide to New Product Development* by Edwin E. Bobrow (New York: Macmillan General Reference, 1997)
See also the "Inventor's Consultant" sources in the "Creative Businesses" chapter.

⊷ ● ⊶

# MISCELLANEOUS SERVICES

❖ Exercise programs and videos—medical studies have shown moderate exercise and weight lifting can slow the rate of bone loss and improve the overall health of people even in their nineties. As the U.S. population ages, so will the demand for moderate-level fitness programs.
❖ Matching service for seniors—running a matching service for mature adults who do not want to live alone and want companionship
❖ Hearing aid repair

# Personal Businesses

*To love what you do and feel that it matters—how could anything be more fun?*

—Katharine Graham

Experts say any business that can save people time and money has a better than average chance of success. Of course, treating people with respect, courtesy, and extra attention will also give you a definite edge over any competitors. Keep this advice in mind as your read the details of the following ventures in this section of personal businesses. As one successful market expert says, "Focus your business efforts on people, not paper."

## ❧ 82 ❧
## ANNOUNCEMENT SERVICES

With greeting card prices soaring, you may find a business niche in creating and designing custom birth, birthday, anniversary, and graduation announcements with coordinating thank-you notes. In creating the cards, you have several options for adding messages and illustrations: compose the messages and draw the illustrations yourself (if you are talented in that way), freelance illustrators and writers (obtain the copyrights), design your own using computer art design software, or use copyright-free designs. This is a competitive business, but if you keep in contact with your customers and give good personal service, you will earn your customers' loyalty.

### Estimated Start-up Costs
$5,000 to $10,000

### Pricing Guidelines
$50 to $75 per customer; includes the personalized design and the cards with envelopes

### Marketing and Advertising Methods and Tips
❖ Ads in publications distributed free to obstetrician and child-birth instruction centers
❖ Referrals from satisfied customers
❖ Ads in local parenting newspapers and publications
❖ Exhibit your samples at baby and children's products trade shows.
❖ Mail-order flyers and brochures of your announcements. Start with one color sheet with an order blank and expand as you get the funds.
❖ Work with owners of gift basket businesses, children's clothing shops, and gift shops to display samples of your announcements.
❖ Advertise in the classifieds or small display ads of baby magazines.
❖ Portfolio of samples
❖ Internet Web site
❖ Business cards

### Essential Equipment
❖ Home office equipment: computer with design and word processing software (mailing list software if you sell via the mail), color printer, and photocopier

❖ Telephone with answering system and fax

## Recommended Training, Experience, or Needed Skills
❖ Need to be a creative person with the ability to customize cards for each of your customers
❖ Business and marketing background helpful
❖ Knowledge of what types of announcement cards are currently on the market, so you can make yours unique or better

## Income Potential
$20,000 to $35,000

## Type of Business
$3/4$ in home designing and producing; $1/4$ marketing your business and making contacts with printers, customers, artists, and writers (if you use freelancers)

## Best Customers
❖ Expecting parents and grandparents
❖ Graduating students
❖ Children of parents who are celebrating anniversaries
❖ Relatives of people commemorating special events and birthdays
❖ Churches, businesses, towns, and organizations that are celebrating anniversaries

## Success Tips
❖ Always look for new ways to differentiate your products and services from commercial announcement enterprises.
❖ Establish a good working relationship with one or more printers who produce your cards. Find printers that will print small runs at reasonable prices.
❖ Foster good customer service by encouraging customers to call with questions, feedback, and ideas. Ship orders promptly.

### Franchises, Distributorships, and Licenses
CardSenders
1201 Eubank Blvd., NE., #6
Albuquerque, NM 87112
Write for information.


### Additional Information
**Recommended Reading**
*What Can I Say? How to Write Greetings and Verse for Every Occasion* by Sadie Harris (New York: Lyons & Burford, 1996)


### Additional Business Ideas
❖ Create "This is the day you were . . . (born, married, graduated)" greetings—compiling the actual news events (and weather, top songs, fashions, etc.) that happened on a customer's commemorative day into an album or a list on a special card
❖ Greeting card business—contact the Greeting Card Association, 1200 G St., NW, #760, Washington, DC 20005, with a SASE for membership information.

### Additional Information
Sandra Louden, P.O. Box 9701, Pittsburgh, PA 15229-0701; send a LSASE for information on how to purchase her greeting card writing tips and a listing of greeting card companies to whom you can submit your writing and illustration ideas.
"Gardening Greetings" offers a Home-Based Greeting Card Kit for $26.50. Those interested can send payment to Sally Silagy, 189a Paradise Circle, Woodland Park, CO 80863, or e-mail her at OGalSal@aol.com for further information.
National Business Library's Small Business Catalog, *"How to Write & Sell Greeting Cards,"* $39.95 + $6.50 for shipping and handling; call (800) 947-7724 for a catalog or credit card orders.

See also the "Greeting Cards" chapter in *101 Best Home-Based Businesses for Women* by Priscilla Y. Huff (Rocklin, CA: Prima, 1995).

## ॐ 83 ॐ

# BUDGET EXPERT

With today's easy credit, both individuals and businesses can often find they have overextended themselves and are having a difficult time keeping up with expenses or, with a business, making a profit. The expertise you will offer to individuals and families will be to analyze their living expenses and income and give them suggestions for living within their budgets. For businesses you can do a breakdown analysis of costs and profits and also make recommendations to cut back on expenses for increased profits.

### Estimated Start-up Costs
$2,000 to $5,000

### Pricing Guidelines
Budget-planning fee for individuals and couples, $200 to $300; for companies, $350

### Marketing and Advertising Methods and Tips
* Classified ads in local newspapers
* Referrals from social service agencies, banks, bookkeepers, and accountants
* Referrals from business owners' associations
* Advertising on cable television classifieds and radio
* Brochures and business cards explaining your services

### Essential Equipment
Home office set up to receive clients; computer with accounting software, laser printer, telephone with answering system and fax, photocopier, and cost-analysis sheets

### Recommended Training, Experience, or Needed Skills
* Finance-related education, training, and experience (bookkeeping, finances, accounting, banking, legal education)

❖ Business management experience
❖ Good and communication and people skills
❖ Licenses and certifications where required

### Income Potential
$20,000 to $40,000

### Type of Business
Full-time in home if you have a home office where you meet with clients

### Best Customers
Newly married couples, families, small business owners, mature adults living on fixed incomes

### Success Tips
❖ Have a number of low-cost strategies your clients can follow and resources they can contact to help them get their finances under control.
❖ Be discreet and confidential.
❖ Teach at local adult evening schools and then offer seminars at community centers to establish your name and business.

### Franchises, Distributorships, and Licenses
Valcor Arbitration Services, Ltd.
Hughes Center
3753 Howard Hughes Pkwy., Suite 200
Las Vegas, NV 89109
Debt arbitration services; write for information.

### Additional Information
#### Recommended Reading
*Budgeting for a Small Business* by Terry Dickey (Menlo Park, CA: Crisp, 1994)

*Downsized but Not Defeated: The Family Guide to Living on Less* by
  Hope Stanley Quinn and Lyn Miller Lachman (Kansas City,
  MO: Andrews & McMeel, 1997)
*Family Budgets That Work* by Larry Burkett (Wheaton, IL:
  Tyndale House, 1988)
*Raising Happy Kids on a Budget* by Patricia Gallagher (1995; Young
  Sparrow Press, Box 265, Worcester, PA 19490)
*10 Minute Guide to Household Budgeting* by Tracy Loungo (New
  York: Macmillan General Reference, 1997)

**Home Study**
  International Correspondence Schools
  925 Oak St.
  Scranton, PA 18515
Associate study in business management with an option in
finance.

### *Additional Business Idea*
Self-publish annual financial-budget workbooks—setting up
customized guidelines for your customers: families, individuals,
professionals, small and home-based businesses

## ‿ 84 ‿
# CONSUMER COMPLAINT LETTERS
Many people feel frustrated today when they are ignored by a
company against which they have a complaint about a product
or service (which is why you will give them the service they
deserve). They may call a company to complain on the telephone, often only to be given "lip service" by a harried employee
or have their call totally ignored. You can offer a letter-writing
service that will compose a complaint letter in clear, concise
English, written to the president or owner of the company and
delivered via certified mail. You will have the satisfaction of helping the forgotten "little person" while earning money and the
reputation for being a consumer champion.

### Estimated Start-up Costs
$3,000 to $5,000

### Pricing Guidelines
$30 to $35 for each initial letter; $15 for a follow-up letter

### Marketing and Advertising Methods and Tips
❖ Press releases to newspapers, wire services, and radio and television stations
❖ Classified ads in local newspapers
❖ Articles in local publications about effective consumer complaining
❖ Referrals from your county consumer complaint office—make an appointment with them to explain your service.

### Essential Equipment
❖ Home office set up to receive clients; computer with word processing software; laser printer; modem and access to the Internet; telephone business system with phone, fax, answering machine combination; and photocopier
❖ Promotional materials: business cards, press releases, and flyers to send to media
❖ Listing of local, state, and federal resources you and/or your clients can contact for assistance

### Recommended Training, Experience, or Needed Skills
❖ Good communication, people, and writing skills
❖ Experience in writing complaint letters and/or working in a consumer affairs office
❖ Ability to write succinctly and with authority
❖ Persistence to find the names and addresses of those who handle consumer complaints for an agency, company, and other groups

### Income Potential
$5,000 to $10,000; you can earn more if you offer this as an

added service with another communication-related business (e.g., secretarial, word processing, resume services).

## Type of Business
Full-time in home, especially if you have a home office to receive customers

## Best Customers
Individuals who do not have the time or knowledge to write effective complaint letters

## Success Tips
❖ Effective complaint letters include the following: a description of your client's problem and how your client would like the problem resolved.
❖ The letter should be as concise and clear as possible.
❖ Do not threaten, yet write politely and with authority.
❖ Include photocopies of all receipts, canceled checks, and other important documentation.
❖ Offer free consultations; if you believe a problem requires the benefit of legal counsel, refer your client to a lawyer's referral service.
❖ Send all letters via certified mail so you have a record.

## Additional Information
### Recommended Reading
*How to Write Complaint Letters That Work: A Consumer's Guide to Resolving Conflicts and Getting Results* by Patricia H. Westheimer and Jim Mastro (Indianapolis: Jist Works, 1994)
*1998 Consumer's Resource Handbook* by U.S. Office of Consumer Affairs, Washington, DC; lists sample consumer complaint letter plus a *Consumer Assistance Directory*. Free (except for $1 postage) is the *Consumer Information Catalog* from the Consumer Information Center, P.O. Box 100, Pueblo, CO 81002.
*Send This Jerk the Bedbug Letter: How Companies, Politicians, and the Mass Media Deal with Complaints and How to Be a More*

*Effective Complainer* by John Bear (Berkeley, CA: Ten Speed Press, 1996)

**Other Sources**
Contact the consumer's advocacy office at your county seat to report a complaint if the business or agency is local. Also register a complaint with the Better Business Bureau if the problem is not resolved to your satisfaction.

### Additional Business Idea
Writing thoughtful sentiments for people—for occasions when people wish to have their feelings put into words for someone special. Use the script font in a desktop publishing program on attractive paper for a finished look.

## ◦❧ 85 ❧◦
## CUSTOMIZED CALENDARS

Walk into any bookstore and you will see a multitude of calendars: animals, babies, artwork, nature scenes, and so on. With this personal business, you take individuals' photos and artwork and arrange them in the order the customer designates. Then you have the calendars printed at your local print shop or office supply store.

Or you can offer to take photos of local businesses' buildings and/or use copies of old photos of a town's historical past and create a calendar to sell to local individuals and businesses.

### Estimated Start-up Costs
$1,000 to $7,000, depending what home office equipment (and camera equipment if you will do your own photography) you will purchase

### Pricing Guidelines
❖ Fees for one calendar (your customers supply the twelve photos—no slides or negatives): $40 to $45

❖ Give customers ten dates they can have highlighted on the calendar for free, and charge 50 cents for each additional date.

## Marketing and Advertising Methods and Tips
❖ Classified ads in parent-targeted publications
❖ Flyers and business cards on community bulletin boards
❖ Referrals from satisfied customers
❖ Press release and article in local newspapers. Start advertising from September on for the holiday rush.
❖ Show samples at local baby and gift and craft shows.
❖ Direct mail to local historical societies followed by a visit with samples
❖ Teach one-day workshops.
❖ Internet Web site

## Essential Equipment
❖ Access to high-quality printer and calendar making supplies. Start by using the reproduction photocopiers at your favorite office supply store, and as your business grows, purchase your own scanner and calendar supplies.
❖ Camera and basic photography equipment if you plan to shoot your own photos

## Recommended Training, Experience, or Needed Skills
❖ Make sample calendars for friends, family members, and organizations to test-market your idea and to get some feedback and a sense of the time and expense that will be involved.
❖ Marketing experience
❖ Photography courses and experience if you plan to take your own photos. Check your local adult evening schools and/or colleges for courses.

## Income Potential
❖ Depends on the costs, your time involved, and the profit margin you need to make

❖ Possibility for making from $10,000 to $30,000 a year

### Type of Business
$\frac{1}{2}$ in home with production and business management; $\frac{1}{2}$ out-of-home meeting with clients, running to office supply and print shops, or taking photos if you go in that direction

### Best Customers
❖ Individuals for gift giving
❖ Schools—create a calendar for elementary schools for a possible fund-raising event.
❖ Businesses for promotional purposes to give to clients and customers
❖ Historical societies for fund-raising or posterity
❖ Local retail stores and gift shops

### Success Tips
❖ This is a customer-oriented business, so satisfaction is a must and depends on your creating a unique product.
❖ Creative marketing and advertising are needed to get your product seen.
❖ Thoroughly test-market your calendars to see what sells.
❖ If you are successful locally, then venture into mail order and advertise in regional and national publications for people to send you their photos and artwork for you to create a personalized calendar. Emphasize, though, that they should not send you originals.
❖ Make sure you have releases granting you the use of another's works or photos if the calendar will be sold to others.
❖ Have customers send photocopies of heirloom photos, not the originals.

### Additional Information
#### Recommended Reading
*Calendar 97: Complete This Calendar with Your Favorite Photos and Make a Personal Craft for a Friend or Relation* (Washington, DC: Elliot & Clark, 1996)

*National Business Library's Small Business Catalog*, "Photography Services"; $39.95 + $6.50 for shipping and handling; call (800) 947-7724 or a catalog or credit card orders.

*Photographer's Market Guide to Photo Submissions and Portfolio Formats* by Michael Williams (1997; Writer's Digest Books, F & W Publications, 1507 Dana Ave., Cincinnati, OH 45207-1005; write for listing of other helpful books for the professional photographer)

**Home Study**
Hemphill Schools
510 S. Alvaredo St.
Los Angeles, CA 90057-2998
Photography and other home-study courses. Write for current course listings and information.

*Additional Ideas*
✤ Sell calendar-making kits.
✤ Sell your photographs to calendar businesses—write directly to the companies that publish calendars to see whether they accept freelance photos and/or ideas and, if so, to request a copy of their submission guidelines. See *1998 Photographer's Market* by Michael Williams, ed. (Cincinnati, OH: Writer's Digest Books, 1998) for over two thousand listings of freelance photo buyers, including calendar companies.

◦◦ 86 ◦◦

# LAUNDRY SERVICE

Many people often seem to have more dirty clothes than clean ones—and the pile usually grows by the end of the week! With this service, your customers leave their bags of laundry with you, you take them to a local Laundromat or a designated area for washing clothes (college washing machines, apartment buildings' washers and dryers), and your customers pick them up at the end of the day, dried and folded. This is a physical job and not very exciting but one that is sure to be in demand. As your business grows, you can hire employees to assist you.

### Estimated Start-up Costs
$1,000 to $3,000 (not including the cost of a van or truck to haul the dirty laundry)

### Pricing Guidelines
- ✤ $10 for large loads of laundry, $7 for small loads
- ✤ Your customers supply the detergent and pretreat any stains with their own stain remover. (Some people are very sensitive to some brands of detergents. If they supply their own, you will not be responsible if they should develop a rash because of a certain soap.)
- ✤ The money needed to operate the washing machines and dryers. You can bill them at the end of the month or whatever period you agree upon.
- ✤ Pick-up and delivery would or would not be charged by the mile, depending on whether you do the wash in the building in which you live or drive to a Laundromat.

### Marketing and Advertising Methods and Tips
- ✤ Flyers at Laundromats, college dormitories, apartment buildings, and senior citizen's housing
- ✤ Ads in college newspapers and community classified newspapers
- ✤ Word-of-mouth referrals

### Essential Equipment
- ✤ Telephone with answering system
- ✤ Rate sheets, terms, guidelines, and questionnaires
- ✤ Release form so you will not be held responsible for any clothing damaged by a machine or dryer
- ✤ Laundry bags with clients' names stenciled on them (they buy them with your service)
- ✤ Vehicle if you drive to a Laundromat

### Recommended Training, Experience, or Needed Skills
- ✤ Ability to be fast and efficient

❖ Basic knowledge of laundry procedures—clothes' and certain fabrics' care and washing instructions
❖ Talk with home economists and manufactures of washing machines and dryers for recommendations on cleaning and washing clothes.
❖ Work experience in a commercial or institutional laundry service

### Income Potential
$500 + a week

### Type of Business
$1/5$ in home for marketing and clients' drop-off and pick-ups, $4/5$ at Laundromats

### Best Customers
College students; single men and women; working women, especially working mothers

### Success Tips
❖ Check to see whether zoning laws permit you to have people dropping off or picking up laundry. Otherwise, you will have to provide this service.
❖ If you decide to do laundry with a machine in your home, you will have to invest in or rent one or two heavy-duty washing machines and dryers as well as check for adequate electrical wiring, water supply, and septic or sewage systems.
❖ Have your lawyer assist you in drawing up releases and your contract.
❖ If you find there is need for this type of service, you may want to think about opening a self-service Laundromat.

### Additional Business Ideas
❖ Dry cleaning pickup and return—meeting people at bus and train stations to take their clothes to be dry cleaned and

meeting them back at the station in one or two days (depending on the dry cleaning businesses with which you work)
* Ironing and simple mending

## ❧ 87 ❧
## MAKEUP ARTIST OR FACIALIST

In this personal business, you give facial treatments as well as counsel people on the proper skin care for them. Additional sidelines to this business are advising (and selling) skin care products you recommend and electrolysis (removal of hair). You can also be a makeup artist with such customers as brides, professionals, and people who make regular public appearances. You can start working part-time with another home-based cosmetology business and then progress to an in-home shop or visit your clients in their homes.

### Estimated Start-up Costs
$7,000 to $15,000 (includes education, training, and specialized equipment costs)

### Pricing Guidelines
$40 to $60 per client (the goal is to have regular appointments with clients)

### Marketing and Advertising Methods and Tips
* Offer complimentary facials.
* Booths at local business shows
* Referrals from beauticians
* Talks to professional women's clubs
* Join and network within Chambers of Commerce and home-based business associations.
* Business cards and flyers on community bulletin boards

## Essential Equipment
✤ Facial-related equipment
✤ Towels
✤ Work area set up for your clients
✤ Home office equipment: business telephone and answering system; computer with desktop publishing software for creating your business cards, brochures, and skin care booklets

## Recommended Training, Experience, or Needed Skills
✤ Education to become a facialist (cosmetician); you will need training (the average is six to nine months), and then you will have to pass the necessary tests to have a state license (which is also needed for electrolysis and/or to be a permanent-makeup artist).
✤ Work in a beauty salon or health and beauty spa to gain experience and practice.

## Income Potential
✤ $20,000 to $40,000
✤ The average number of clients a facialist sees a day is four to five. To see more, you will need to hire an assistant.
✤ A makeup session can run $20 to $35.

## Type of Business
Full-time in home, or $1/2$ spent in the homes of your clients

## Best Customers
✤ Professional men and women
✤ Speakers and those whose careers often bring them in front of the public or other professionals
✤ Do makeup for brides, teenagers going to proms, and people with skin discolorations who prefer to hide them with makeup.

## Success Tips
✤ Practice and study until you are skilled at your service.

❖ Be personable as well as a good teacher and listener.
❖ Stay current with the latest science of the industry and make-up trends.
❖ Be a good example—your skin should look healthy and "glowing."
❖ Confer with dermatologists to get tips on skin care, and refer clients to them if you suspect a client has a skin problem that may be hazardous to her health.

### Franchises, Distributorships, and Licenses
Avon Products, Inc.
9 West 57th St.
New York, NY 10019-2683
http://www.avon.com

Mary Kay Cosmetics
6702 Ports o'Call Drive
Rowlett, TX 75088-6221; http://www.MaryKay.com

### Additional Information
#### Recommended Reading
*Dermascope Magazine,* 4447 McKiney Ave., Dallas, TX 75205; $35/year
*Five-Minute Facelift* by Robert Thé (New York: Sterling, 1997)
*How to Start and Manage a Cosmetology Business* by Jerre G. Lewis and Leslie D. Renn (Lewis and Renn Associates, 10315 Harmony Dr., Interlochen, MI 49643); $14.95 + $3 shipping and handling
*Skin Inc.,* Circulation Dept., 362 S. Schmale Rd., Carol Stream, IL 60188; $46/year
*The Technique of the Professional Make-up Artist* by Vincent J.R. Kehoe (Stoneham, MA: Focal, 1995)

#### Organization
Aestheticians International Association
3939 E. Highway 80, Suite 408
Mesquite, TX 75150-3355
Includes information for the wellness industry, make-up artists, aestheticians, and so forth.

### Additional Business Ideas

❖ Permanent-makeup artist—becoming licensed to do micropigmentation, which is a form of tattooing to imitate makeup (i.e., eyeliner, lipstick, eyebrows). Some of the people who would use this service are those who are allergic to cosmetics, have visual limitations or pigment disorders, are models, and others.

❖ Theater makeup artist—offering your services to local community theater and musical groups. See *The Complete Make-Up Artist: Working in Film, Television, and Theatre* by Penny Delmar (Evanston, IL: Northwestern University Press, 1995)

❖ Selling your beauty products—see *The Skin Care Book: Simple Herbal Recipes* by Kathlyn Quatrochi (Loveland, CO: Interweave, 1997); herbal recipes, bath preparations, massage oils rinses, and more

### ৵৵ 88 ৵৵
# NAIL SALON/MANICURIST

Nail art and unusual shades of nail polishes have rocketed in popularity over the past few years. Entrepreneurs have started companies with new designs, colors of nail polishes, and artificial nails. For example, Susan had been working at such jobs as tree climber, waitress, and fish filleter, but when she got married, her husband, a business owner, suggested she start her own business.

Susan had always enjoyed getting manicures and so decided to go to cosmetology school to take courses to be a licensed manicurist. When she obtained her license, she worked at a beauty salon, but she liked the idea of working from her home. Susan's husband helped her build a shop attached to their home, and she started out slowly with some former clients from the salon. Susan's business grew from word-of-mouth referrals and the business cards she placed around the community. Three years later, she has more customers than she can schedule, plus an on-call waiting list of clients that want to be notified immediately if Susan should have a cancellation. Susan says she checked with her township officials before she opened her salon to see whether she was permitted to have customers and parking at her home.

## Estimated Start-up Costs
$4,000 to $20,000 or more (if you build an addition or refurbish a room, garage, etc.)

## Pricing Guidelines
❖ $40 to $60 + for artificial nails or nail art
❖ $15 to $20 for a basic manicure or pedicure

## Marketing and Advertising Methods and Tips
❖ Referrals from beauticians and salons
❖ Referrals from satisfied customers
❖ Your customers' nails—they are "advertising" themselves for your business!
❖ Flyers on community bulletin boards
❖ Yellow Pages
❖ Front-yard sign

## Essential Equipment
❖ Industry-related equipment: table, lights, polishes, brushes, files, clippers, and so forth
❖ Comfortable chairs
❖ Parking space available for clients
❖ Shop or room with separate entrance

## Recommended Training, Experience, or Needed Skills
❖ Training: look in your Yellow Pages for listings of cosmetology schools.
❖ License or certificate: check with your state's regulations.
❖ Good listening and people skills
❖ Artistic sense and creativity if you are a nail artist
❖ Work for a salon to get started and gain experience.

## Income Potential
$35,000 to $50,000

## Type of Business
Full-time, in home

## Best Customers
❖ Teenagers
❖ Models
❖ Women and men whose professions and jobs involve using their hands in front of the public (e.g., bank tellers, receptionists, secretaries and word processors, executives)

## Success Tips
❖ Offer something distinctive with your salon. Susan specializes in hand-painted art, which has become her "trademark."
❖ Have additional services such as pedicures, nail repairs, and so forth.
❖ Offer to work at girls' birthday parties.
❖ Follow all the necessary regulations required by your state and any local zoning restrictions.
❖ Stay current with the latest trends in the industry by attending trade shows and reading trade publications.

## Additional Information
### Recommended Reading
*Nails Magazine* (210615 S. Western Ave., Torrance, CA 90501); (310) 376-8788; http://www.nailsmag.com; $38/year
*National Business Library's Small Business Catalog*, "Nail Salon"; $39.95 + $6.50 for shipping and handling; call (800) 947-7724 for catalog or credit card orders.

### Organization
World International Nail and Beauty Association
606 West Katella
Orange, CA 92667

For professionals in nail and skin care; trade show, other programs, trade magazine.

### Additional Business Idea
Create new types of polishes or adornments for nails.

## ఆ 89 ఆ
## SPIRITUALITY COUNSELOR

Sociologists and trend experts have noted in recent years a movement in our country to reach our "inner spirit" through meditation, books about spirituality, exercise, nonviolence, religion, astrology, psychics, wellness spas, genealogy, and other areas. They claim we are trying to deal with the stress in our lives while also trying to find peace and purpose. If you have pertinent background, knowledge, and/or training, you may want to venture into giving lessons or consulting with clients in these areas.

### Estimated Start-up Costs
$1,000 to $3,000

### Pricing Guidelines
$20 to $45 an hour, or $70 + fee for a four- to six-week course of ongoing sessions

### Marketing and Advertising Methods and Tips
* Classified and display ads in free fitness and wellness publications distributed at grocery stores
* Teaching courses at senior citizens' centers, retirement homes, health and wellness centers, spas, and YMCAs; adult evening classes held at schools, colleges, and learning centers
* Referrals from satisfied clients

❖ Exhibits and demonstrations at health and exercise trade shows

### Essential Equipment
❖ Mats
❖ Exercise room
❖ Music equipment to play tapes if you hold the classes in your home

### Recommended Training, Experience, or Needed Skills
❖ Train and apprentice with experts in the fields in which you are interested.
❖ Attend courses and related conferences.
❖ Read trade publications and attend conferences to stay up with the current information.

### Income Potential
$10,000 to $20,000, depending on whether you hold your own classes in your home and/or work for another business or organization

### Type of Business
Full-time if you conduct classes from your home; $1/4$ in home, $3/4$ out of home if you teach at other places

### Best Customers
❖ Middle- and upper-income individuals
❖ Businesses that wish to offer stress-related exercise and meditation classes to their employees
❖ Women's groups

### Success Tips
❖ Be physically fit, have a good personality, and enjoy teaching.
❖ Be on the lookout for new ways to market your programs.
❖ Offer other items to your students, like videos and T-shirts.

## Additional Information
### Recommended Reading

*The American Yoga Association's New Yoga Challenge: Powerful Workouts for Flexible Strength, Energy and Inner Discovery* by Alice Christensen (Lincolnwood, IL: NTC/Contemporary Books, 1997)

*The Complete Book of T'Ai Chi* by Stewart McFarlane and Mew Hong Tan (New York: Dorling-Kindersly, 1997)

*Complete Meditation* by Stephen Kravette (Atglen, PA: Schiffer, 1997)

*The New Yoga for People over 50: A Comprehensive Guide for Midlife and Older Beginners* by Suza Francina (Deerfield Beach, FL: Health Communications, 1997)

*Tai Chi Handbook: Exercise, Meditation, and Self-Defense* by Herman Kauz (New York: Doubleday, 1987)

### Organizations

Heart of Yoga Association
971 Manzanita Pl.
Los Angeles, CA 90029
Send a LSASE for membership information.

Patience T'ai Chi Association (PTCA)
P.O. Box 350532
Brooklyn, NY 11235
Videos, seminars, courses; send a LSASE for more information.

Also do a Web search for "yoga" to find many sites.

## Additional Business Ideas

✤ Florigrapher—telling your customers with what flower their name is associated and also the floral symbol that is related to their particular profession

✤ Teaching tarot card reading—$60 for a one-time, two-hour course

✤ Teaching meditation and stress management—$70 for three two-hour sessions

⊰⚫⊱

# MISCELLANEOUS PERSONAL BUSINESSES

❖ How-to instructor—teaching women in their homes how to do wallpapering, painting, small household repairs, or a specific skill with the handicrafts, sewing, cooking, and so forth

❖ Personal coach—this is one of the hottest and fastest-growing professions in the country. More and more individuals are turning to personal coaches to help them discover their life purpose, set goals and priorities, and stay focused. Personal coaches are often consultants, managers, mentors, entrepreneurs, and therapists who can augment their services with personal coaching. They enjoy personal development while earning good money helping others reach their potential.

❖ Personal document adviser—helping people organize their documents and important papers

❖ Pager rentals and sales—marketing to parents and families with busy schedules who need to keep in touch with one another

❖ Tracing lost heirs—helping families find heirs mentioned in wills to help settle estates

# Specialty Travel Services

*Always somebody goin' away, somebody gettin' home.*

—John Joy Bell

Experts are predicting that the number of U.S. scheduled air passengers will increase 59 percent by 2007 to more than 900 million a year (*Newsweek*, January 27, 1997), while today the travel and tourism industry is the third largest retail business, accounting for more than $430 billion in sales (*Income Opportunities*, June 1996). With such popularity and predictions for continued growth, tourism is expanding into new, smaller business opportunities. Here are just a few of the new niches in this huge industry.

## ❧ 90 ❧
## EMERGENCY TRAVELERS' SERVICE

Last summer my husband and I were vacationing in a little town surrounded by farmland in upstate Pennsylvania. Our new car developed a serious engine breakdown, and we spent the next two hours trying to get someone to look at it. When we did, we were told it was dangerous to drive it. As this was a Saturday afternoon, everything had closed down in the small town and we could not rent a car, take ours to a local dealer, or even get roadside service from our car's manufacturer to find a dealer within a hundred miles! We were too far from home to have it towed.

There are traveler's automobile assistance companies like AAA (which we now have!), but what about other possible crises like experiencing a medical emergency, losing money, needing a rental car on a Saturday night or Sunday, or coping with some other unexpected concern? With an emergency traveler's service, you would provide referrals to emergency rooms, doctors, dentists, other professionals, mechanics, food establishments, and any other service a traveler (and stranger) would need.

You could put together an annual directory for your town, city, or county and receive payments from the businesses and professionals for their listing or commissions from any service that was used and paid for by the traveler(s). If the business is successful, you could expand your directories into other areas.

### Estimated Start-up Costs
$3,000 to $7,000

### Pricing Guidelines
❖ Charge for the listing in your directory, or charge a commission for each referral your service makes.
❖ Offer simple classified ads or display ads.
❖ Sell your directory at local stores and establishments.

### Marketing and Advertising Methods and Tips
❖ Press releases to local newspapers, radio stations, and cable television studios
❖ Direct mail to motels, bed and breakfasts, medical groups and associates, church leaders, taxi owners, auto mechanics and garages, locksmiths, auto rental agencies, small food shops, pharmacies, pet shops, travel agencies, Chambers of Commerce, and local law enforcement agencies

### Essential Equipment

Home office: two-line business telephone with conferencing capabilities, voice mail, and fax; computer with desktop publishing, travel, and database software; printer and scanner

### Recommended Training, Experience, or Needed Skills

* Good organization skills
* Knowledge of self-publishing procedures and distribution
* Database of services and resources available for travelers in each of your target areas

### Income Potential

$10,000 to $50,000 +, depending on the number of communities with which you deal

### Type of Business

$\frac{1}{2}$ in home compiling the directories and conducting business, $\frac{1}{2}$ marketing and interviewing new referrals

### Best Customers

* Travelers and people on vacations
* Motels and hotels
* Bed and breakfasts
* Food shops, grocery stores, and pharmacies
* Travel agencies
* Chambers of Commerce
* Restaurants and gas stations

### Success Tips

* Resort towns, cities that hold numerous conventions and conferences, college towns, campsites and parks, and other areas that regularly have visitors are good places to establish a service like this.
* Establish an 800 number with twenty-four-hour access for each directory so travelers can call if they have additional questions.

## Additional Information
### Recommended Reading
*The Family Vacation Health and Safety Guide* by Linda R. Bernstein (New York: Berkley, 1995)

*Pocket Guide to Auto Maintenance and Emergency Car Repair* by Wally Stewart and Ned Hawkins (Helena, MT: Greycliff, 1995)

*Traveler's Self-Care Manual: A Self-Help Guide to Emergency Medical Treatment for the Traveler* by William W. Forgey (Washington, DC: ICS, 1990)

## Additional Business Idea
Publish self-guided tour guides for visitors to towns in your area.

## ∽ 91 ∾
# HOMESTAY

A homestay is similar to a bed and breakfast but on a much smaller scale. A homestay may have only one to three guests or a small family at a time. You may have one to three rooms available, preferably with a private bath and possibly a separate entrance. Areas best for homestays would be tourist areas; convention towns, and college towns; towns near large hospitals (so that visiting families could be nearby while a relative is recuperating), large family amusement parks, sporting events centers, automobile race tracks; and so forth. You could offer a continental breakfast for free or for a small fee.

## Estimated Start-up Costs
$2,000 for new bedding, furnishings, and advertising

## Pricing Guidelines
$20 to $50 a room, depending on your area and the services you provide

### Marketing and Advertising Methods and Tips
* Ads in Chamber of Commerce booklets, local tourist guides, and bed-and-breakfast guides
* Ads in programs, promotional brochures, and guides published by the resorts, sports centers, amusement parks, convention centers, and so forth
* Signs in your yard
* Referrals from travel agents, real estate agents, and hospitals that have long-distance visitors
* Advertising on restaurant placemats

### Essential Equipment
* Furnished room and amenities
* Access to telephone, private bath, and washing machine and dryer
* Small refrigerator and microwave oven for each room
* Directory of local businesses and restaurants

### Recommended training, Experience, or Needed Skills
* Training in hospitality
* Work in a motel, hotel, and/or bed and breakfast
* Ability to cook
* Enjoyment in meeting new people

### Income Potential
$3,000 to $8,000 a year

### Type of Business
In home, full-time unless you run it in conjunction with another traveler's service (like the previously mentioned emergency travelers' service)

### Best Customers
Emergency travelers, businesspeople, vacationers, and people attending events

*Success Tips*
* ❖ This is a part-time business that can be run like a mini–bed and breakfast in conjunction with another business you might have.
* ❖ Check with local authorities and food licensing offices to see what permits and food handling licenses you may need.
* ❖ Make sure this type of business—having strangers in your home—will not interfere with your family (or vice versa).
* ❖ Also check with your insurance agent for liability insurance and your lawyer for liability concerns.

*Additional Information*
**Recommended Reading**
*How to Open and Operate a Bed and Breakfast,* 5th ed., by Jan Stankus (Old Saybrook, CT: Globe Pequot, 1997)
*Start Your Own Bed and Breakfast: Earn Extra Cash for Your Extra Room* by Beverly Matthews (New York: Pocket Books, 1985); check your library if out of print or hard to find.

**Home Study**
Echols International Tourism Institute
676 N. Clair St., Suite 1950
Chicago, IL 60611
Diploma courses in airline, travel, hospitality training, and others. Write for a current catalog.

*Additional Business Idea*
Paper, coffee, and doughnuts to go—delivering newspapers, coffee, and doughnuts or muffins to people on weekends, holidays, and vacation days

### ⊷ 92 ⊷
# INDEPENDENT TRAVEL SALES REP
As an independent travel sales rep, you can refer clients to travel agencies with which you work and receive a commission for this

referral. You can also work with the clients, making arrangements and bookings but having the agency get the tickets. With some full-service agencies, you will pay a small fee to use their name, take the bookings, and fax them the information. They, in turn, will process the tickets for you (because you are not permitted to do so).

### Estimated Start-up Costs
$2,500 to $6,000

### Pricing Guidelines
10 to 65 + percent commission

### Marketing and Advertising Methods and Tips
❖ Word-of-mouth referrals
❖ Flyers on community bulletin boards
❖ Coupon advertising with other businesses
❖ Networking within home-based business associations
❖ Business cards
❖ Booth at home shows
❖ Local newspaper advertisements
❖ Write a short travel column for your local paper—a short ad and information piece (you pay).

### Essential Equipment
❖ Home office: computer and related software, with Internet access for searching for travel sites and researching, business telephone with conference calling capabilities and voice mail, fax machine, and photocopier
❖ Assorted travel brochures

### Recommended Training, Experience, or Needed Skills
❖ Travel agent training, education, and experience
❖ Knowledge of the travel industry
❖ Check to see whether you need any required certificates or

licenses (as an independent agent) and permits (to operate from your home).

### Income Potential
$25,000 to $50,000

### Type of Business
$3/_4$ in home conducting business, $1/_4$ meeting in clients' homes and the agencies with which you work

### Best Customers
People who like your tours and vacations

### Success Tips
❖ With the travel industry breaking into so many different avenues, you may want to specialize in an aspect of tourism in which you have both knowledge and travel experience.
❖ You may want to add travel planning or consulting to your service.

### Franchises, Distributorships, and Licenses
Eagle Travel Service
8647 Hall Blvd.
Loxahatchee, FL 33470
Write for information.

### Additional Information
#### Recommended Reading
*Entrepreneur's Small Business Development Catalog*, "Travel Agency"; $69.50 + $ 7.95 for shipping and handling; call (800) 421-2300 for a catalog or credit card orders.
*Home-Based Travel Agent* by Kelly Monaghan (New York: Intrepid Traveler, 1997)
*How to Start and Manage a Travel Agency Business* by Jerre G. Lewis and Leslie D. Renn (Lewis and Renn Associates, 10315 Harmony Dr., Interlochen, MI 49643); $14.95 + $3

*National Business Library's Small Business Catalog,* "Travel Agency"; $49.95 + $6.60 for shipping and handling; call (800) 947-7724 for catalog or credit card orders.
*Specialty Travel Index,* Alpine Hanse, #313, 305 San Anselmon Ave., San Anselmo, CA 94960

**Organization**
National Association of Commissioned Travel Agents
P.O. Box 2398
Valley Center, CA 92082-2398
http://www.nacta.com
Send a LSASE for membership and other inquiries. "Represents the interests of independent travel entrepreneurs."

**Home Study**
There are quite a few home study, travel career training courses. For a brochure listing these (and other home study career studies), write to the National Home Study Council, 1601 18th St., NW, Washington, DC 20009.

*Additional Business Idea*
Travel gift baskets—taking orders from travel agents who will give your gift baskets to clients; preparing custom-made baskets to fit the vacation destination. See *101 Best Home-Based Businesses for Women,* "Gift Baskets," by Priscilla Y. Huff (Rocklin, CA: Prima, 1995).

## ⊸ 93 ⊷
# WOMEN'S SELF-DEFENSE INSTRUCTOR

With so many women working or going to school at all hours of the day or traveling long-distances, they need to be aware of (1) how to avoid potentially dangerous situations and (2) how to defend themselves and survive should they be in a physically threatening position. Just knowing how to react automatically from practice in self-defense courses can often give a woman those few seconds that will make a definite difference in her life.

Start teaching your courses at YMCAs and community centers until you feel confident and have the funds to start your own independent venture.

### Estimated Start-up Costs
$1,000 (not including the fees for courses you take yourself)

### Pricing Guidelines
* Fees for courses
* Prices of your personal protection devices if you decide to sell these, too

### Marketing and Advertising Methods and Tips
* Classified ads in newspapers
* Notices in women's publications
* Flyers at health centers, health clubs, and beauty salons
* Word-of-mouth referrals
* Community talks to women's groups, high schools, and colleges

### Essential Equipment
* Mats
* Booklets and manuals you self-publish or provide
* Personal protection devices if you sell these as part of your business

### Recommended Training, Experience, or Needed Skills
* Certificates, courses, and training in self-defense methods
* Background in law enforcement
* Physical agility and coordination
* Ability to teach and communicate well

### Income Potential
$20,000 to $40,000, depending on the density of the population where you live

## Type of Business
$1/2$ in home if you have a room and parking area for students, $1/2$ out of home holding classes in individuals' homes or other locations

## Best Customers
Women and teenagers who drive, walk, or travel at times by themselves

## Success Tips
❖ Take the courses needed to qualify you as an instructor of self-defense for women.
❖ Take courses and pay attention to studies of why and how women have become victims in different situations; consult with experts and law enforcement officers who are specialists and experienced in these areas so you can better develop effective tactics and strategies for students to use. Have some of these experts (and women who have survived attacks and situations) speak to your groups.
❖ Offer classes in your home if you have facilities or in your clients' homes with a group of their women relatives and friends.
❖ Develop self-defense, street-wise, and survival tactics for older women who may not be as agile as younger women.
❖ Offer safety tips for women traveling to strange cities.

## Additional Information
### Recommended Reading
*Martial Arts for Women: A Practical Guide for Women* by Jennifer Lawler (Wethersfield, CT: Turtle, 1998)
*Street Smarts: A Personal Safety Guide for Women* by Louise Rafkin (New York: Harper, 1996)

## Additional Business Idea
Office etiquette coach—being a consultant to professional women on how to handle themselves in office "politics" and pro-

cedures, including some workplace "survival" tips. See *201 Ways to Say No Gracefully and Effectively (Quick-Tip Survival Guide)* by Alan Axelrod and Jim Holtje (New York: McGraw-Hill, 1997) for ideas on how to dodge work overload, bad ideas, prying questions, nuisances, bullies, and so forth.

<ce>•

# MISCELLANEOUS SPECIALTY TRAVEL SERVICES

✤ Local biking and walking tours
✤ Luggage rental
✤ Travel newsletter—targeted toward a specific industry or audience

# Word Businesses

*I have all the attributes of a writer: denial, pain, and self-abuse.*
— Buzz Bissinger, author of *A Prayer for the City*

### Resources for Writers
**Recommended Reading**
*A Beginner's Guide to Getting Published* by the editors of Writer's
   Digest (Cincinnati, OH: Writer's Digest Books, 1994)
*Freelancers Marketplace: The Freelance Writer's Guide to the Markets,*
   10308 Oso Grande NE, Albuquerque, NM 87111; $59/
   eighteen issues per year
*How to Be Your Own Literary Agent* by Martin P. Levin (Berkeley,
   CA: Ten Speed Press, 1997)
*How to Make Money Publishing from Home* by Lisa Shaw (Rocklin,
   CA: Prima, 1997)
*How to Start a Home-Based Communications Business: An
   Unabridged Guide* by Louann Nagy Werksma (Old Saybrook,
   CT: Globe Pequot, 1995)
*How to Start a Home-Based Writing Business,* 2nd ed., by Lucy V.
   Parker (Old Saybrook, CT: Globe Pequot, 1997)

*National Writers Union Guide to Freelance Rates and Standard Practice* by National Writer's Union (Cincinnati, OH: Betterway, 1994)

*Net Gain: Expanding Your Book's Markets through Virtual Communities* by John Hagel III and Arthur G. Armstrong (Boston: Harvard Business School Press, 1997)

*1001 Ways to Market Your Books*, 5th ed., by John Kremer (1998; Open Horizons, P.O. Box 205, Fairfield, IA 52556-0205)

*Radio-TV Interview Report*, Bradley Communications Corporation, 135 E. Plumstead Ave., P.O. Box 1206, Lansdowne, PA 19050-8206; publication in which to advertise your books; sent to radio and television producers, journalists, and publication editors. Write for advertising costs.

*The Writer*, 120 Boylston St., Boston, MA 02116-4615; $28/year

*Writer's Digest* Magazine, P.O. Box 2124, Harlan, IA 51593-2313; $23.96/twelve issues

*Writer's Guide to Book Editors, Publishers, and Literary Agents, 1997-1998* by Jeff Herman (Rocklin, CA: Prima, 1997)

*Writer's Journal*, 3585 N. Lexington Ave., Suite 328, Arden Hills, MN 55126-8056; $14.97/one issue per year

*The Writer's Lawyer: Essential Legal Advice for Writers and Editors in all Media* by Ronald Goldfarb and Gail Ross (New York: Time Books, 1989)

*Writer's Market*, book and CD (1998; Writer's Digest Books, 1507 Dana Ave., Cincinnati, OH 45207-1005); call (800) 289-0963 for credit card orders.

*writers.net* by Gary Gach (Rocklin, CA: Prima, 1997); Internet resources for writers

*Writing for Money*, 526 Boston Post Rd., Wayland, MA 01778-1833; $89/seventeen issues

Writer's Digest Book Club (see address under "Home Study" on page 372) offers many monthly choices on all writing genres. Writer's Digest Books publishes the following annual market books: *Children's Writer's and Illustrator's Market, Novel and Short Story Writer's Market, Poet's Market*, and others. It also publishes the following sourcebooks: *Mystery Writer's Sourcebook, Romance Writer's Sourcebook*, and *Science Fiction and Fantasy Writer's Sourcebook*.

**Organizations**
    American Society of Journalists and Authors
    1501 Broadway, Suite 302
    New York, NY 10036

    American Writer's Institute
    26 Lazy Eight Dr.
    Daytona Beach, FL 32124
Presents "Writing for Dollar$" seminars.

    Many national and international writers' groups and organizations are listed in the *Literary Market Place* and *International Literary Market Place* (New Providence, NJ: Bowker, both published annually), which you can find in the reference section of most libraries. You can also look in *Gale's Directory of Associations* (Detroit, MI: Gale Research, annual; http://www.gale.com). For local writers' groups, contact your public librarians, who often know of other writers and groups with whom you can network.

**Home Study**
    Writer's Digest School
    1507 Dana Ave.,
    Cincinnati, OH 45207

    NRI Schools
    4401 Connecticut Ave., NW
    Washington, DC 20008
Offers "Fiction Writing," "Nonfiction Writing," and "Word Processing"; write for catalog.

## ∽ 94 ∾
# ABSTRACTING SERVICE

An abstracting service involves reading articles, journals, magazines, and other publications for a particular field or industry and writing a condensed version of these pieces for storage as computer data. The average length of an abstractor's synopsis will run ten to fifteen sentences. Abstracting provides secondary information about published works, including bibliographical data and summaries of content. The data are in standard computer format and can be uploaded to electronic databases, such as CD-ROMs, or downloaded by Internet users.

In abstracting you must answer the questions of who, what, where, when, and how. Professional abstractors recommend that an abstractor "use an economy of words" and be similar to a "newswire" story that presents the abstracted information in a "terse, informative, and critical" manner. A well-written abstract will avoid the use of jargon, abbreviations, and acronyms.

If you have expertise in a profession and/or a specific industry, enjoy reading and writing, and have good comprehension skills, this may be a good business for you.

### Estimated Start-up Costs
$3,000 to $9,000

### Pricing Guidelines
❖ $20 to $30 an hour, or a fee of $7 to $18 for each article
❖ Follow the industry guidelines (see "Organizations" on page 375).

### Marketing and Advertising Methods and Tips
❖ Direct mail and contact to database publishers and those in the industry who are looking for professional abstractors
❖ Ads in trade publications
❖ Referrals from clients
❖ Look in *Gale Directory of Databases*, 2 vols. (Detroit, MI: Gale Research, 1997), in the reference section of larger public libraries.

### Essential Equipment
❖ Home office: computer and peripherals: hard drive, back-up system, fax, printer, software, modem, and access to Internet

❖ Promotional materials: business cards, samples of your work, and resume of your expertise and experience in the industry in which you hope to specialize
❖ Your own reference library

### Recommended Training, Experience, or Needed Skills
❖ Knowledge in your field
❖ Ability to read, organize, and write about the essentials of what you are abstracting

### Income Potential
$20,000 to $35,000

### Type of Business
Full-time in your home

### Best Customers
❖ Publishers of databases and CD-ROMs
❖ Corporation libraries

### Success Tips
❖ You have to possess an understanding and knowledge of the field in which you are abstracting.
❖ You must be able compose and highlight the main points of the article as it deals with the material.
❖ Network with other abstractors.
❖ Keep current with industry trends and terms.

### Additional Information
**Recommended Reading**
*Directory of Indexing and Abstracting Courses, 1992;* available from American Society of Indexers for $15
*The Information Broker's Handbook,* 2nd ed., by Sue Rugge and Alfred Glossbrenner (New York: McGraw-Hill, 1995)

**Organizations**
   American Society of Indexers
   P.O. Box 48267
   Seattle, WA 98148-0267
Publishes the *Key Words* newsletter and has other publications
for sale; send a LSASE for more information.

   National Federation of Abstracting and Information Services
      (NFAIS)
   1518 Walnut St., Suite 307
   Philadelphia, PA 19102
Offers information, workshops, books, and a newsletter; send a
LSASE for more information.

*Additional Business Idea*
Indexing (see "Organizations" above)

## ◌ 95 ◌
# BOOK PACKAGER

Book packaging is touted as being the publishing business in the
coming years. It is one of the best methods for small publishers
to make money. A book packager may offer to larger commercial
book publishers the services of writing, editing, typesetting,
composition, document and cover design, illustration, and pre-
press and production tasks. The best job a packager can get is to
be hired as a substitute publisher. Here you suggest an idea or
concept for a book (or a series) and then go through all the steps
of having it written and produced.

   Book packagers are finding a demand in specialized markets and CD-ROM interactive products. There is a growing trend
for large commercial book publishers to contract parts or entire
projects out to book packagers and independent contractors. For
example, freelance writers could be hired to write books for a
popular children's series. If you have experience and knowledge in both book marketing and a specialized industry or
field, you could possibly have a lucrative home business with
this idea.

### Estimated Start-up Costs
❖ $4,000 to $10,000
❖ You may have long periods of no income until a project is completed and sales profits begin to come in, so be prepared to cover your expenses through savings or other work.

### Pricing Guidelines
❖ Charge by the project: in your contract you would ask for half upfront with the balance paid upon completion. To arrive at a project fee, you could charge $25 to $30 per page or $40 to $45 an hour (about $10,000 for a book of four hundred pages).
❖ Typesetting charges would be higher per page for a newsletter, flyer, and similar smaller pieces.

### Marketing and Advertising Methods and Tips
❖ Direct mail and follow-up calls to major publishers in your area of specialization
❖ Networking within the book publishing industry and contacts by attending book publishing conventions and fairs
❖ Referrals from publishers with which you have worked

### Essential Equipment
Home office equipment: computer, laser printer, fax, modem, desktop publishing and word processing software, and telephone with answering system

### Recommended Training, Experience, or Needed Skills
❖ Work experience as a project editor or as a book packager for a larger publisher
❖ English or journalism degree and/or experience in book marketing
❖ Knowledge of desktop publishing and design
❖ Ability to negotiate bids that will give you a good profit, even if you have to subcontract some of the work
❖ Excellent organizational skills
❖ Concept of how long a project can take to complete

## Income Potential
$40,000 to $85,000 (when you have been established as a well-known book packager)

## Type of Business
Mostly at home handling the details of your current project—tending to a myriad of tasks and assigning ones you cannot handle, making many telephone calls, sending items through a cross-country delivery service or U.S. mail

## Best Customers
Large publishing houses that publish books in your field(s) of specialization

## Success Tips
❖ Look for undiscovered niches in the industry with which you are familiar.
❖ Get firsthand experience in the process of designing, compiling, production, handling writers and photographers, and selling and marketing books. Working in the publishing business will also help you make contacts for possible future business assignments.
❖ Try to presell your book to cover the expense of printing.
❖ Remember, a book packager needs ideas and a specialized market niche.
❖ Be prepared to travel to some of the cities that are publishing centers (e.g., New York) to meet with your clients.

## Additional Information
### Recommended Reading
*Editing, Design, and Book Production* by Charles Foster (Chicago: Pluto, 1993)
*Making Books: A Step-by-Step Guide to Your Publishing* by Gillan Chapman and Pam Robson (Brookfield, CT: Millbrook, 1994)

**Organization**
American Book Producer's Association
160 5th Ave., Suite 604
New York, NY 10010-7880
Send a LSASE for information.

**On-line Source**
For general desktop publishing information: http://www.
DesktopPublishing.com

*Additional Business Idea*
Home-based publisher (see Lisa Shaw's book cited on page 370)

## ❧ 96 ☙
## CHILDREN'S WRITER

Anyone who likes reading has a special children's book or story they remember reading or having read to them as a child. Classics such as *Good Night, Moon,* the Curious George series, Nancy Drew mysteries, *The Black Stallion, The Secret Garden,* and many, many other favorites will continue to enthrall young readers. Writing for children and teenagers has changed quite a bit over the last years with the introduction of paperback series like The Babysitter's Club and Goosebumps in addition to horror stories for older children. Publishing, like any other industry, follows trends and often is market driven.

If you want to succeed as a children's and/or teenager's writer, you have to do the following:

1. Love and respect children.
2. Decide for which age group you would like to write.
3. Learn what that age group likes and dislikes. Volunteer at a school or work with that age group in a community organization to get to understand them and their patterns of speech.
4. Start writing stories and/or short articles for submission to children's publications.

5. Study the market books, what children like to read, and what books are being published; and look for a subject that is not being covered, or present it in a different slant (join writer's groups and subscribe to industry publications to gather this information).

6. Perfect your writing skills, take courses, and learn the proper submission procedures in preparing your manuscript for a children's publication and/or book publisher.

### Estimated Start-up Costs
$2,500 to $6,000

### Pricing Guidelines
❖ For magazine articles, $50 to $500 + depending on the publication's rates, whether you are a regular contributor, and other points
❖ For books, advances run from nothing to several thousand dollars.

### Marketing and Advertising Methods and Tips
❖ Study the markets for which you are writing by using market guides, obtaining a copy of the catalog of a publisher (so you can see what kinds of books they are publishing), and reading their books so you get an idea about length and their audience. Then, if you believe your article or book idea is something that "fits" their line, send a SASE to request a copy of their writer's or author's submission guidelines.
❖ Get some writing credits (stories, articles published in small publications or presses).

### Essential Equipment
❖ Home office equipment: computer with word processing software (use the same programs your publishers use so you can submit your manuscript on disk), printer, and modem; assorted supplies (mailing labels, envelopes of various sizes, manuscript boxes, protected mailers for photos, computer disks, and slides)

❖ Writing reference and how-to books
❖ Quality stationery with your name, address, and telephone and fax numbers

### Recommended Training, Experience, or Needed Skills
❖ Writing courses at adult evening schools and colleges
❖ Good grammar, writing, and communication skills
❖ Ability to be creative in both fiction and nonfiction writing
❖ Persistence! If you really want to be a writer, you have to keep on writing and searching for the market(s) that work best for your writing.

### Income Potential
$5,000 to $20,000 +. It takes a long time (though not always) to earn enough money to support yourself full-time. You can diversify as a writer, writing articles, stories, and books. One popular children's writer tours elementary schools and gives two forty-five-minute programs for $1,200. She visits an average of sixty schools each year, plus she receives royalties twice a year from sales of her children's books.

### Type of Business
$3/4$ in home writing and marketing, $1/4$ (or more) out marketing your books

### Best Customers
First write a good story or article for the age of the children you prefer; then submit to the markets that publish writing similar (subject, audience, genre, etc.) to yours.

### Success Tips
❖ Article writing: study back issues of a children's publication (at least a year's worth) to see what has and has not been covered. Follow its writer's guidelines. Know which rights you should sell (or not sell).

❖ Books: treat each book like a new business, complete with business plan and marketing strategies. You have to be active in promoting your book through talks, school presentations, and so on.

❖ Write more than one book so you develop a loyal readership among children.

❖ Learn about contracts and your rights as a writer.

## Additional Information
### Recommended Reading

*Children's Writer* newsletter; Institution of Children's Literature, 95 Long Ridge Rd., West Redding, CT 06896-1124; $24/year; specialized newsletter with tips and markets for your children's writing; contests

*The Children's Writer's Word Book* by Alijandra Mogilner (Cincinnati, OH: Writer's Digest Books, 1992)

*National Business Library's 1998 Small Business Catalog*, "How to Write and Sell Children's Books"; $39.95 + $6.50 for shipping and handling; call (800) 947-7724 for a catalog or credit card orders.

*1997 Children's Writer's and Illustrator's Market* by Alice P. Buening, ed. (Cincinnati, OH: Writer's Digest Books, annual)

*SCBWI Bulletin;* bimonthly newsletter of the Society of Children's Book Writers and Illustrators

*Ten Steps to Publishing Children's Books* by Berthe Amoss and Eric Suben (Cincinnati, OH: Writer's Digest Books, 1997)

*Writing with Pictures: How to Write and Illustrate Children's Books* by Uri Shulevitz (New York: Watson-Guptill, 1997)

### Organization

Society of Children's Book Writers and Illustrators (SCBWI)
345 North Maple Drive, Suite 296
Beverly Hills, CA 90210
http://www.scbwi.org

Offers children's book writers and illustrators information on seminars, conferences, critique groups, and an informative bimonthly newsletter. Regional chapters also hold conferences and publish newsletters.

**Home Study**
The Institute of Children's Literature
93 Long Ridge Rd.
West Redding, CT 06896-1124
Write for course details.

*Additional Business Idea*
Children's book illustrator—see these additional resources: *How to Write and Illustrate Children's Books* by Treld Pelkey Bicknell and Felicity Trotman, eds. (Cincinnati, OH: North Light Books, 1988); *The Very Best of Children's Book Illustration* by Society of Illustrators (Cincinnati, OH: North Light Books, 1993); and *Picturebook* (3911 10th Ave., S., Birmingham, AL 35222), a directory in which illustrators advertise (one-page ad starts at $1,800) that is sent to art directors, publishers, and editors of children's books.

## ✑ 97 ✑
# FREELANCE MAGAZINE WRITER
When you think of all the newsletters, magazines, and on-line sites—all with editors needing writers—you can well imagine that many markets exist for freelance writers. While all those publications need writers, you still have to follow guidelines and procedures before any editor will even look at your article, let alone publish it. If you are planning to be a professional writer, you have to expect payment and accept rejection.

Often rejections by magazine editors have little to do with the actual writing itself but rather with the fact that the writer did not research the magazine she was querying to see whether her idea was appropriate for the publication. Here are some pointers to becoming a paid magazine writer:

1. Research your markets; review at least a year's worth of back issues for the subjects covered.
2. Send a publication a SASE for a copy of its writers' guidelines.

3. Keep a master plan of potential magazine markets. In the event your work or query is rejected, you can send it right out, again.

4. Your query letter should include your title, a specific topic, the rights you are selling, the estimated word length, your credentials for writing the article, and copies of your writing clips (photocopies of your previously published articles).

5. If you are given the go-ahead, make sure either you or your editor makes a contract stipulating the payment, the rights, the word length, expenses the magazine will pay, the deadline, and any other pertinent information. This is the time to ask questions—not the day before your deadline!

### Estimated Start-up Costs
$3,000 to $5,000

### Pricing Guidelines
❖ Most magazines have standard rates for articles, but if you become a regular contributor, you can ask for more money per article.
❖ Rates can range from payment "in copies" to $2,000 for a major magazine article. Just do not give your writing away for free.

### Recommended Marketing and Advertising Methods and Tips
❖ Research the audience, topics, slant, and so forth, of the magazines for which you want to write, and send them a query letter (a letter to the editors to interest them in your proposed article). Do not call editors or fax them about an article idea. Some do accept e-mail queries, but do so only if they state that in their market listing or writers' guidelines.
❖ Trade and hobby magazines are often easier to break into with publishing, especially if you have experience with their topics.

## *Essential Equipment*

❖ Home office equipment: computer with word processing software (use the same programs your editors use so you can submit your manuscript on disk), printer, and modem; assorted supplies (mailing labels, envelopes of various sizes, manuscript boxes, protected mailers for photos, computer disks, and slides)

❖ Writing reference and how-to books

❖ Quality stationery with your name, address, and telephone and fax numbers

## *Recommended Training, Experience, or Needed Skills*

❖ Writing courses at adult evening schools or colleges

❖ Good grammar, writing, and communication skills

❖ Ability to be creative in both fiction and nonfiction writing

❖ Persistence! If you really want to be a writer, you have to keep on writing and searching for the market(s) that work best for you writing.

❖ Professionalism—send out only your best writing and perfect-looking manuscripts.

## *Income Potential*

❖ $1,000 to $25,000 +

❖ Have a goal to try new markets each year and maybe to write a book. Most writers have other jobs, but if you can market your ideas and keep your queries circulating, you can increase your earnings each year.

## *Type of Business*

Full-time in home

## *Best Customers*

❖ Magazines and publications to which you subscribe

❖ Magazines and publications for which you have already written before. Most editors prefer to establish a good working relationship with writers they like, to the point they may call you with regular assignments.

✤ Magazines and publications in which you have knowledge about the industry

## Success Tips

✤ Deliver your articles on time and according to the specifications in your contract or agreement.

✤ Always check (and double-check) your facts, quotes, and other information with your sources and any persons you quoted.

✤ Having photos (yours or a professional's) to accompany a piece helps sell an article idea to an editor (make sure you have a photo release signed by featured individuals).

✤ Have an "idea box" in which you put thoughts for possible future articles.

✤ Perfect your writing style—listen for your own "voice."

✤ Study the different forms of articles: the list, true-life dramas, food/recipe, travel, women's issues, how-to (most popular), round-up, personal, and the essay.

## Additional Information

### Recommended Reading

*The Magazine Article: How to Think It, Plan It, Write It* by Peter P. Jacobs (Bloomington: Indiana University Press, 1997)

*Magazine Writing That Sells* by Don McKinney (Cincinnati, OH: Writer's Digest Books, 1994)

*Writer's Digest Handbook of Making Money Freelance Writing* by Amanda Boyd and Thomas Clark, editors of *Writer's Digest* Magazine (Cincinnati, OH: Writer's Digest Books, 1997)

## Additional Business Ideas

✤ Teaching freelance writing—if you have a degree in English, writing, and/or journalism, teach writing courses at colleges and universities. If you are a published writer, you can teach an adult evening school class.

✤ Start your own magazine—see *Handbook of Magazine Publishing*, 2nd ed., by Folio Publishing Group, Nashville, TN (1983); this book may be out of print, so check your local library system for a copy or Amazon.com on the Internet.

## ☙ 98 ❧
# LEGAL DIGESTING SERVICE

A legal digesting service is also known as a deposition digesting service. As a legal digester, you summarize depositions as well as a variety of statements that have been taken by legal professionals from parties involved in litigation transactions. If you have experience in being a transcriptionist and/or a knowledge of legal terminology, you might consider specializing in this type of service, especially if you live near a county seat or federal court offices.

### Estimated Start-up Costs
$5,000 to $9,000

### Pricing Guidelines
$30 to $45 an hour, or go by industry recommendations

### Marketing and Advertising methods and Tips
✤ Contact legal firms for which you have worked or with which you made contacts.
✤ Classified ads in local legal publications, the journal of the trial lawyers' association, and your state's bar journal
✤ Referrals from lawyers with whom you have worked
✤ Direct mail followed by calls for an appointment to new lawyers setting up legal practices
✤ Direct mail to local district courts

### Essential Equipment
✤ Promotional materials: business cards and pamphlets describing your services, experience, and qualifications

❖ Home office: computer and related software, printer, modem for Internet access and e-mail transmissions; telephone and answering system; fax; dictation and transcription equipment
❖ Legal reference books

## Recommended Training, Experience, or Needed Skills
❖ Training programs in legal transcription (see "Additional Information" below)
❖ Experience working in a legal firm
❖ Ability to understand legal terminology
❖ Good typing and spelling skills
❖ Knowledge of word processing, dictation, and transcription equipment
❖ Excellent listening and comprehension skills, writing ability

## Income Potential
$30,000 to $40,000

## Type of Business
$3/4$ in home, $1/4$ marketing and meeting with your clients

## Best Customers
❖ Law firms that are doing serious litigation
❖ Paralegal services that subcontract legal digesting services
❖ Local courts

## Success Tips
❖ Strive for accuracy and a fast turnaround time.
❖ Be professional and discreet with the information you handle.
❖ Work or volunteer in a public defender's office for experience.

## Additional Information
### Recommended Reading
*Basics of Legal Document Preparation* by Robert R. Cummins (Albany, NY: Delmar, 1996)

*Expert Legal Writing* by Terri Leclercq (Austin: University of Texas Press, 1995)

*Legal Analysis and Writing for Paralegals* by William Putnam (New York: Van Nostrand Reinhold, 1997)

*Legal and Paralegal Businesses on Your Home-Based PC* by Kathryn Sheehy Hussey and Rick Benzel (Blue Ridge Summit, PA: Windcrest/McGraw-Hill, 1994)

*Legal Terminology and Transcription* by Marilyn K. Wallis (Upper Saddle River, NJ: Prentice Hall, 1996)

*Micrososft Work: Quick Start for Legal Professionals* by Penny Smalley (Upper Saddle River: Prentice Hall, 1997)

**Home Study**
At-Home Professions
2001 Lowe St.
Fort Collins, CO 80525
Legal transcription course; write for information.

Hillside Digesting Services
P.O. Box 288
Fallbrook, CA 92088
(800) 660-3376
Write or call for information about the variety of training courses, samples, and marketing manuals offered for this type of legal service.

### *Additional Business Ideas*
❖ Independent paralegal—for home study options to earn a paralegal certificate, write Graduate School, USDA, Room 129, 600 Maryland Ave., SW, Washington, DC 20078-0952.
❖ Scopist—see "Court Services" in *101 Best Small Businesses for Women* by Priscilla Y. Huff (Rocklin, CA: Prima, 1997)

## ৵৹ 99 ৵৹
# POETRY-ON-DEMAND—
# CUSTOM RHYMES FOR EVERY TIME
It is very difficult to earn money as a poet. Most of the time, it is hard to get poetry published unless you publish it yourself;

establish a name for yourself; have a degree in literature, English, or journalism; and are a professor or well-known celebrity. However, in addition to having a poem published by newsletter, magazine, or book publishers, you can also try some creative and fun entrepreneurial ventures with your poetry.

Consider Esther Fox, for example. By day, she is a full-time secretary to a school superintendent. By night (and on her days off), she writes custom-designed poems for special occasions: wedding anniversaries, high school graduation, birthdays, retirement celebrations, and other special occasions. She also will compose poems for eulogies (though she usually does not charge for these).

In her business, "Fox Tales," customers contact Esther with details about the occasion and the person(s) for whom the poem(s) are to be written. Then she writes a draft of a poem(s) according to the information she is given. Esther will ask her customers to proofread the poem(s) for accuracy and any changes they wish her to make. She will make final copies printed from her computer on prebordered paper chosen by her customers. Framing adds to Esther's fees.

For tips on writing custom poems for money, send $2 and a LSASE to Esther Fox, "Fox Tales", 412 Philmont Ave., Feasterville, PA 19053.

### Estimated Start-up Costs
$1,000 to $3,000

### Pricing Guidelines
$25 to $50 per poem—usually eight to ten stanzas (four lines); a short rhyme (as for a card) may be less; framing and paper will add to your price.

### Marketing and Advertising Methods and Tips
✤ Volunteer to write poems for occasions of family members and friends.
✤ Classified ads in local publications and free newspapers

* Referrals from satisfied customers and others who hear and read your poems
* Press releases for an unusual business
* Radio ads
* Start a poetry group at your local library.

## Essential Equipment
* Home office: computer with desktop publishing design, lettering, and word processing software; color inkjet or laser printer; answering system and phone
* Assorted prebordered, colored paper and assorted frames

## Recommended Training, Experience, or Needed Skills
* Talent and creative ability to write poetry
* Good communication skills
* Knowledge of framing techniques
* Take poetry-writing courses at local adult evening classes or colleges.

## Income Potential
$5,000 to $7,500 a year—more if you attend craft fairs on a regular basis and sell your mounted poems

## Type of Business
$3/4$ in home writing and marketing, $1/4$ consulting with your clients or attending craft shows

## Best Customers
Family and friends of people having birthdays; new parents, graduates, retirees; or those who are celebrating anniversaries, holidays, Father's and Mother's Days, and so forth

## Success Tips
* Enjoy the poetry writing process.

❖ Enjoy people and trying to get their sentiments into your poems.

### Additional Information
**Recommended Reading**
*1997 Poet's Market* by Christine Martin and Chantelle Bentley, eds. (Cincinnati, OH: Writer's Digest Books, annual)
*Poets and Writers Magazine,* 72 Spring St., New York, NY 10012; $14.97/year
*Poet's Guide: How to Publish and Perform Your Work* by Michael J. Bugeja (Brownsville, OK: Story Line Press, 1995)
*The Poet's Handbook* by Judson Jerome (Cincinnatti, OH: Writer's Digest Books, annual)

### Organizations
American Academy of American Poets
584 Broadway, Suite 1208
New York, NY 10012-3250
http://www.poets.org

Poetry Society of America
15 Gramercy Park
New York, NY 10003

### Additional Business Ideas
Writing advertising slogans for small and home-based businesses

## ∝ 100 ∾
## PUBLIC RELATIONS SPECIALIST

A public relations specialist's role is to take her client's mission and theme to the public to educate and attract more customers and markets to her client's business or organization. Your work can involve promoting onetime events and new products, writing regular press releases and information pieces to the media, and hopefully being hired on a retainer basis. Your work could also involve writing case histories, speeches, papers, reports, manuals, newsletters, audiovisual scripts, and proposals as well as editing work of trainees, partners, agencies, freelancers, and employers. It is a highly competitive and challenging field but one that is always busy and exciting.

With more companies downsizing and home businesses starting and needing publicity, you should be able to find a selection of markets for your public relations business.

### Estimated Start-up Costs
$3,000 to $10,000

### Pricing Guidelines
* $50 to $90 an hour or $200 to $1,500 a day, as well as per-project and retainer fees
* Go by your industry rates and standards and the budgets your clients have for your type of work.

### Marketing and Advertising Methods and Tips
* Decide what industry and size of businesses you prefer and whether you want to specialize in just one area of public relations (i.e., newsletter editor, press release and media contact specialist, etc.), and then design your promotional materials to highlight and target the potential clients with which you wish to work.
* Promotional materials: can be composed in a kit to send or deliver directly to clients and then followed up with a telephone call to make a personal appointment
* Volunteer for nonprofit groups to get referrals and experience (you may also be hired by them in the future).
* Join local Chambers of Commerce and home business associations.
* Direct mail to new businesses
* Yellow Pages
* Ads in trade industry publications

### Essential Equipment
❖ Home office equipment: computer, modem, hard drive, laser printer, photocopier, public relations software, desktop publishing software; business telephone with teleconferencing capabilities and an answering system; fax machine; eventually a cellular phone
❖ Promotional materials: portfolio of samples of your public relations writing
❖ Professional attire

### Recommended Training, Experience, or Needed Skills
❖ Courses/education in communications, marketing, and advertising
❖ Experience working in these areas and working or volunteering in the public relations field
❖ Helps to have an understanding in the industry in which you will want to work
❖ Must be a talented and skillful writer who can inform as well as persuade and convince your audience of your clients' credibility and worthiness
❖ Have to be energetic, outgoing, and straightforward in dealing with your clients and obtaining clients for them

### Income Potential
$30,000 to $50,000 +

### Type of Business
$1/2$ in home working and conducting your business, $1/2$ meeting with your clients and marketing your business

### Best Customers
❖ Businesses that do not have a public relations firm and whose service and products need to be presented periodically to the public and/or their particular industry
❖ Other home-based and microbusinesses
❖ Nonprofit organizations that regularly seek contributions

❖ Larger companies striving to communicate and foster better employee relations with management and other workers
❖ Public and private school districts
❖ Museums and science centers
❖ Recreational parks

## Success Tips

❖ Get experience and on-the-job training and experience before you advertise for your first client.
❖ You have to build trust both with your clients and their customers.
❖ Be creative (and appropriate) in your work.
❖ Develop good communications and working relationships with your clients.

## Additional Information
### Recommended Reading

*Dartnell's Public Relations Handbook*, 4th ed., by Robert L. Dilenschneifer (Chicago: Dartnell, 1996)

*Getting Publicity: The Very Best for Your Small Business*, 2nd ed., by Tana Fletcher and Julia Rockler (Bellingham, WA: Self-Counsel Press, 1995)

*Handbook for Public Relations Writing* by Thomas Bivins (Lincolnwood, IL: NTC Business Books, 1996)

*How to Start a Home-Based Public Relations Business*, 2nd ed., by Louann Nagy Werksma (Old Saybrook, CT: Globe Pequot, 1997)

*Public Relations News*, 127 E. 80th St., New York, NY 10021

### Organization

Public Relations Society of America
33 Irving Place, 3rd Floor
New York, NY 10003

## Additional Business Idea

Specialize in promotional newsletters for businesses—contact the Newsletter Publishers Association, 1401 Wilson Blvd., Suite

207, Arlington, VA 22209; $395 membership includes discounts on insurance, supplies, newsletter, and such books as *How to Launch a Newsletter* and *Success in Newsletter Publishing,* plus a current directory of members and industry supplies.

## ❧ 101 ❧
## TECHNICAL WRITER

A technical writer presents scientific and technical data in an understandable form that can be comprehended by readers who are not scientists or engineers. Technical writers help scientists, engineers, and experts communicate their information and instructions to their readers so that the readers in turn can put the information to practical use. Having a specialization in fields or areas that you will be writing for is usually what qualifies you to be hired; few attempt to write in a field with which they have little experience. Your writing may also involve organizing and writing reports about new discoveries and theories in your field.

### Estimated Start-up Costs
$4,500 to $9,000

### Pricing Guidelines
$35 to $80 per hour, depending on the grade of complexity and type of readership

### Marketing and Advertising Methods and Tips
+ Referrals from contacts made while working as a technical writer for a company or agency
+ Direct mail to companies in your specialized industry
+ Business cards and samples of writing projects in which you have had input (manuals, reports, etc.)
+ Networking with other members of a trade or professional association
+ Ads in trade journals and/or publications

### Essential Equipment
* Home office: computer with industry-related and word processing software, printer, modem, photocopier, and telephone/fax combination
* Samples of your writing

### Recommended Training, Experience, or Needed Skills
* Degree in the area in which you plan to specialize
* Technical writers for print publications must have excellent verbal communication skills to interact with experts.
* The ability to turn technical jargon into clear and understandable language for the layperson. The technical writer for on-line documentation is challenged to understand all the technical aspects of a topic or program and be able to write documentation that the user will be able to understand and implement.
* Along with a degree, journalism and writing courses are also helpful.

### Income Potential
$25,000 to $75,000 a year

### Type of Business
3/4 in home, 1/4 out of home consulting and meeting with companies and businesses

### Best Customers
* Computer software companies
* U.S. government branches (defense, agriculture, etc.)
* Pharmaceutical firms
* Hospitals
* Colleges and universities
* Electronics industries, food-processing plants, or chemical manufacturers

❖ Research laboratories
❖ Communications firms

## Success Tips

❖ Find the type of technical writing you enjoy and are the most adept at writing.
❖ If possible, get feedback from your readers or users to better understand what information they can and cannot grasp.
❖ Write with the knowledge of the expert but with the understanding of what the reader needs to know to easily use the information presented.

## Additional Information

### Recommended Reading

*The American Management Association (AMA) Style Guide for Business Writing* (New York: AMACON, 1996)

*Basic Technical Writing* by Herman M. Weisman (New York: Macmillan, 1994)

*The Essentials of Technical Writing* by Gary Blake and Robert Bly (New York: Macmillan, 1995)

*Making Money in Technical Writing* by Peter Kent (New York: ARCO, 1997)

### Organization

Society for Technical Communication
901 N. Stuart St., Suite 904
Arlington, VA 22031-1854
Web site: http://www.stc-va.org
e-mail: membership@stc-va.org

## Additional Business Idea

Speechwriting—for information on the home study course "Introduction to Speechwriting" (eleven lessons), write to Graduate School, USDA, Room 129, 600 Maryland Ave., SW, Washington, DC 20078-0952.

# Glossary of Business Terms

*Accounts payable* is the liability of a company and the balances due to suppliers of services or goods.

*Accounts receivable* is the sum owed for services or goods that have been furnished. It is a business's assets.

*Ad allowance* is the contribution of money by the vendor toward the cost of advertising.

*Advertising* is the informing of people in your marketing community of the features and advantages of your service or product.

*Asset* is a single item of value, tangible or intangible, to its owner.

*Assets* are the total of an individual's or business' resources, such as ownership of property, buildings, money, fixtures, and so forth.

*Bartering* is the exchange of your services for something of value to you from your client.

*Break-even point* is the dollar amount your business must make to break even; that is, sales income must equal costs. To stay in business, you need to make a profit, so the price you charge must be higher than the cost of providing the service or product.

*Business interruption insurance* covers a business's continuing expenses, such as taxes and payroll, as well as loss of net profit.

*Business plan* is a written description and strategic plan that includes a definition of the business's products and/or services, financial strategies, organization, summation of overhead, start-up and operating costs, potential markets, and the people involved in making the business operate and succeed.

*Capital* is a business's net worth—the assets minus the liabilities.

*COD* stands for collect (or cash) on delivery. It means payment must be made on goods when they are received or delivered.

*Corporation* is a legal entity that functions somewhat like an individual, legally and for tax purposes. Liabilities are held by the corporation, minimizing the personal liability for owners.

*Cost* is the price charged by the maker for merchandise.

*Credit* is the power or ability to obtain goods in exchange for a pledge to pay later.

*Cybermall* is a collection of business-related Web sites. http://www.cybermall.com

*DBA* stands for "doing business as." If you include your legal name as part of your business, you can skip this step in most states. However, if you are planning to conduct business using a fictitious name, you will be expected to file a DBA so the public knows you are launching a business using a name other than your own. You can generally file a DBA at your county clerk's office or with an attorney.

*Depreciation* is a deduction that can be written off the value of property (i.e., office equipment, etc., but not land because it is not expendable) over a period of time. Check with your accountant for the latest information on business deductions.

*Disaster recovery* is the service offered by specialized firms, including the large computer manufacturers, to help businesses avoid the loss of vital computer data.

*Double-entry accounting* is a system in which the total of all the entries on the left side are balanced by an equal number of entries on the right-side. Debits pertain to the left-side entries; credits, to right-side entries. A credit or debit can be applied to any general ledger account, whether it is an expense, asset, liability, capital, or income.

*EIN* stands for a federal employer identification number. If you are a sole proprietor, you can use your social security number instead, but many business forms require an EIN, so all business owners should consider applying for one. Contact your closest U.S. Small Business Administration branch office, or call the IRS for the appropriate form.

*Expense* is the cost of a good or service—the money spent to run your business.

*Fixed expenses* are those that generally do not change from month to month (i.e., rent, taxes, etc.).

*"Flaming"* is being inundated with hate mail in your electronic mailbox (e-mail) in retaliation for not following the unwritten rules of Internet etiquette.

*Franchise* is a business contract that gives you the right to sell a product or service within a certain area.

*Franchisee* (you, the licensee) is the person who pays a royalty and often a franchise fee for the right to sell and distribute the franchisor's products and use its trade name or trademark.

*Franchisor* (the owner of the franchise; also the licensor) is the person who sells his or her trade name and business system to a franchisee.

*General ledger* is the primary records of the expenses, income, assets, and liabilities of a business.

*Gross income* usually pertains to a business's income before deductions. With your home office, gross income is your business's income minus the expenses that do not relate to your home use. Contact your accountant or local IRS office for "business use of your home" deductions.

*Income* is money received for goods and/or services as well as from other sources such as rents, investments, and so forth.

*Invoice* is a list of itemized statements from a manufacturer showing the charges for the merchandise. It should agree with the price shown on the purchase order.

*Liability* concerns debts or monetary obligations to another party.

*Limited liability corporation* is a business structure in which income and income taxes are distributed among partners, but the partners are not personally liable for debts.

*LSASE*—see SASE.

*Marketing* is all the activities involved in the buying and selling of a product or service.

*Market niche* is a defined group of customers who are particularly suited for your product or service.

*Market share* is the percentage of the total available market that your business returns in profits.

*Net income* means profit remaining after business expenses have been taken out.

*Networking* is a sharing of information and work experiences by a like group of people (entrepreneurs) within a specific business or trade industry.

*Overhead* is the overall cost of running a business other than the cost of equipment, materials, and production.

*Partnership* is an association of two or more people working as co-owners of a business with the intent of making a profit. Both individuals are liable for the business, and general partners can share unlimited liability, with each usually responsible for the acts of the other. It is advisable to talk to a business attorney to have an agreement drawn up between both partners that covers such aspects as what happens if one partner dies or wants to dissolve the partnership and other related matters.

*Price* is the value placed on what is exchanged.

*Purchase order* is the record of agreement made with the manufacturer that includes costs, discount terms, and the shipping process.

*Retail* is selling directly to your customer.

*ROI* stands for return on investment.

*SASE* stands for self-addressed, stamped envelope, often required by associations and publishers when more information is requested or manuscripts are sent for submission. Most often, a #10 envelope (a long business-size envelope, or LSASE) should be sent with the information request or manuscript.

*S corporation* a unique type of corporation that provides the advantages of a corporation but, unlike a corporation, is treated for income tax purposes as a flow-through entity.

*Sole proprietorship* is the form of your business if you start it yourself—a business owned by one individual. It is the fastest way to start a business. Check with a knowledgeable attorney about licensing or other legal requirements. Profits and losses are simply included on your individual tax returns. On the downside, if someone sues your business, he or she may be able to sue you personally, and your personal assets are subject to those claims.

*"Spamming"* is transmitting advertisements actively through talk groups or by unsolicited e-mail, which is an infraction of the unwritten code of business etiquette on the Internet.

*Suite software* are computer programs that offer full-featured, software applications all in one package for your business.

*Testimonial* is a compliment from a customer. With customers' permission, you should use testimonials as part of your advertising and in your promotional materials.

*The Thomas Register of Manufacturers* is a massive multivolume directory, organized by subject matter, that lists thousands of North American manufactures of everything from office equipment to chairs. Its listing includes both light and heavy industry and can be found in the reference section of most libraries.

*Trade association* is a group of people formed to promote the information and guidelines of a particular industry (e.g., secretarial services, crafters, consultants, etc.).

*URL (uniform resource locator)* is a string of keyboard characters that designates the exact address of every page, graphic image, and file on the World Wide Web. Each address starts with http://.

*Value* is the worth of your product, service, or expertise. It is the sole justification for the prices you charge.

*Variable expenses* are also known as variable costs. Costs will increase with your volume of sales and income.

*Wholesale* is selling directly to a store or dealer who, in turn, adds her profit margin and sells directly to the customer.

# Frequently Asked Questions (FAQs)

**Q: What are some characteristics of a good idea for a business?**
A: With both the husband and wife working today in most families, any business that (1) saves people time and (2) solves a problem of some sort has a good chance to succeed.
**Q: How can I find the best business for me?**
A: Here are a few tips from successful entrepreneurs:

1. List all the things you like to do (and have some experience with) and all the things you think you would like to do.
2. Read business books and publications to get a list of business ideas that could combine your experiences, skills, and the work you would really like to do.
3. Find out which businesses from your idea list exist in your surrounding communities, and see how your business idea would compare; or if there is not a business that you might like to start currently in your area, do some preliminary research to see whether there are potential customers to sustain your business.
4. Narrow your choice down to two or three businesses, and learn all you can about running such businesses—take a course, work in the industry, talk to women entrepreneurs

in similar businesses (in your area or in a noncompeting area), draw up business plans, and so forth. Then—and only then—when you feel you are ready and have had all your questions answered to your satisfaction, open for business!

**Q: How do I know whether I have a business or a hobby?**
A: If you do not already have an accountant, you should consult one who specializes in working with home-based and small businesses. He or she can help you make the distinction. Here are some guidelines from the IRS:

1. Is your intent of your venture to make a profit?
2. An owner of a business keeps meticulous business records.
3. Do you declare reasonable losses?
4. Do you document any loans and money you have invested in your business?
5. A business shows a profit in three of five consecutive years.
6. Can you prove you are advertising for more customers?
7. Does your home business qualify for home office deductions?
8. Do you keep separate business and personal records?

**Q: Can I start more than one business?**
A: Yes, one man in my neighborhood owns eighteen businesses! Do not limit yourself; if you have skills and experience in more than one area, go ahead. One woman in my community does custom sewing and also has a soap-making business. Some businesses are seasonal (e.g., growing herbs, landscaping, etc.), so you could fill in the winter months with some other business (teaching skiing, tutoring, writing, etc.).

**Q: What if my local zoning laws do not permit a home-based business?**
A: Many times local ordinances do not mention (specifically) home-based business restrictions (they usually deal with commercial zoning); however, some do restrict conducting business from your home. First, it is best to be honest and find out what your zoning laws state. If there are restrictions, see whether

you can file a variance to get a "special use" permit and learn to whom you should address your request.

Put your request in the form of a professional-looking proposal that describes your business, including whether you will need customer parking, have regular deliveries, and the like. You may be required to notify your neighbors (officials often do not question a home business location until complaints are made by other residents). If the board rejects your proposal, you may want to seek an attorney's advice (or do so even before you approach your local officials). Most of the time the officials will grant a variance, though you may be required to pay a permit fee and/or an annual business tax.

If you need more support, having other home-based business owners' and an association's support will help. In any case, it is best to be honest and let your local officials know of your business intentions. You may "break new ground" in your community in educating your officials about the benefits of home-based businesses.

**Q: How do I organize my office?**

A: First, set up a business filing system so that you can easily access the business information you need at any time. If you are having difficulty, contact a professional organizer or ask other home-based entrepreneurs about their organizing systems. Books like *Office Clutter Cure* by Don Aslett (Cincinnati, OH: Betterway, 1995) can also give helpful tips.

**Q: What kinds of documents related to my business should I save?**

A: Check with your bookkeeper and/or accountant for the items they want you to save. It is generally recommended to save the following: all tax returns, canceled checks, deposit slips, invoices (copies), receipts for cash paid out, any type of record or receipt that backs up knowledge about your business's record-keeping systems, sales slips, receiving reports, mileage log and receipts for vehicle maintenance, health insurance payments (if you pay for coverage), and receipts for major equipment purchases.

**Q: Should I tell my customers and other businesses with which I deal that my business is home based?**

A: I always believe in being honest with your customers, but there really is no need to tell others you work from home, unless you believe that it is advantageous in promoting your business. It is more important to run your business as professionally as you would run a business conducted from an office building. It is better to concentrate on providing the best product and/or service that you can to your customers. If you do this, your customers really will not care where you conduct business!

Q: How can I project a professional image about my business even though it is home based?

A: First, your promotional materials will help sell your image. Create these with your own desktop publishing software and printers: business stationery and envelopes, business cards, brochures, and pamphlets. All should contain your logo (if you have one), your business's name, your name as president and/or owner, address, telephone and fax numbers, and your E-mail and/or Web site address. Look at others' cards and designs to help you create ones that best describe your own business and the image you want to convey. Set up your fax sheets also to contain your business information.

Second, act like a professional: have a telephone line that is answered by you or an answering system; return telephone messages promptly; keep appointments; dress appropriately when you meet with clients; handle business matters with confidence.

Q: Is it important I have my business on a "budget," and why?

A: Yes, it is very important to have a budget, which is really a financial plan that is a formal, written summary of your goals and plans in terms of dollars and cents. Having a budget and financial plan offers the following advantages to your business:

❖ It helps you evaluate early on in your business start-up how your business's revenue and expenses compare with the projected income that was stated in your original business plan. Then you can adjust the running of your business accordingly.

❖ Creating a budget also forces you to plan ahead and set goals. Business experts suggest after you analyze your business's first-year expenses, you should do a cost analysis on each service or product and concentrate on promoting the areas that are the most profitable.

❖ You can plan to seek a balance between your fixed and variable expenses (variable expenses are often more difficult to predict than fixed ones—see the glossary for more explanation).

❖ After you analyze your budget, you can also check with such organizations as Dun & Bradstreet, Moody's, and Standard & Poor's that compile financial ratings of businesses. Review businesses in your industry and their averages for income to see how your business's earnings compare.

**Q: My home-based business is not equipped to receive clients. Is there a place I can go if I have an important meeting?**

A: Yes, check to see whether there is a small business incubator or an executive suite office building in your area that allows entrepreneurs to rent offices by the hour or day. Contact the National Business Incubation Association or the Executive Suite Association (see the "Miscellaneous Sources of Help" chapter). If not, you may want to network with other business owners, schools, universities, or business organizations to make arrangements to use any of their empty offices for your meetings.

**Q: Should I have a separate telephone line for my business?**

A: Ideally, you should get a separate telephone line for your business as soon as you can afford one for several reasons: for tax deduction purposes; for a listing in your telephone company's business listing; to have an answering system to take business calls when you are not accessible; and for ordering information. If you cannot afford another phone line at the present time, you can make arrangements to have your current telephone line receive business calls designated by a different number of rings. Talk to your telephone company's business office for additional special services it may offer small businesses.

**Q: Should I get an 800 number for my business?**

A: If you take orders in your business, 800 numbers are very useful. Some areas have run out of numbers and are now using 888. Take note that not all customers like it when businesses use letters instead of numbers in their phone listings, so you should put the numbers in parentheses for convenience—for example, "1(888)555-BOOK (1-888-555-2665)."

Q:  I am enjoying being the owner of my own thriving business and the independence it gives me. Do you think my business can benefit from forming alliances with other small businesses like the big businesses do?

A:  Working with other small business owners gives a person the opportunity to have a small company but still complete the projects, do the work, and meet customer needs. One of the best books on this growing business trend is *Teaming Up* by Paul and Sarah Edwards with Rick Benzel (New York: Putnam's, 1997).

Q:  What is the best way to approach an agreement with a customer, supplier, contractor, and others?

A:  The best way is to have a written agreement or contract. It should specify such things as delivery dates of products or completed services, prices, the responsibilities of both parties, and anything else pertaining to the transaction. Some industries have standard contracts you can follow, or you can ask your lawyer to draw one up for you to use in your business.

Q:  How do I know whether I need to charge a sales tax, and how do I collect sales tax for my state?

A:  Most states charge a sales tax. You should contact your state department of revenue or commerce to apply for a "seller's permit" and to receive a sales tax number. A deposit or bond will be requested from you, which the state will keep if you do not pay the taxes you collect. Then you will file monthly or quarterly sales tax returns with your state agency. If you sell a retail product directly to the consumer, you will have to charge sales tax (check with your state for items that are sales tax exempt and about collecting sales tax from out-of-state customers).

Q:  I am interested in exporting my product to other countries. Where can I find information about this?

A:  You can write or call the International Trade Administration, The U. S. Department of Commerce, Herbert C. Hoover Bldg., 14th Street & Constitution Avenue, NW, Washington, DC 20230,

(202) 482-2000; or call the Export Opportunity Hotline at (800) 243-7232, which answers questions on overseas trade.

Q: How can I sell my products to catalog houses?

A: Contact the catalog houses to which you wish to sell your products, ask for the name of the person in charge of buying products, and inquire about the procedure for submitting a sample of your product for consideration. Most buyers want a one-page fact sheet along with a photo or sample of your product. After submitting your package, follow up with a phone call. See also *How to Sell to Catalog Houses* ($10 + $2.50 for shipping and handling; Success Publications and Ballard Books, Box 263, Warsaw, NY 14569). Also check the reference section of your public library for *The National Directory of Catalogs*, published by Oxbridge Communications and distributed by Gale Research.

Q: What considerations should I keep in mind about the products I submit to catalog houses?

A: One buyer told me, pick your best-selling products to submit, ones that are unusual or unique, and, most important, ask yourself whether you would be able to mass-produce your items in the allotted time if demand for your product becomes high and you receive many orders.

Q: I'm interested in starting a 900-number business. How do I find out more information?

A: One source of information that you can contact about the 900-number field is the Teleservices Industry Association, 777 Alexander Rd., Princeton, NJ 08540. You can also write for the basic resource guide published by the Interactive Services Association, 8403 Colesville Rd., #865, Silver Spring, MD 20910; or read *900 Know-How: How to Succeed with Your Own 900 Number Business* by Robert Mastin (Newport, RI: Aegis, 1996).

Q: Is a consulting business easier to start than other businesses?

A: To have a successful consulting venture you need to follow all the steps for a business start-up: getting capital, attracting prospective clients, establishing networking contacts, forming a marketing plan, testing your market, and timing when you will begin to consult full-time. A good source to read is *Consulting on the Side* by Mary Cook (New York: Wiley, 1996).

# Women's Business Centers

These federally funded women's business centers offer various business start-up programs and guidance, including training seminars, one-on-one counseling, speakers, and workshops. The national office's address is as follows:

U.S. Small Business Administration
Office of Women's Business Ownership
Women's Business Centers
409 3rd St. SW, 6th Floor
Washington, DC 20416
(202) 205-6673
http://www.onlinewbc.org

## Alabama
Women's Business Assistance Center (WBAC), 1301 Azalea Rd., Suite 201-A, Mobile, AL 36693

## California
West Company, 367 N. State St., Suite 201, Ukiah, CA 95482
Women Business Owners Corporation, 18 Encanto Dr., Palos Verdes, CA 90274-4215

Women's Enterprise Development Corporation (WEDC) [previously known as California AWED], 100 W. Broadway, Suite 500, Long Beach, CA 90802

Initiative for Self Employment (WI), 450 Mission St., Suite 402, San Francisco, CA 94102

## Colorado
Mi Casa Business Center for Women, 700 Knox Ct., Denver, CO 80204

## Connecticut
American Woman's Economic Development Corporation (AWED), 2001 W. Main St., Suite 140, Stamford, CT 06902

## District of Columbia
National Women's Business Center, 1250 24th St., NW, Suite 350, Washington, DC 20037

## Florida
Women's Business Development Center (WBDC), EAS 2611, University Park, Miami, FL 33199

## Georgia
Women's Economic Development Agency (WEDA), 1417 Peachtree St., NE, Suite 404, Atlanta, GA 30309

## Illinois
Women's Business Development Center, 8 S. Michigan Ave., Suite 400, Chicago, IL 60603

## Louisiana
Women Entrepreneurs for Economic Development, Inc. (WEED), 1683 N. Claiborne Ave., New Orleans, LA 70116

Women's Business Center, 2245 Peters Rd., Harvey, LA 70050

## Maine
Coastal Enterprises, Inc. (CEI), Women's Business Development Program (WBDP), P.O. Box 268, Wiscasset, ME 04578

## Massachusetts
Center for Women and Enterprise, Inc., 45 Bromfield St., 6th Floor, Boston, MA 02108

## Michigan

Ann Arbor Community Development Corporation, Women's Initiative for Self-Employment (WISE), 2008 Hogback Rd., Suite 2A, Ann Arbor, MI 48105

Grand Rapids Opportunities for Women (GROW), 25 Sheldon SE, Suite 210, Grand Rapids, MI 49503

## Minnesota

Women in New Development (WIND) [a division of Bi-County Community Action Programs, Inc.], P.O. Box 579, Bemidji, MN 56601

Women's Business Center, White Earth Reservation Tribal Council, 202 S. Main St., P.O. Box 478, Mahnomen, MN 56557

## Mississippi

Mississippi Women's Economic Entrepreneurial Project (MWEEP), 106 W. Green St., Mound Bayou, MS 38762

National Council of Negro Women, 633 Pennsylvania Ave., NW, Washington, DC 20004. The NCNW established an economic-entrepreneurial center in the cities of Mound Bayou and Ruleville and in Bolivar County, Mississippi. This area has been designated as a rural Enterprise Zone by the government.

## Missouri

National Association of Women Business Owners (NAWBO) St. Louis, 7165 Delmar, Suite 204, St. Louis, MO 63130

## Montana

Montana Women's Capital Fund, 54 N. Last Chance Gulch, P.O. Box 271, Helena, MT 59624

Women's Opportunity and Resource Development, Inc., 127 N. Higgins, Missoula, MT 59802

## Nevada

Nevada Self-Employment Trust (NSET), 560 Mill St., Reno, NV 89502

Nevada Self-Employment Trust (NSET), 1600 E. Desert Inn Rd., #209E, Las Vegas, NV 89109

## New Jersey

New Jersey NAWBO EXCEL, 225 Hamilton St., Bound Brook, NJ 08805-2042.

## New Mexico

Women's Economic Self-Sufficiency Team (WESST Corp.), 414 Silver Southwest, Albuquerque, NM 87102

WESST Corp. Farmington, 500 W. Main, Farmington, NM 87401

WESST Corp. Las Cruces, 691 S. Telshor, Las Cruces, NM 88001

## New York

American Women's Economic Development Corporation (AWED), 71 Vanderbilt Ave., Suite 320, New York, NY 10169

## North Dakota

Women's Business Institute (WBI), 320 N. Fifth St., Suite 203, P. O. Box 2043, Fargo, ND 58107-2043

## Ohio

EMPOWER Pyramid Career Services, 2400 Cleveland Ave., NW, Canton, OH 44709

Enterprise Center/Women's Business Center, 1864 Shyville Rd., Piketon, OH 45661

Glenville Development Corporation's Women's Development Center, 540 E. 105th St., Cleveland, OH 44108

Greater Columbus Women's Business Initiative, 37 N. High St., Columbus, OH 43215-3065

Northwest Ohio Women's Entrepreneurial Network, Toledo Area Chamber of Commerce, 5555 Airport Highway, Suite 210, Toledo, OH 43615

Women Entrepreneurs Inc., Bartlett Bldg., 36 E. 4th St., Cincinnati, OH 45202

Women's Business Center, 42101 Griswold Rd., Elyria, OH 44035

Women's Business Resource Network (OWBRN), 77 S. High St., 28th Floor, Columbus, OH 43266

Women's Business Resource Program of Southeast Ohio, Technology and Enterprise Bldg., Suite 190, 20 E. Circle Dr., Athens, OH 45701

Women's Organization for Mentoring, Enterprise, and Networking (WOMEN), 526 S. Main St., Suite 221, Akron, OH 44313

## Oklahoma

Working Women's Money University (WWMU), 3501 NW 63rd, Suite 609, Oklahoma City, OK 73116

## Oregon

Organization of Native American Business and Entrepreneurial Network (ONABEN), 520 Southwest 6th Ave., Suite 914, Portland, OR 97204

Southern Oregon Women's Access to Credit (SOWAC), 33 N. Central, Suite 209, Medford, OR 97501

## Pennsylvania

Women's Business Development Center, 1315 Walnut St., Suite 116, Philadelphia, PA 19107

## South Dakota

The Entrepreneur's Network for Women (ENW), 100 S. Maple, P.O. Box 81, Watertown, SD 57201

## Texas

Center for Women's Business Enterprise (CWBE), 508 Ladin Ln., Austin, TX 78734

North Texas Women's Business Development Center, Inc. (NTWBDC), 1402 Corinth St., Dallas, TX 75215-2111

## Utah

Utah Technology Finance Corporation, 177 E. 100 South, Salt Lake City, UT 84111

## Washington

Organization of Native American Business Entrepreneur Network (ONABEN)—see "Oregon."

## Wisconsin

Wisconsin Women's Business Initiative Corporation (WWBIC), 1915 N. Dr. Martin Luther King Jr. Dr., Milwaukee, WI 53212

Wisconsin Women's Business Initiative Corporation (WWBIC), Madison Office, 16 N. Carroll St., Suite 310, Madison, WI 53703

# Miscellaneous Sources of Help

## Associations for Women

Send a LSASE for information, unless stated otherwise, for all of these groups.

American Mothers at Home
914 S. Santa Fe, Suite 297
Vista, CA 92084

American Women's Economic Development Corporation
(AWED)
71 Vanderbilt Ave., Suite 320
New York, NY 10169

Founded in 1976, AWED is the premier national, not-for-profit organization committed to helping entrepreneurial women start and grow their own businesses, with additional offices in southern California, Connecticut, and Washington, D.C. Since its inception, AWED has served over a hundred thousand women to increase the start-up, survival, and expansion rates of small businesses.

Association of Enterprising Mothers
6965 El Camino Real, Suite 150-612
Carlsbad, CA 92009

At-Home Mothers' Resource Center
406 E. Buchanan
Fairfield, IA 52556
Offers information and resources for work-at-home mothers.
Publishes the *At-Home Motherhood Resource Catalog* and *At-Home
Mothering* magazine.

Formerly Employed Mothers at the Leading Edge (FEMALE)
P.O. Box 31
Elmhurst, IL 60126
http://femalehome.org
A network helping home-based mothers keep in touch with
other professional women and providing parents support
through local networking opportunities and newsletters.

Home-Based Working Moms (HBWM)
P.O. Box 500164
Austin, TX 78750
http://www.hbwm.com
A national organization for moms (and dads) who work at home
and those who would like to. Membership benefits include a
monthly newsletter, networking opportunities, resource guides,
support information, membership directory, discounted advertising, and more. Dues are $34/year.

Mothers' Access to Careers at Home (MATCH)
P.O. Box 123
Annandale, VA 22003
A support, networking, and advocacy group for women trying to
balance their families and careers by working from home. It is
based in the Washington, D.C., metro area and offers a subscription to its newsletter and a resource directory for sale.

Mothers' Home Business Network
P.O. Box 423
East Meadow, NY 11554
http://www.mhbn.com

Home business guidance, especially for mothers. Also offers a newsletter and resource guide.

> The National Association of Women Business Owners (NAWBO)
> 110 Wayne Ave., Suite 830
> Silver Spring, MD 20910-5603
> http://www.nfwbo.org

"The premier source of information on women-owned businesses . . . worldwide." Its research branch is the National Foundation for Women Business Owners (NFWBO).

> National Chamber of Commerce for Women: The Home-Based Business Committee
> 10 Waterside Plaza, Suite 6H
> New York, NY 10010

"Publishes updated job descriptions and pay comparisons for business-owners and for job holders; also provides *Home-Based Business of the Year* guidelines for opportunity-seekers."

> National Women's Business Council (NWBC)
> 409 3rd St., SW, Suite 5850
> Washington, DC 20024

Its mission "is to promote bold initiatives, policies, and programs designed to foster women's business enterprise at all stages of development in the public and private sectors of the marketplace." Counsels the President, Congress, and the Interagency Committee on Women's Business Enterprise on the effectiveness of government programs that foster women's entrepreneurship. Publishes the quarterly newsletter *The Partnership* and such reports as *Women Succeed in Business: Success Guide for Women Entrepreneurs* (1996) and *Expanding Business Opportunities: Report to the President and Congress* (January 1996).

> Women Incorporated
> 1401 21st St., Suite 310
> Sacramento, CA 95814

A national network of women in business with over twenty-five thousand members. Benefits include access to loans, group health benefits, and discounts on travel and business products.

Offers for sale *The Busy Woman's Guide to Business Plans, The Busy Woman's Guide to Marketing Plans,* and *The Busy Woman's Guide to Successful Self-Employment.* Membership is $29 a year.

### Other Associations for Home-Based and Small Businesses
Remember to send along a LSASE when you write these groups for more information.

American Association of Home-Based Businesses, Inc.
P.O. Box 10023
Rockville, MD 20849-0023
http://www.ahbb.org
"A national, nonprofit association dedicated to the support and advocacy of home-based businesses." AAHBB does not sell or endorse any business opportunities.

American Entrepreneurs Association (AEA)
2392 Morse Ave.
Irvine, CA 92614

American Home Business Association
4505 S. Wasatach Blvd.
Salt Lake City, UT 84124-9918
http://www.homebusiness.com
Offers many benefits and discounts to members.

Home Business Institute
P.O. Box 301
White Plains, NY 10605-0301
Offers home business liability protection, group medical insurance, and life insurance.

Home Office and Business Opportunities Association
92 Corporate Park, Suite C-250
Irvine, CA 92714

Home Office Association of America
909 Third Ave., Suite 990
New York, NY 10022-4731

Offers new marketing ideas, member benefits, business information, and networking opportunities.

Independent Business Alliance
111 John St., 27th Floor
New York, NY 10038

National Association for the Cottage Industry
P.O. Box 14850
Chicago, IL 60614

National Association for the Self-Employed (NASE)
2121 Precinct Line Rd.
Hurst, TX 76054
(800) 232-NASE

Provides benefits and advocacy for the self-employed. Health insurance plans are available.

National Association of Home-Based Businesses
10451 Mill Run Circle, Suite 400
Owings Mills, MD 21117

National Home Office Association (NHOA)
3412 Woolsey Dr.
Chevy Chase, MD 20815

Small Office/Home Office Association (SOHOA)
1765 Business Center Dr., #100
Reston, VA 22090

Offers a range of insurance programs.

## Books
### General Business
Look for these at your public library or order through Amazon Books (Internet: http://www.amazon.com) or your local bookstore.

*Bootstrapper's Success Secrets: 151 Tactics for Building Your Business on a Shoestring Budget* by Kimberly Stanséll (Franklin Lakes, NJ: Career Press, 1997); excellent source for starting and running a business efficiently and profitably on a budget

*Home Business Made Easy* by David Hanania (Grants Pass, OR: Oasis, 1992)

*Homemade Money*, 5th rev. ed., by Barbara Brabec (Cincinnati, OH: Betterway, 1997); one of the best in home-business information

*How to Start and Manage a Home Based Business: A Practical Way to Start Your Own Business* by Jerre G. Lewis and Leslie D. Renn (1996; Lewis and Renn Associates, 10315 Harmony Dr., Interlochen, MI 49643); step-by-step guide in an easy-to-read, easy-to-understand format for $14.95 + $3 postage and handling. Also ask for a listing of their numerous specific business guides (word processing, bookkeeping, gift baskets, etc.)

*Money-Smart Secrets for the Self-Employed: Make More and Keep More When You Work for Yourself!* by Linda Stern (New York: Random House Reference and Information Publishing, 1996)

*Start and Run a Profitable Home-Based Business*, 3rd ed., by Edna Sheedy (Bellingham, WA: Self-Counsel Press, 1997)

*Starting a Home-Based Business* (The Complete Idiot's Guide series) by Barbara Weltman (New York: Alpha, 1997)

*The SOHO Desk Reference* by HarperCollins Publishers (New York: HarperCollins, 1997); comprehensive handbook for small office/home office business owners

*Teaming Up: The Small Business Guide to Collaborating with Others to Boost Your Earnings and Expand Your Horizons* by Paul and Sarah Edwards and Rick Benzel (New York: Putnam's, 1997)

*The Whole Work Catalog;* many books on self-employment and careers; The New Careers Center, 1515 23rd St., Box 339-CT, Boulder, CO 80306

*The Women's Business Resource Guide: A National Directory of Over 800 Programs, Resources and Organizations to Help Women Start or Expand a Business* by Barbara Littman (Lincolnwood, IL: NTC/Contemporary Books, 1997)

### Other Books on Self-Employment
*Home-Based Business Guide* by Rosalie Marcus; advertising specialties; Lasting Impressions, 1039 Wellington, Rd., Jenkintown, PA 19046

*The Road to Self-Employment* by Gerri Norington, executive director, Women's Business Training Center, 530 Broadway, Suite 910, San Diego, CA 92101; send a SASE for ordering information.

*Gale's Reference Books* (Detroit, MI: Gale Research, annual); look in the library reference section for these titles:

*Encyclopedia of Associations: National Organizations of the U. S.*

*Encyclopedia of Business Information Sources, 1997-98*

*National Directory of Women-Owned Firms*

*Small Business Sourcebook*

## Publications
### Home-Based and Small Business

*Business @ Home Magazine*, John Knowlton, editor, 619 SW Broadway, Suite 200, Portland, OR 97205; $9.95/year, quarterly

*Business Start-Ups*, Subscription Dept., P.O. Box 50347, Boulder, CO 80323-0347; http://www.entrepreneurmag.com

*Entrepreneurial Edge Magazine*, 921 Penllyn Blue Bell Pike, Blue Bell, PA 19422; $14.95 for four issues

*Entrepreneur's Home Office*, Subscription Dept., P.O. Box 53784, Boulder, CO 80323-3784 http://www.entrepreneurmag.com

*Home Business Communique*, Carol Tober, publisher/editor, P.O. Box 3644, Lakewood, CA 90711-3644; features news from various home-based businesses throughout the United States

*Home Office Computing*, P.O. Box 53543, Boulder, CO 80323-3543; $16.97 for twelve issues/year; http://www.smalloffice.com

*Income Opportunities*, P.O. Box 55207, Boulder, CO 80323-5207; $11.97/year for twelve issues

*PROFIT$ Online* magazine, http://profitsonline.com

*Self-Employed Professional*, 462 Boston St., Topsfield, MA 01983-9917; $18/year for six issues

*Small Business Opportunities*, Harris Publications, Inc., 1115 Broadway, NY 10160-0397; $9.97/year for six issues

*Working at Home*, P.O. Box 5484, Harlan, IA 51593-2984; $11.97/year for four issues; http://www.successmagazine.com

## Business Kits

*Dun & Bradstreet's Business Solutions in a Box* includes how-to guides, a free Web site, business insurance services, educational tools, networking opportunities, and other small business products and industry services. Call (800) 266-5269, ext. 1599, for more information.

*Home-Based Business Kit* (#78); includes "Selling by Mail Order," "How to Create Your Own Brochure," "Teenage Money Making Guide," "Making Money at Arts & Crafts Shows," and others. Send a LSASE to Success Publications, 3419 Dunham, Box 263, Warsaw, NY 14569, for a listing of publications.

## Government

### Local

#### Cooperative Extension Services

Every county in the United States has such an office, sponsored by the U.S. Department of Agriculture (USDA). These offices work in affiliation with state universities, and in some states, they sponsor courses and programs for home business owners. Contact your local office (in the white or blue pages of your telephone directory), or visit the USDA Web site (http://www.reeusda.gov), which provides links to cooperative extensions.

#### Libraries

Your public library should be one of the first places you visit in your search for home-based business information. Some colleges and universities that offer business-related degrees have libraries with extensive business sections that you may consult.

#### Local Business Associations

Check with your local government offices to see whether the following organizations exist nearby:

Local Chamber of Commerce groups (some have branches for women business owners)

Home-based business associations—visit the Web site compiled by Paul and Sarah Edwards on the "Working from Home Forum," http://www.homeworks.com, which contains a home business directory of associations and publications.

### Local High Schools and Vo-Tech Schools
Check for continuing education business start-up courses.

### Postal Business Centers (PBCs)
PBCs show small and medium-sized businesses how to use the U.S. Postal Service at the best rates.

### State
Also see *Bootstrapper's Success Secrets* by Kimberly Stanséll (cited on page 419), which lists a "Directory of State Resources for Small Businesses" in the appendix.

### State Chamber of Commerce
Chambers of Commerce provide start-up kits, information about state legislation affecting small business, and numerous publications for entrepreneurs.

### State Legislators
Contact the offices of your state representatives and senators for information about your state's resources for small business information. Pennsylvania, for example, has a free book, *Starting a Small Business in Pennsylvania,* which discusses business structures, tax requirements, licenses, procedures on doing business with the state government, and other important information for businesses in Pennsylvania. Your also may find information on selling your products and/or services to your state government.

### States' Web Sites
Begin by using this address: http://www.yahoo.com/Government/U_S_ _States.

### Federal
### Business Information Centers (BICs)
Approximately 40 BICs in the United States, sponsored by the Small Business Association (SBA), provide the latest technology to help small businesses get started and grow. Its "Start, Run, Grow" program has a package of technology tools entrepreneurs can use for free. Call (800) 8-ASK-SBA, or see the SBA Web site, http://www.sba.gov.

http://www.sba.gov.

### Consumer Information Catalog
This is a catalog of free and low-cost federal publications, including the *Resource Directory for Small Business Management*, which lists publications for small and home business start-up and management. Write P.O. Box 100, Pueblo, CO 81002 (http:// www.pueblo.gsa.gov) for a catalog, or e-mail at cic.info@ pueblo.gsa.gov and write "SEND INFO" in body of message.

### Doing Business with the U.S. Government
*Commerce Business Daily*—$297/year; a daily publication that lists available contracts for bidding. Found in some public libraries, or write United Communications Group, P.O. Box 90608, Washington, DC 20090-0608.

*United States Government: New Customer!* by Robert Sullivan (Great Falls, VA: Information International, 1997)

### International Trade
SBA Office of International Trade
409 3rd St., SW, 8th Floor
Washington, DC 20416
(202) 205-6720

### Internet Sites
Government Information Locator Service: http://www.sba.gov/ gils

IRS: http://www.ires.ustreas.gov; other state and federal tax forms: http://www.securetax.com

Small Business Administration (SBA): http://www.sba.gov/

> Office of Women's Business Ownership
> 409 Third St., SW, 6th Floor
> Washington, DC 20416
> http://www.sba.gov/womeninbusiness
> Advice from loans to free counseling.

SCORE (Service Corps of Retired Executives)—a group of volunteers who offer management counseling and advice to small-business owners. Contact the SBA at 409 3rd St., SW,

Small Business Development Centers—see the SBA Web site for offices near you, or look in your telephone directory under "Small Business Development Center." SBDCs usually work in conjunction with universities or SBA branch offices and are available in forty-six states, the District of Columbia, Puerto Rico, and the Virgin Islands. They provide free services, counseling, and low-cost seminars to prospective and existing business owners. Call (703) 448-6124 for information.

U. S. Business Advisor: http://www.business.gov

U. S. Census Bureau: women-owned business statistics—http://www.census.gov

U.S. Small Business Administration (SBA): http://www.sba.gov; the Answer Desk: (800) 8-ASK-SBA

Women's Bureau: http://www.dol.gov/dol/wb/welcome.html

## *Entrepreneurship Education*

Center for Entrepreneurial Leadership, Inc.
Ewing Marion Kauffman Foundation
4900 Oak St.
Kansas City, MO 64112-2776
http://www.emkf.org

Nonprofit organization dedicated to encouraging entrepreneurs. Write for details about the programs available in your area.

Edward Lowe Foundation
51990 Decatur Rd.
Cassopolis, MI 49031
(800) 232-LOWE

Provides information services, research, and educational experiences that support small business people and the free enterprise system. Call for a free information packet. (See also smallbizNet under "Internet Resources" on page 428 and *Entrepreneurial Edge Magazine* in "Publications" on page 421.)

Krypton Institute
120 N. Wall St., 3rd Floor
Spokane, WA 99201

Intensive five-day course. Write for tuition costs.

Michael Dingman Center for Entrepreneurship
The Maryland Business School, University of Maryland
College Park, MD 20742-1815
Sponsors annual conference for women's entrepreneurship.

## Home Study

The following organizations offer business and career courses.
Write for current catalog listings.

Graduate School USDA (U.S. Department of Agriculture)
Room 129
600 Maryland Ave, SW
Washington, DC 20078-0952
Courses on accounting, elderlaw, paralegal, communications,
computers, and more. Write for a current catalog.

National Home Study Council
1601 18th St., NW
Washington, DC 20009
Write for the *Directory of Accredited Home Study Schools,* which
lists many home study schools that are accredited. Some of
those listed are the following:

Foley-Belsaw Institute
6301 Equitable Rd.
Kansas City, MO 64120-9957

International Correspondence Schools
925 Oak St.
Scranton, PA 18540-9888

NRI Schools
4401 Connecticut Ave., NW
Washington, DC 20078-3543

Professional Career Development Institute
6065 Roswell Rd., Suite 3118
Atlanta, GA 30328-4044

Stratford Career Institute Inc.
233 Swanton Rd., Suite 121
St. Albans, VT 05478-9911

## Resources for People with Disabilities

Disabled Businesspersons Association (DBA)
9625 Black Mountain Rd., Suite 207
San Diego, CA 92126-4564

National Organization on Disability
910 16th St., NW, Suite 600
Washington, D.C. 20006

Alliance for Technology Access
2175 East Francisco Blvd, Suite L
San Rafael, CA 94936
(415) 455-4575
e-mail: atainfo@ataccess.org
A nonprofit organization that refers people to local centers that offer resources for technology for persons with disabilities. Does not have information on self-employment. Call for the location of a center near you, or access its Web site: http://ataccess.org.

### On-line Source

The Boulevard, http://www.blvd.com, is a Web site containing information on products, resources, publications, employment opportunities for the disabled, and more.

## Internet Resources

### Women's Business

http://www.abwahq.org—American Business Women's Association

http://women.aswe.org/aswe/—American Society of Women Entrepreneurs

http://www.fodreams.com—Field of Dreams; network of women's businesses, on-line newsletter

http://www.mbemag.com—*The Women's Business Exclusive,* a newsletter for minority and women business owners

http://www.momwork.com—National association for stay-at-home moms and others who desire to work at home

http://www.nfwbo.org—National Foundation for Women Business Owners http://www.bizymoms.com—women's business information; author of *The Stay-At-Home Mom's Guide to Making Money* (Rocklin, CA: Prima, 1997)

## Small Business

http://www.lowe.org/smallbiznet—a service of the Edward Lowe Foundation, smallbizNet includes a four-thousand-document Digital Library, content-rich Internet links, a small business bookstore, and monthly small business features.

http://www.isbc.com—International Small Business Consortium

http://www.anincomeofherown.com—"An Income of Her Own," a site for teen women to learn about and find valuable resources for becoming entrepreneurs

### *Mail-Order Business Information*

*How to Start a Home-Based Mail Order Business* by Georgeanne Fiumara; $15.95 + $3 shipping and handling. Order from Mother's Home Business Network (see address under "Organizations" on page 416)

*National Directory of Mailing Lists* by Ken Barry, ed (New York: Oxbridge Communications, 1998)

### *Expos, Trade Shows, and Conferences*

http://www.tscentral.com—trade shows

*Entrepreneur Magazine's Small Business Expos,* 2392 Morse Ave., Irvine, CA 92614; national shows featuring franchises, business opportunities, business products, and services. Write for a schedule or pick up the latest issue of *Entrepreneur Magazine,* which lists its expo dates.

SOHO Business Expos, Miller Freeman Expositions, Inc., Fort Lee Executive Park, 1 Executive Dr., 3rd Floor, Fort Lee, NJ 07024; national expos featuring exhibits for the home-based and small office.

### *Small Business Incubators*

National Business Incubation Association
20 E. Circle Dr., Suite 190
Athens, OH 45701
(614) 593-4331
info@nbia.org and http://www.nbia.org

Members of this association are located throughout the country with the purpose of assisting small businesses grow and become independent. Write, call, or send an e-mail message for the location of a business incubator nearest to you. Also offers an extensive publications library (also on-line) that contains a section devoted to books for businesses and business libraries.

### Supplies and Equipment
**Paper**
Earth Care Paper, Inc., P.O. Box 14140, Madison, WI 53714-14140
Paper Direct, 100 Plaza Dr., Secaucus, NJ 07094-3606

**Computer Forms**
NEBS, Inc., 500 Main St., Groton, MA 01471

**Office Products**
Lefty's Corner, P.O. Box 615, Clarks Summit, PA 18411; sells writing supplies and many other items for left-handers. Send $3 for catalog, refundable with first purchase.
Quill Monthly Office Products Catalog, 100 Schelter Rd., Lincolnshire, IL 60069-3621. Quill also offers inexpensive and helpful booklets on saving money on office supplies, compiling a mailing list, customer service, and more.
Viking Office Products, 13809 S. Figueroa St., P.O. Box 6114, Los Angeles, CA 90061-0144

### Miscellaneous Sources
D-U-N-S, Number
Dun & Bradstreet
899 Eaton Ave.
Bethlehem, PA 18025
(800) 333-0505
Call for information about getting a D-U-N-S, Number for your business (among other things, it is needed to gain a federal contract).

Executive Suite Association
438 E. Wilson Bridge Road, Suite 200
Columbus, OH 43085
Office space to rent and business support service (for home-based and small business owners when they need to meet

formally with clients, conduct business in an office setting, etc.). Write for information about office suites located near you.

### Radio

CBS: *Home Office Computing's Small Business Minute;* log on to http://www.cbsradio.com to find a station in your area.

Paul and Sarah Edwards's *Working from Home Show;* Business News Network, (719)-528-7040, Sundays from 10 to 11 P.M. ET.

### Television

CNN's financial network, CNN's *Take It Personally,* hosted by John Metaxas and Beverly Schuch. *Home Office Computing*'s editors appear every other Tuesday between 3 and 4 P.M. ET to discuss current small business issues and answer questions.

*Working from Home* With Paul and Sarah Edwards, a weekly, half-hour series on the Home & Garden Television network; (423) 694-2700

Television Shopping Networks: Write for an application about selling your product.

Home Shopping Network
1 HSN Dr.
St. Petersburg, FL 33729

QVC/Vendor Relations
1385 Enterprise Dr.
West Chester, PA 19380

### *How to Contact the Author*

If you have any comments, questions, or business ideas you would like to see profiled in upcoming business books, please send them to Priscilla Y. Huff, Box 286, Sellersville, PA 18960, or send e-mail to pyhuff@cynet.net, or visit my Web site at http://www.littlehse.com.

# Index

**431**